Teresa Y. Neely
Kuang-Hwei (Janet) Lee-Smeltzer
Editors

Diversity Now: People, Collections, and Services in Academic Libraries

Diversity Now: People, Collections, and Services in Academic Libraries has been co-published simultaneously as *Journal of Library Administration*, Volume 33, Numbers 1/2 and 3/4 2001.

Pre-publication
REVIEWS,
COMMENTARIES,
EVALUATIONS . . .

"COVERS A BROAD RANGE OF IDEAS AND BEST PRACTICES IN DIVERSITY. The sections on recruitment retention and job satisfaction describe practical, successful programs. . . . A well-rounded view of diversity issues."

Joan Giesecke, DPA
Dean of Libraries
University of Nebraska-Lincoln

The Haworth Information Press
An Imprint of The Haworth Press, Inc.

Diversity Now:
People, Collections,
and Services
in Academic Libraries

Diversity Now: People, Collections, and Services in Academic Libraries has been co-published simultaneously as *Journal of Library Administration*, Volume 33, Numbers 1/2 and 3/4 2001.

The *Journal of Library Administration* Monographic "Separates"

Below is a list of "separates," which in serials librarianship means a special issue simultaneously published as a special journal issue or double-issue *and* as a "separate" hardbound monograph. (This is a format which we also call a "DocuSerial.")

"Separates" are published because specialized libraries or professionals may wish to purchase a specific thematic issue by itself in a format which can be separately cataloged and shelved, as opposed to purchasing the journal on an on-going basis. Faculty members may also more easily consider a "separate" for classroom adoption.

"Separates" are carefully classified separately with the major book jobbers so that the journal tie-in can be noted on new book order slips to avoid duplicate purchasing.

You may wish to visit Haworth's Website at . . .

http://www.HaworthPress.com

. . . to search our online catalog for complete tables of contents of these separates and related publications.

You may also call 1-800-HAWORTH (outside US/Canada: 607-722-5857), or Fax 1-800-895-0582 (outside US/Canada: 607-771-0012), or e-mail at:

getinfo@haworthpressinc.com

Diversity Now: People, Collections, and Services in Academic Libraries, edited by Teresa Y. Neely, PhD, and Kuang-Hwei (Janet) Lee-Smeltzer, MS, MSLIS (Vol. 33, No. 1/2/3/4, 2001). *Examines multicultural trends in academic libraries' staff and users, types of collections, and services offered.*

Leadership in the Library and Information Science Professions: Theory and Practice, edited by Mark D. Winston, MLS, PhD (Vol. 32, No. 3/4, 2001). *Offers fresh ideas for developing and using leadership skills, including recruiting potential leaders, staff training and development, issues of gender and ethnic diversity, and budget strategies for success.*

Off-Campus Library Services, edited by Ann Marie Casey (Vol. 31, No. 3/4, 2001 and Vol. 32, No. 1/2, 2001). *This informative volume examines various aspects of off-campus, or distance learning. It explores training issues for library staff, Web site development, changing roles for librarians, the uses of conferencing software, library support for Web-based courses, library agreements and how to successfully negotiate them, and much more!*

Research Collections and Digital Information, edited by Sul H. Lee (Vol. 31, No. 2, 2000). *Offers new strategies for collecting, organizing, and accessing library materials in the digital age.*

Academic Research on the Internet: Options for Scholars & Libraries, edited by Helen Laurence, MLS, EdD, and William Miller, MLS, PhD (Vol. 30, No. 1/2/3/4, 2000). *"Emphasizes quality over quantity. . . . Presents the reader with the best research-oriented Web sites in the field. A state-of-the-art review of academic use of the Internet as well as a guide to the best Internet sites and services. . . . A useful addition for any academic library." (David A. Tyckoson, MLS, Head of Reference, California State University, Fresno)*

Management for Research Libraries Cooperation, edited by Sul H. Lee (Vol. 29, No. 3/4, 2000). *Delivers sound advice, models, and strategies for increasing sharing between institutions to maximize the amount of printed and electronic research material you can make available in your library while keeping costs under control.*

Integration in the Library Organization, edited by Christine E. Thompson, PhD (Vol. 29, No. 2, 1999). *Provides librarians with the necessary tools to help libraries balance and integrate public and technical services and to improve the capability of libraries to offer patrons quality services and large amounts of information.*

Library Training for Staff and Customers, edited by Sara Ramser Beck, MLS, MBA (Vol. 29, No. 1, 1999). *This comprehensive book is designed to assist library professionals involved in presenting or planning training for library staff members and customers. You will explore ideas for effective general reference training, training on automated systems, training in specialized subjects such as African American history and biography, and training for areas such as patents and trademarks, and business subjects.* Library Training for Staff and Customers *answers numerous training questions and is an excellent guide for planning staff development.*

Collection Development in the Electronic Environment: Shifting Priorities, edited by Sul H. Lee (Vol. 28, No. 4, 1999). *Through case studies and firsthand experiences, this volume discusses meeting the needs of scholars at universities, budgeting issues, user education, staffing in the electronic age, collaborating libraries and resources, and how vendors meet the needs of different customers.*

The Age Demographics of Academic Librarians: A Profession Apart, by Stanley J. Wilder (Vol. 28, No. 3, 1999). *The average age of librarians has been increasing dramatically since 1990. This unique book will provide insights on how this demographic issue can impact a library and what can be done to make the effects positive.*

Collection Development in a Digital Environment, edited by Sul H. Lee (Vol. 28, No. 1, 1999). *Explores ethical and technological dilemmas of collection development and gives several suggestions on how a library can successfully deal with these challenges and provide patrons with the information they need.*

Scholarship, Research Libraries, and Global Publishing, by Jutta Reed-Scott (Vol. 27, No. 3/4, 1999). *This book documents a research project in conjunction with the Association of Research Libraries (ARL) that explores the issue of foreign acquisition and how it affects collection in international studies, area studies, collection development, and practices of international research libraries.*

Managing Multicultural Diversity in the Library: Principles and Issues for Administrators, edited by Mark Winston (Vol. 27, No. 1/2, 1999). *Defines diversity, clarifies why it is important to address issues of diversity, and identifies goals related to diversity and how to go about achieving those goals.*

Information Technology Planning, edited by Lori A. Goetsch (Vol. 26, No. 3/4, 1999). *Offers innovative approaches and strategies useful in your library and provides some food for thought about information technology as we approach the millennium.*

The Economics of Information in the Networked Environment, edited by Meredith A. Butler, MLS, and Bruce R. Kingma, PhD (Vol. 26, No. 1/2, 1998). *"A book that should be read both by information professionals and by administrators, faculty and others who share a collective concern to provide the most information to the greatest number at the lowest cost in the networked environment." (Thomas J. Galvin, PhD, Professor of Information Science and Policy, University at Albany, State University of New York)*

OCLC 1967-1997: Thirty Years of Furthering Access to the World's Information, edited by K. Wayne Smith (Vol. 25, No. 2/3/4, 1998). *"A rich-and poignantly personal, at times-historical account of what is surely one of this century's most important developments in librarianship." (Deanna B. Marcum, PhD, President, Council on Library and Information Resources, Washington, DC)*

Management of Library and Archival Security: From the Outside Looking In, edited by Robert K. O'Neill, PhD (Vol. 25, No. 1, 1998). *"Provides useful advice and on-target insights for professionals caring for valuable documents and artifacts." (Menzi L. Behrnd-Klodt, JD, Attorney/Archivist, Klodt and Associates, Madison, WI)*

Economics of Digital Information: Collection, Storage, and Delivery, edited by Sul H. Lee (Vol. 24, No. 4, 1997). *Highlights key concepts and issues vital to a library's successful venture into the digital environment and helps you understand why the transition from the printed page to the digital packet has been problematic for both creators of proprietary materials and users of those materials.*

The Academic Library Director: Reflections on a Position in Transition, edited by Frank D'Andraia, MLS (Vol. 24, No. 3, 1997). *"A useful collection to have whether you are seeking a position as director or conducting a search for one." (College & Research Libraries News)*

Emerging Patterns of Collection Development in Expanding Resource Sharing, Electronic Information, and Network Environment, edited by Sul H. Lee (Vol. 24, No. 1/2, 1997). *"The issues it deals with are common to us all. We all need to make our funds go further and our resources work harder, and there are ideas here which we can all develop." (The Library Association Record)*

Interlibrary Loan/Document Delivery and Customer Satisfaction: Strategies for Redesigning Services, edited by Pat L. Weaver-Meyers, Wilbur A. Stolt, and Yem S. Fong (Vol. 23, No. 1/2,

1997). *"No interlibrary loan department supervisor at any mid-sized to large college or university library can afford not to read this book." (Gregg Sapp, MLS, MEd, Head of Access Services, University of Miami, Richter Library, Coral Gables, Florida)*

Access, Resource Sharing and Collection Development, edited by Sul H. Lee (Vol. 22, No. 4, 1996). *Features continuing investigation and discussion of important library issues, specifically the role of libraries in acquiring, storing, and disseminating information in different formats.*

Managing Change in Academic Libraries, edited by Joseph J. Branin (Vol. 22, No. 2/3, 1996). *"Touches on several aspects of academic library management, emphasizing the changes that are occurring at the present time. . . . Recommended this title for individuals or libraries interested in management aspects of academic libraries." (RQ American Library Association)*

Libraries and Student Assistants: Critical Links, edited by William K. Black, MLS (Vol. 21, No. 3/4, 1995). *"A handy reference work on many important aspects of managing student assistants. . . . Solid, useful information on basic management issues in this work and several chapters are useful for experienced managers." (The Journal of Academic Librarianship)*

The Future of Resource Sharing, edited by Shirley K. Baker and Mary E. Jackson, MLS (Vol. 21, No. 1/2, 1995). *"Recommended for library and information science schools because of its balanced presentation of the ILL/document delivery issues." (Library Acquisitions: Practice and Theory)*

The Future of Information Services, edited by Virginia Steel, MA, and C. Brigid Welch, MLS (Vol. 20, No. 3/4, 1995). *"The leadership discussions will be useful for library managers as will the discussions of how library structures and services might work in the next century." (Australian Special Libraries)*

The Dynamic Library Organizations in a Changing Environment, edited by Joan Giesecke, MLS, DPA (Vol. 20, No. 2, 1995). *"Provides a significant look at potential changes in the library world and presents its readers with possible ways to address the negative results of such changes. . . . Covers the key issues facing today's libraries . . . Two thumbs up!" (Marketing Library Resources)*

Access, Ownership, and Resource Sharing, edited by Sul H. Lee (Vol. 20, No. 1, 1995). *The contributing authors present a useful and informative look at the current status of information provision and some of the challenges the subject presents.*

Libraries as User-Centered Organizations: Imperatives for Organizational Change, edited by Meredith A. Butler (Vol. 19, No. 3/4, 1994). *"Presents a very timely and well-organized discussion of major trends and influences causing organizational changes." (Science Books & Films)*

Declining Acquisitions Budgets: Allocation, Collection Development and Impact Communication, edited by Sul H. Lee (Vol. 19, No. 2, 1994). *"Expert and provocative. . . . Presents many ways of looking at library budget deterioration and responses to it . . . There is much food for thought here." (Library Resources & Technical Services)*

The Role and Future of Special Collections in Research Libraries: British and American Perspectives, edited by Sul H. Lee (Vol. 19, No. 1, 1993). *"A provocative but informative read for library users, academic administrators, and private sponsors." (International Journal of Information and Library Research)*

Catalysts for Change: Managing Libraries in the 1990s, edited by Gisela M. von Dran, DPA, MLS, and Jennifer Cargill, MSLS, MSed (Vol. 18, No. 3/4, 1994). *"A useful collection of articles which focuses on the need for librarians to employ enlightened management practices in order to adapt to and thrive in the rapidly changing information environment." (Australian Library Review)*

Integrating Total Quality Management in a Library Setting, edited by Susan Jurow, MLS, and Susan B. Barnard, MLS (Vol. 18, No. 1/2, 1993). *"Especially valuable are the librarian experiences that directly relate to real concerns about TQM. Recommended for all professional reading collections." (Library Journal)*

Monographic "Separates" list continued at the back

Diversity Now: People, Collections, and Services in Academic Libraries

Selected Papers from The Big 12 Plus Libraries Consortium Diversity Conference

Teresa Y. Neely
Kuang-Hwei (Janet) Lee-Smeltzer
Editors

Diversity Now: People, Collections, and Services in Academic Libraries has been co-published simultaneously as *Journal of Library Administration*, Volume 33, Numbers 1/2 and 3/4 2001.

The Haworth Information Press
An Imprint of
The Haworth Press, Inc.
New York • London • Oxford

Published by

The Haworth Information Press®, 10 Alice Street, Binghamton, NY 13904-1580 USA

The Haworth Information Press® is an imprint of The Haworth Press, Inc., 10 Alice Street, Binghamton, NY 13904-1580 USA.

Diversity Now: People, Collections, and Services in Academic Libraries has been co-published simultaneously as *Journal of Library Administration*™, Volume 33, Numbers 1/2 and 3/4 2001.

Cover design by Amy Genner, Kevin Rundblad, and Callise Denney

Library of Congress Cataloging-in-Publication Data

Big 12 Plus Libraries Consortium Diversity Conference (2000 : University of Texas at Austin)
    Diversity now : people, collections, and services in academic libraries : selected papers from the Big 12 Plus Libraries Consortium Diversity Conference / Teresa Y. Neely, Kuang-Hwei (Janet) Lee-Smeltzer, editors.
        p. cm.
    Co-published simultaneously as Journal of library administration, vol. 33, nos. 1/2 and 3/4 2001.
        Includes bibliographical references and index.
        ISBN 0-7890-1696-6 (alk. paper) -- ISBN 0-7890-1697-4 (pbk. : alk. paper)
        1. Minority librarians–Employment–United States–Congresses. 2. Diversity in the workplace–United States–Congresses. 3. Academic libraries–United States–Personnel management–Congresses. 4. Minority librarians–Recruiting–United States–Congresses. 5. Academic libraries–Services to minorities–United States–Congresses. 6. Library education–United States–Congresses. 7. Libraries and minorities–United States–Congresses. I. Neely, Teresa Y. II. Lee-Smeltzer, Kuang-Hwei. III. Journal of library administration. IV. Title.

Z682.4.M56 B54 2002
023'.9–dc21
                                                                                            2002017175

Indexing, Abstracting & Website/Internet Coverage

This section provides you with a list of major indexing & abstracting services. That is to say, each service began covering this periodical during the year noted in the right column. Most Websites which are listed below have indicated that they will either post, disseminate, compile, archive, cite or alert their own Website users with research-based content from this work. (This list is as current as the copyright date of this publication.)

Abstracting, Website/Indexing Coverage . . . . Year When Coverage Began

- *Academic Abstracts/CD-ROM* 1993
- *Academic Search: data base of 2,000 selected academic serials,*
  updated monthly: EBSCO Publishing 1995
- *Academic Search Elite (EBSCO)* 1993
- *AGRICOLA Database (AGRICultural OnLine Access)*
  <www.natl.usda.gov/ag98> 1991
- *BUBL Information Service: An Internet-based Information Service*
  for the UK higher education community
  <URL: http://bubl.ac.uk/> 1999
- *Business ASAP* 1993
- *CNPIEC Reference Guide: Chinese National Directory*
  of Foreign Periodicals 1995
- *Current Articles on Library Literature and Services (CALLS)* 1992
- *Current Awareness Abstracts of Library & Information*
  Management Literature, ASLIB (UK) 1998
- *Current Cites [Digital Libraries] [Electronic Publishing] [Multimedia &*
  Hypermedia] [Networks & Networking] [General] 2000
- *Current Index to Journals in Education* 1997
- *Educational Administration Abstracts (EAA)* 1991
- *FINDEX <www.publist.com>* 1999
- *FRANCIS. INIST/CNRS <www.inist.fr>* 1999
- *General BusinessFile ASAP <www.galegroup.com>* 1993
- *General Reference Center GOLD on InfoTrac Web* 1984
- *Higher Education Abstracts, providing the latest in research theory in more*
  than 14 major topics 1991

(continued)

Special Bibliographic Notes related to special journal issues (separates) and indexing/abstracting:

- indexing/abstracting services in this list will also cover material in any "separate" that is co-published simultaneously with Haworth's special thematic journal issue or DocuSerial. Indexing/abstracting usually covers material at the article/chapter level.
- monographic co-editions are intended for either non-subscribers or libraries which intend to purchase a second copy for their circulating collections.
- monographic co-editions are reported to all jobbers/wholesalers/approval plans. The source journal is listed as the "series" to assist the prevention of duplicate purchasing in the same manner utilized for books-in-series.
- to facilitate user/access services all indexing/abstracting services are encouraged to utilize the co-indexing entry note indicated at the bottom of the first page of each article/chapter/contribution.
- this is intended to assist a library user of any reference tool (whether print, electronic, online, or CD-ROM) to locate the monographic version if the library has purchased this version but not a subscription to the source journal.
- individual articles/chapters in any Haworth publication are also available through the Haworth Document Delivery Service (HDDS).

Diversity Now: People, Collections, and Services in Academic Libraries

CONTENTS

ABOUT THE EDITORS

Teresa Y. Neely, MLS, PhD, is Head of Reference at the University of Maryland, Baltimore County. She was most recently a reference librarian and assistant professor at Colorado State University Libraries, Fort Collins. Dr. Neely's publications include "Effects of Diversity on Black Librarianship: Is Diversity Divergent?" in *The Revised Handbook of Black Librarianship, Second Editon;* "Diversity in Conflict" (*Law Library Journal*); her doctoral dissertation, forthcoming as a monograph from Scarecrow Press, Inc. titled *Information Literacy in Higher Education: A Sociological and Psychological Framework* (Spring, 2002); and "Instruction and Outreach at Colorado State University Libraries" (*The Reference Librarian*), co-authored with colleagues from CSU Libraries. Dr. Neely also led the effort to edit *Culture Keepers III: Making Global Connections-Proceedings of the Third National Conference of African American Librarians, Winston-Salem, NC, 1997;* and is a reviewer for the Children's Bookshelf section of *The Black Issues Book Review*. Dr. Neely's research interests include diversity, information literacy, staff training and development, management, and reference services.

Kuang-Hwei (Janet) Lee-Smeltzer, MS, MSLIS, is Catalog Librarian at the Harris County Public Library in Houston, Texas. She most recently held the positions of metadata librarian at Questia Media in Houston and coordinator, bibliographic control and electronic resource services at Colorado State Unviersity Libraries, Fort Collins. Recent publications include "Cataloging in Three Academic Libraries: Operations, Trends, and Perspectives" (*Cataloging & Classification Quarterly*); "Finding the Needle: Control Vocabularies, Resource Discovery, and Dublin Core" (*Library Collections, Acquisitions, and Technical Services*); and "Report on OCLC CORC meeting, November 3-4, 1999, Dublin, Ohio" (*DataLink: The Alliance Newsletter*). Ms. Lee-Smeltzer's professional activities include the ALCTS Creative Ideas in Technical Services Discussion Group (co-chair), and the *Library Collections, Acquisitions, and Technical Services* editorial board. Her research interests include trends, development, and implementation of metadata for digital information resources.

Both editors served on the program committee for The Big 12 Plus Diversity Now Conference, held in Austin, Texas, April 3-4, 2000, where these papers originated as presentations.

Introduction

Teresa Y. Neely
Kuang-Hwei (Janet) Lee-Smeltzer

On April 3rd and 4th, 2000, The Big 12 Plus Libraries Consortium sponsored "Diversity Now: People, Collections, and Services in Academic Libraries."[1] This conference was modeled after and continues the tradition of the "Challenge to Change" diversity conference held at Pennsylvania State University Libraries 1998.[2] Hosted by the University of Texas at Austin, the conference sought to bring together best practices in diversity in academic libraries in the areas of people, collections, and services. More than fifty contributed papers, panel discussions, table talks and poster sessions were represented, as well as keynote speeches by five outstanding leaders from library education, university administration, and American jurisprudence.

The sixteen papers included here represent the wide spectrum that is encompassed by the conference theme areas. We have divided this issue into four sections. The first section, People: Recruitment and Retention, explores partnerships between academic research libraries and campus agencies that work directly with students and are charged with building a diverse campus community (Janice Simmons-Welburn and William C. Welburn); introduces a model retention program for junior faculty of color (Camila A. Alire); clarifies the role of librarians in adopting and promoting domestic partner benefits for university employees who are unmarried same- and opposite-sex couples (Polly Thistlethwaite); promotes professional development in retaining underrepresented academic librarians, using the University of Minnesota Training Institute as a model (Eric Kofi Acree, Sharon K. Epps, Yolanda Gilmore, and Charmaine Henriques); and provides effective retention strategies for diverse employees (Linda R. Musser).

[Haworth co-indexing entry note]: "Introduction." Neely, Teresa Y., and Kuang-Hwei (Janet) Lee-Smeltzer. Co-published simultaneously in *Journal of Library Administration* (The Haworth Information Press, an imprint of The Haworth Press, Inc.) Vol. 33, No. 1/2, 2001, pp. 1-3; and: *Diversity Now: People, Collections, and Services in Academic Libraries* (ed: Teresa Y. Neely, and Kuang-Hwei (Janet) Lee-Smeltzer) The Haworth Information Press, an imprint of The Haworth Press, Inc., 2001, pp. 1-3. Single or multiple copies of this article are available for a fee from The Haworth Document Delivery Service [1-800-HAWORTH, 9:00 a.m. - 5:00 p.m. (EST). E-mail address: getinfo@haworthpressinc.com].

2 Diversity Now: People, Collections, and Services in Academic Libraries

In the second section, People: Institutional and Organizational Culture, Johnnieque B. (Johnnie) Love presents her unique research perspective on assessment and diversity integration into the academic library workplace; Bertie Greer, Denise Stephens and Vicki Coleman deconstruct the interaction of cultural diversity and gender role spillover in the workplace; and Joyce Thornton reports on the job satisfaction of African American women in librarianship. This section also includes an article from Joan S. Howland, whose article had been previously accepted by the editor of the *Journal of Library Administration* but was awaiting a home. Her article fits in perfectly with the conference papers. She outlines six critical challenges for working in a multicultural environment, from the perspective of an experienced administrator.

The third section, Collections and Access, includes an article inspired by John Mark Tucker's *Untold Stories: Civil Rights, Libraries, and Black Librarianship*. In her paper, Irene Owens examines the historical context of the establishment of library collections on the history, literature, and art of persons of African descent in Historically Black Colleges and Universities (HBCUs) against the backdrop of "separate and unequal" practices, and the unintended fall out of the *Morrill Land Grant Acts of 1860 and 1890*. Elaina Norlin and Patricia Morris also examine HBCU libraries, but discuss the present state and future prospects and offer suggestions on how all librarians can strengthen connections with these institutions.

The fourth and final section is titled Instruction and Library Education and includes an article on communication and teaching, which also discusses how the scholarship associated with communication theory can assist in facilitating learning about diversity among those who will be expected to contribute to the success of their employing organizations (Mark D. Winston); and one on incorporating service learning experiences in the library and information science curriculum (Loriene Roy). A librarian from the University of Colorado at Boulder shares her experience in developing and teaching a full credit course in the Department of Ethnic Studies (Yem S. Fong); storytelling is exemplified as an instructional tool and the use of multicultural literature to support instruction for pre-service teacher training in an article about the Multicultural Storytelling Project at the Texas A&M University Libraries (Johnnieque B. (Johnnie) Love, Candace Benefiel, and John B. Harer); and an MLIS research project from the University of Alberta, Edmonton, Canada explores the information needs and library use of Aboriginal students in Canada (Deborah A. Lee).

Although the conference was geared toward best practices, the articles in this volume go beyond the predictable formula of "this is what we did, and this is how well it worked." Authors transformed their presentations into papers which reveal the utilization of the best practice with other theoretical models or integrated national trends, with the practice as an example. We are proud of the papers presented here, and although the title notes these are selected papers, the decision to contribute to this volume was strictly voluntary in favor of the authors themselves.

The next diversity conference, sponsored by the Committee on Institutional Cooperation (CIC) is scheduled to be held April 4th-6th at the University of Iowa, Iowa City, Iowa.[3] It is our hope as co-editors, and members of the program committee for "Diversity Now," that this tradition continues to identify and disseminate the best practices for diversity in academic research libraries.

NOTES

1. For information on presentations and programs, visit the conference Web site [online] *http://carbon.cudenver.edu/public/library//diversitynow/index.html* [cited 8 May 2001].

2. For information on presentations and programs, visit the conference Web site [online] *http://www.libraries.psu.edu/divers/conf/* [cited 8 May 2001].

3. For conference information, contact co-chairs of the program committee, Janice-Simmons Welburn, University of Iowa at *j-simmons-welburn@uiowa.edu* or Bonnie MacEwan, Penn State University at *bjm13@psu.edu* or visit the official conference Website *<http://www.lib.uiowa.edu/cicdiversity/>*.

PEOPLE:
RECRUITMENT AND RETENTION

Cultivating Partnerships/Realizing Diversity

Janice Simmons-Welburn
William C. Welburn

SUMMARY. Academic librarians should not only seek methods for continuous learning about an increasingly diverse college student body, they are encouraged to pursue partnerships with campus agencies that work directly with students, especially those charged with building a diverse community of students. The authors present two examples to illustrate strategies-in-action. *[Article copies available for a fee from The Haworth Document Delivery Service: 1-800-HAWORTH. E-mail address: <getinfo@ haworthpressinc.com> Website: <http://www.HaworthPress.com> © 2001 by The Haworth Press, Inc. All rights reserved.]*

KEYWORDS. College students, information literacy, TRIO programs, summer undergraduate research programs, partnerships, academic libraries

Janice Simmons-Welburn is affiliated with the University of Iowa Libraries, Iowa City, IA (E-mail: *j-simmons-welburn@uiowa.edu*).

William C. Welburn is affiliated with the University of Iowa, Graduate College, Iowa City, IA (E-mail: *william-welburn@uiowa.edu*).

|Haworth co-indexing entry note|: "Cultivating Partnerships/Realizing Diversity." Simmons-Welburn, Janice, and William C. Welburn. Co-published simultaneously in *Journal of Library Administration* (The Haworth Information Press, an imprint of The Haworth Press, Inc.) Vol. 33, No. 1/2, 2001, pp. 5-19; and: *Diversity Now: People, Collections, and Services in Academic Libraries* (ed: Teresa Y. Neely, and Kuang-Hwei (Janet) Lee-Smeltzer) The Haworth Information Press, an imprint of The Haworth Press, Inc., 2001, pp. 5-19. Single or multiple copies of this article are available for a fee from The Haworth Document Delivery Service |1-800-HAWORTH, 9:00 a.m. - 5:00 p.m. (EST). E-mail address: getinfo@haworthpressinc.com|.

INTRODUCTION

As the overall population of the United States continues to change in its ethnic constitution,[1] the nation's colleges and universities are challenged to create strategies that enhance access and expand the educational opportunities for an increasingly diverse citizenry.[2] The nation's populations have always been, to paraphrase historian Stephanie Grauman Wolf,[3] as varied as its lands, yet only in the past three decades-following the tumultuous movement for civil rights-have colleges and universities adopted new approaches that respond to anticipated increases in enrolling diverse populations of students.[4]

These strategies intend to assure success among students seeking access to associate, baccalaureate, graduate, and professional degree and certification programs in a society imagined to be ever widening in its scope of opportunities.[5] The educational continuum through which today's students pass resembles, as William Bowen and Derek Bok put it, a river:

> It is more helpful to think of the nurturing of talent as a process akin to moving down a winding river, with rock-strewn rapids and slow channels, muddy at times and clear at others. Particularly when race is involved, there is nothing simple, smooth, or highly predictable about the education of young people.[6]

Along the winding river, many colleges and universities continue to devise initiatives administrators hope will respond to the educational needs of emerging populations and, in particular, minority and low income/first-generation students. They intend to reduce the effects of disparities in educational background and performance, improve institutional climate, and encourage minority and low income/first-generation students to stay in the rush of the water, persisting not only through the baccalaureate degree but also to pursue advanced graduate and professional study.[7] Such initiatives are abundant-at community and liberal arts colleges and at public and private research universities alike-and when successful yield favorable results.[8]

An examination of the potential for cultivating partnerships between academic libraries and campus academic or academic support services provides a backdrop for further consideration of the value of realizing diversity in American institutions of higher learning.[9] The support that academic libraries can give to programs designed to develop traditionally underrepresented students in higher education is worth cultivating, realizing that opportunities to collaborate across the complex institutional structures of colleges and universities are often difficult to accomplish. Yet becoming information literate can be an integral part of higher learning, and accordingly can serve to be an integral part of the responsibility of an institution in enabling students' pursuit of success in reaching goals well beyond the academy.[10]

THE INTELLECTUAL ECOSYSTEM
OF UNDERGRADUATE EDUCATION

Despite the observable differences between types of colleges and universities-size, affiliation, resource support, degree offerings, to name a few-there are important threads that tie one sector of higher education to the others.[11] While findings in the 1998 Boyer Commission report on reinventing undergraduate education are intended to challenge research universities, they are applicable to all of higher education. Particularly noteworthy is the Commission's characterization of the campus as an intellectual ecosystem:

> The interaction of many kinds of stimuli creates at a university a special kind of intellectual environment, with the health of the whole a manifestation of the health of each part. That environment should become an *intellectual ecosystem* [emphasis added]. Universities are communities of learners, whether those learners are astrophysicists examining matter in the far reaches of space or freshmen new to an expanded universe of learning. The shared goals of investigation and discovery should bind together the disparate elements to create a sense of wholeness.[12]

Today's academic libraries are challenged to articulate a role in the campus ecosystem for student learning and academic development. Academic library leaders can begin by promoting continuous learning among staff about how college affects undergraduate students both in and out of the classroom. No effort will be made here to review the substantial body of research and commentary on college student development;[13] yet, two important questions rise to the surface of the following discussion about student diversity:

- What are the transitions and impediments that shape the river for minority and low income/first-generation college students, given the complexities of the campus intellectual ecosystem?

- What opportunities exist for collaboration between academic libraries and other agencies of diversity on college and university campuses that shape a more effective institutional response to the requirements for student learning in an information age?

What follows is an attempt to join issues common to higher educational institutions, regardless of differences in academic or organizational mission, environment or culture, that focus on the learning experiences of undergraduates. It is an attempt at setting a stage to think about what opportunities exist for partnerships between academic libraries and academic support services. This paper argues that collaborative work will ensure a sustainable presence for information literacy in academic support services programs. Two examples will be given from experiences at the University of Iowa as evidence of the value of partnerships and collaborative work between units in academic settings as a way of supporting institutional goals.

The Effect of College on Students

Researchers often point to disparities in academic preparedness of students seeking entry into higher education. Disparities are quite often attributed to individual or family-related experiences, or to educational background and experience in schools.[14] Some researchers have found connections between academic achievement and access to Advanced Placement (AP) and honors courses, and involvement in extracurricular activities.[15] Researchers from the American College Testing Program (ACT) relate such factors to "students' choices of high school course work and grades they earn in those courses, which, in turn, are strongly related to ACT scores,"[16] still a major determinant of selectivity in college admissions. A U.S. Department of Education study found that "the impact of a high school curriculum of high academic intensity and quality on [baccalaureate] degree completion is far more pronounced-and positively-for African-American and Latino students than any other pre-college indicator of academic resources."[17] They continued:

> Academic Resources . . . produce a much steeper curve toward bachelor's degree completion than does socioeconomic status. Students from the lowest two SES (Socioeconomic Status) quintiles who are also in the highest Academic Resources quintile earn bachelor's degrees at a higher rate than a majority of students from the top SES quintile.[18]

Socioeconomic disparities define the reality of K-12 education, of what Jonathan Kozol called the savage inequalities of American school systems, and race still seems to matter in access to quality schooling even when controlled for socioeconomic status.[19] According to student development scholar Patrick Terenzini, first-generation college students differ:

> In a number of ways from that of their traditional peers, and the differences suggest potential learning problems ahead for first-generation students . . . [who are] more likely to come from low-income families, to be Hispanic, to have weaker cognitive skills [in reading, math, and critical thinking], to have lower degree aspirations, and to have been less involved with peers and teachers in high school . . . [moreover they] tend to have more dependent children, expect to take longer to complete their degree programs, and report receiving less encouragement from their parents to attend college . . . the combined portrait is one of students at academic risk.[20]

Part of the road ahead in resolving disparities in academic preparation is a required shift in attention to the transitions from high schools to colleges and from two- to four-year institutions. Bridging programs or collaborations between high schools, community colleges, and four-year colleges, take on special significance as they provide systematic and comprehensive academic support and build connections between students and faculty.[21] Some initiatives in higher education that have been funded by federal agencies, such as the U.S. Department of Education's TRIO Programs,[22] the National Science Foundation's Alliance for Minority Participation in Science (AMPS), and the National Institutes of Health bridging programs, give special attention to educational needs of first-generation college students.

Persistence-especially among students of color-also appears to be related to climate and aspirations. Research by Sylvia Hurtado on the institutional climate for Latino students concluded that an improved institutional climate, one that is aware and knowledgeable of Latino culture and is less hostile to the presence and expressions of Latino students, faculty and staff, is strongly associated with successful educational attainment among Latino students. Latino students possessing academic strengths do appear to seek acceptance, and therefore are most receptive to a welcoming climate.[23] Alberto Cabrera and his colleagues found that for all students, "exposure to a campus climate of prejudice and intolerance lessens commitment to the institution and, indirectly, weakens decisions to persist."[24] In other words, a chilly climate affects all students and is detrimental to their academic progress.

There is also a general perception that minority and low income/first-generation undergraduates are especially hampered by lower aspirations than other students, that ill-focused aspirations affect persistence, graduation rates, and decisions to pursue graduate education. Viewed another way, the perception of low aspirations closely resembles what psychologist Claude Steele refers to as *stereotype threat*, a "situational threat that . . . can affect the members of any group about whom a negative stereotype exists."[25] The perception of lower aspirations among both minority and low-income/first-generation students may obfuscate self-doubt affecting both groups, doubt that leaves a misperception about educational goals and aspirations.

Mentoring, a "dynamic reciprocal relationship in a work environment between an advanced career incumbent and a beginner aimed at promoting the career development of both,"[26] can be an effective method of redressing low aspirations. Academic mentoring programs for minority students are commonplace, especially among selective colleges and universities that wish to establish relationships between undergraduate students and faculty in students' chosen areas of academic interest, thereby favorably contributing to students' socialization in a given discipline.[27] Bowen and Bok also maintain that institutional interventions, such as undergraduate research and intensive academic programs, boost the efforts of colleges and universities to increase the number of students of color who choose graduate or professional study.[28] Results of mentoring programs, such as the Mellon Minority Undergraduate Program, the Myerhoff Scholars Program at the University of Maryland-Baltimore County, and the Committee on Institutional Cooperation's (CIC) Summer Research Opportunities Programs (SROP), all point to successful outcomes, including higher involvement in graduate education.[29]

Additionally, the U.S. Department of Education, Office of TRIO Programs has expanded its menu of federally funded academic support services programs for low income/first-generation students by developing Ronald McNair Scholars Programs serving 3,641 students on 156 college and university campuses. McNair scholars are undergraduate students who receive the individual attention of faculty mentors, who also work with the students on research projects.[30]

A Typology of Institutional Initiatives

Colleges and universities have responded to factors with different initiatives designed to reduce if not eliminate disparities.[31]

- *Pre-college programs.* Programs for middle and high school students, designed to encourage college enrollment and, in some cases, science majors. Such programs include Howard Hughes Life Sciences Programs, high school summer science training programs, and Upward Bound.
- *Bridging programs.* Programs designed to assist in both academic and social transition from high school to college. Examples include Upward Bound, AMPS, and other transition programs that work primarily if not exclusively with low income/first-generation students.
- *Educating undergraduates.* Programs that combine "rigor and optimism"[32] to not only improve performance but inspire students to pursue graduate study. Examples include Mellon Minority Undergraduate Programs at private colleges and universities, the Meyerhoff Academy at the University of Maryland-Baltimore, SROP at Big 10 universities, and Ronald E. McNair Scholars programs.
- *Predoctoral programs.* Programs that prepare new graduate students for the rigor of graduate education. Examples can be found at the Universities of Michigan and Illinois.

HOW LIBRARIES CAN RESPOND: CULTIVATING PARTNERSHIPS

Unfortunately, neither the role of the academic library nor the quest for an information literate student body figures prominently in discussions on the effect of college on students' cognitive growth and academic success. Terms such as libraries, library instruction, information seeking, or information literacy do not appear in the index to Terenzini and Pascarella's 800 page review of twenty years of research on the development of college students.[33] Yet, students enroll in colleges and universities with far ranging pre-college educational experiences and academic preparation, and their exposure to academic resources varies substantially. Likewise, their access to information in support of education varies by resources available, including access to libraries and to resources available via the Internet. School systems across the United States vary substantially, and many are without the resources to provide their students with what Carol Kuhlthau called an information-age school library.

> The central goal of the restructured library media program is to develop ability in the process of learning from a variety of sources of information in each subject in the curriculum . . . this is the essential piece to the puzzle that is missing in many efforts to restructure education of the twenty-first century. Failing to prepare students for learning in an information-rich environment is to fail to meet the challenge of education today.[34]

An information literate student is "one who can recognize when information is needed and has the ability to locate, evaluate, and effectively use the needed information."[35] If the purpose of instructional activities in academic libraries is to enhance the quality of student learning by incorporating information literacy, then how do libraries intersect information literacy with the requirements for student learning? The answer to this question must also take into account disparities in exposure to information resources and other academic resources that compose the mosaic of educational and sociocultural experiences of today's undergraduates.

We propose that libraries cultivate partnerships with those campus programs that are directly responsible for diversifying our student bodies. Libraries can have a significant impact on preparing students for their desired futures by first recognizing the importance of programmatic interventions, then persuading program administrators of the benefits of exposure to information-rich environments to students' academic training.

Cultivating Partnerships at the University of Iowa: Two Examples

Two examples-one involving a program for high school students and the other a summer undergraduate research program-illustrate how the University of Iowa Libraries has worked with other offices on campus to cultivate partnerships and introduce information literacy.

Upward Bound

In the first example, University of Iowa Libraries staff were able to negotiate an information literacy component to the university's Upward

Bound program. Upward Bound is one of eight outreach and academic support programs known as TRIO and administered by the U.S. Department of Education designed to reach middle and high school students from low-income households and encourage their participation in higher education. Created by the 1964 Educational Opportunity Act and reauthorized under subsequent Higher Education Acts, Upward Bound specifically prepares high school students for college.

Many college and university libraries have developed limited engagement with Upward Bound. At the University of Iowa, however, the Libraries moved beyond traditional, short-term instruction to develop a more integrated program with Upward Bound staff that would employ concepts of information literacy. The Libraries' goal in revising its pedagogical strategy was fundamentally epistemic; each session and each assignment represented a step toward greater knowledge and awareness of how to seek out, evaluate, and use information.

In practical terms, the Libraries had grown accustomed to offering a brief orientation and tour to Upward Bound students. In the early 1990s, the Libraries' diversity librarian began engaging Upward Bound staff in dialogue over the benefits of developing the information seeking skills of academically high-risk students, and as more library staff became involved, the partnership between Upward Bound and the Libraries in teaching the use of various information resources evolved. The Libraries first guided Upward Bound students through a series of skill-building experiences in information seeking using library resources over several sessions using the Information Arcade, the Libraries' technology-based teaching-learning center.

As library and Upward Bound staff worked together, instruction evolved from a library session to course-integrated teaching combined with library training sessions for Upward Bound teaching staff. The emphasis in the revised approach shifted from teaching library use to providing grounds for building individual knowledge on locating information in support of class assignments and other academic activities, independently analyzing results and refining search strategies, and seeking out sources to aid in using chosen information. Students gained exposure to a variety of accessible information resources, including the Libraries online information system and catalog, the Web, and printed sources found among the Libraries holdings.

The benefits of this partnership are manifold, yet three stand out. First, TRIO programs are strongly encouraged to involve students in new technologies. Given that much of the Libraries' mode of instructional delivery and goals of information literacy involves the use of information technologies, the Libraries' instructional design greatly enhances the Upward Bound program's charge. Second, Upward Bound can add to its arsenal of methods for supporting students in their transition from high school to college exposure not only the vastness of a college or university library but also how academic library systems can be effectively exploited to support coursework.[36]

Finally, by participating in Upward Bound and other TRIO programs, the Libraries became an active agency in academic socialization for students transitioning from high school to college. Libraries became actively involved in the lives and success of a significant number of students of color or low-income, first-generation pre-college students. As the Council for Opportunity in Education has observed,

> Students in the Upward Bound program are four times more likely to earn an undergraduate degree than those students from similar backgrounds who did not participate in TRIO.

> Nearly 20 percent of all Black and Hispanic freshmen who entered college in 1981 received assistance through the TRIO Talent Search or EOC programs.

> Students in the TRIO Student Support Services program are more than twice as likely to remain in college than those students from similar backgrounds who did not participate in the program.[37]

Summer Research Opportunities Program (SROP)

Upward Bound is but one case in point of a program that has successfully bridged numerous students into higher education. The SROP is an example of an effort to encourage students to go higher in education by pursuing advanced graduate work, preferably research doctoral degrees. SROP, an idea that began in 1980 at Purdue University and was expanded to include other Big 10 schools, is now commonplace not only among research universities but also among liberal arts colleges and other types of institutions of higher education.[38] Summer research program student participants are matched with faculty mentors to actively engage in the mentors' research. While largely concentrated in scientific disciplines (the sciences, engineering, and mathematics), summer research programs invite advanced undergraduate students from all disciplines where there are substantive research opportunities for an eight to ten week program that includes a research component as well as programming intended to prepare students for graduate school admissions.

Most student participants in the University of Iowa's SROP are not enrolled at the University; rather, they are working toward degrees at smaller, teaching-centered colleges with more limited access to the resources of a research university. As a second illustration of the value of collaboration, the Libraries began working with the University of Iowa Graduate College-the campus host of SROP-to incorporate elements of information literacy as a part of the student participants' experience. Given that students' time was largely consumed by research assignments, the Libraries and Graduate College sought a method of collaboration that would be relatively unobtrusive yet sustainable. Dispensing with a tour of the Main Library-which did not serve the interests of the science students-librarians created a Web site tailored to support the needs of student participants, including access to an array of discipline-specific, scholarly information resources on the Internet and in the Libraries, along with names, areas of expertise, and contact information for librarians covering the students' subject interests. A librarian introduced the Web page during the program's seminar, and the program director and teaching assistant prepared subsequent writing assignments that required use of the Web page and its various links. The Web page is retained during the course of the subsequent academic year to enable students to continue to use it as an information resource.

Unlike the first example, the Libraries accepted that there was little time available to present in-depth instruction to SROP students. Yet traditional methods such as tours only inadequately prepared students for seeking information. In this illustration, linking resources in a form that is available to students when they need it and where they have access to it-in labs, the library, or from the computer cluster in the residence hall-resolved the dilemma.

Both examples illustrate how libraries learn to cultivate partnerships on campus in support of student learning. They show the importance of negotiating the library's role in programs designed to foster campus diversity using innovative pedagogical and technological approaches contingent upon different programmatic goals.

CONCLUSION

When one views the college campus as an intellectual ecosystem, there are numerous opportunities to cultivate partnerships between the library and campus agencies that can be enriched by teaching students strategies for locating, evaluating, and using information in response to a vast array of academic, professional, and personal needs. This is clearly understood by the academic library community, though less understood or accepted elsewhere in colleges and universities. Yet the disparity throughout the American K-12 educational system creates unequal footing at the doors of higher education. There is great benefit to enriching not only students' science and math skills, but also to increase students' capacity to use the information around them. Partnerships between libraries and other academic-centered programs may serve as agencies to, as historian Tom Holt wrote, "think for themselves and think creatively."[39]

NOTES

1. Jennifer Cheeseman Day, *Population Projections of the United States by Age, Sex, Race, and Hispanic Origin 1995-2050*, U.S. Bureau of the Census, Current Population Reports, P25-1130 (Washington, DC: GPO, 1996).

2. Eugene Y. Lowe, "Promise and Dilemma: Incorporating Racial Diversity in Selective Higher Education," in *Promise and Dilemma: Perspectives on Racial Diversity in Higher Education*, ed. Eugene Y. Lowe (Princeton, NJ: Princeton University Press, 1999), 3. See also *Does Diversity Make a Difference? Three Research Studies on Diversity in College Classrooms* (Washington, DC: American Council on Education and American Association of University Professors, 2000), 1-2; *Reaching the Top: A Report of the National Task Force on Minority High Achievement* (New York: The College Board, 1999).

3. Stephanie Grauman Wolf, *As Various as Their Lands: The Everyday Lives of Eighteenth Century Americans* (New York: HarperCollins, 1993); Martha Farnsworth Richie, in a study for the Population Reference Bureau wrote, "The U.S. population has always been multiracial, and it is becoming even more diverse now than it was at its founding two centuries ago," see "America's Diversity and Growth: Signposts for the 21st Century," *Population Bulletin* 55 (2) (June 2000).

4. *Does Diversity Make a Difference?* 1.

5. The College Board, *Reaching the Top*, 11-12. See also Patricia Gandara and Julie Maxwell-Jolly, *Priming the Pump: Strategies for Increasing the Achievement of Underrepresented Minority Undergraduates* (New York: The College Board, December 1999).

6. William G. Bowen and Derek A. Bok, *The Shape of the River: Long-Term Consequences of Considering Race in College and University Admissions* (Princeton, NJ: Princeton University Press, 1998), 14.

7. Gandara, *Priming the Pump*; for an example of a program, see Uro Treisman, "Studying Students Studying Calculus: A Look at the Lives of Minority Mathematics Students in College," *College Mathematics Journal* 23 (November 1992): 362-72.

8. For instance, the Council for Opportunity in Education reported "over 1,900 TRIO Programs currently serve nearly 700,000 low-income Americans between the ages of 11 and 27." *What is Trio*, Council of Educational Opportunity Programs [online] available from http://www.trioprograms.org/home.html [cited 25 October 2000]. Bowen and Bok also describe exemplary programs at selective schools, see Bowen and Bok, *Shape of the River*, 86-90.

9. By academic support services, the authors refer to those non-academic units that administer or host academic programs for students. These include student support services programs, tutoring programs, and programs designed for academically at-risk students.

10. According to the American Library Association, Presidential Commission on Information Literacy, "To be information literate, a person must be able to recognize when information is needed and have the ability to locate, evaluate, and use effectively the needed information." American Library Association. Presidential Committee on Information Literacy. *Final Report* (Chicago: American Library Association, 1989) [online] available from http://www.ala.org/acrl/nili/ilit1st.html [cited 25 October 2000].

11. The Carnegie Foundation's *Classification of Institutions of Higher Education*, under revision at the time of this writing, provides one method of understanding the differences between types of colleges and universities. It is heavily based on degrees granted, affiliation, mission and other institutional characteristics. [online] available from http://www.carnegiefoundation.org/Classification/index.htm.

12. The Boyer Commission on Educating Undergraduates. *Reinventing Undergraduate Education: A Blueprint for America's Research Universities*, 1998 [online] available from http://notes.cc.sunysb.edu/Pres/boyer.nsf [cited 25 October 2000].

13. See Patrick Terenzini and Ernest Pascarella, *How College Affects Students: Findings and Insights from Twenty Years of Research* (San Francisco: Jossey-Bass, 1991).

14. Laura J. Horn and Xianglei Chen, *Toward Resiliency: At-Risk Students Who Make it to College* (Washington, DC: U.S. Department of Education, Office of Research and Improvement, May 1998); Laura Horn, *Confronting the Odds: Students at Risk and the Pipeline to Higher Education* (Washington, DC: National Center for Educational Statistics, 1997); Clifford Adelman, *Answers in the Tool Box: Academic Intensity, Attendance Patterns, and Bachelor's Degree Attainment* (Washington, DC: US Department of Education, Office of Educational Improvement, 1999); Patrick T. Terenzini, Leonard Springer, Patricia M. Yaeger, Ernest T. Pascarella, and Amaury Nora, "First-Generation College Students: Characteristics, Experiences, and Cognitive Development," *Research in Higher Education* 37 (February 1996): 16-17.

15. Julie Noble, Mark Davenport, Jeff Schiel, and Mary Pommerich, "Relationships Between the Noncognitive Characteristics, High School Course Work and Grades, and Test Scores of ACT-Tested Students," *ACT Research Report* 99-4, 1999; Julie Noble, Mark Davenport, Jeff Schiel, and Mary Pommerich, "High School Academic and Noncognitive Variables Related to the ACT Scores of Racial/Ethnic and Gender Groups." *ACT Research Report* 99-6, 1999.

16. Noble et al., "Relationships Between the Noncognitive Characteristics."

17. Adelman, *Answers in the Tool Box*, ix.

18. Ibid.

19. Jonathan Kozol, *Savage Inequalities: Children in America's Schools* (New York: HarperPerennial, 1992).

20. Terenzini et al., "First-Generation College Students."

21. The College Board, *Reaching the Top*, 31-32; Charles Woolston, Freeman A. Hrabowski, and Kenneth I. Maton, "The Recruitment and Retention of Talented African Americans in Science: The Role of Mentoring," *Diversity in Higher Education* 1 (1977): 103-14; L. Scot Miller, "Promoting High Academic Achievement among Non-Asian Minorities," in *Promise and Dilemma*, 74-81.

22. The TRIO programs include eight outreach and support programs targeted to help disadvantaged students progress from middle school to postbaccalaureate programs. TRIO began with Upward Bound, which emerged out of the Economic Opportunity Act of 1964; in 1965, Talent Search, the second outreach program, was created as part of the Higher Education Act; in 1968, Student Support Services, which was originally known as Special Services for Disadvantaged Students, was authorized by the Higher Education Amendments and became the third in a series of educational opportunity programs. By the late 1960s, the term "TRIO" was coined to describe these federal programs. See Federal TRIO Programs [online] available from http://www. ed.gov/offices/OPE/HEP/trio/ [cited 6 November 2000].

23. Sylvia Hurtado, "The Institutional Climate for Talented Latino Students," *Research in Higher Education* 35 (February 1994): 21-41; see also Sylvia Hurtado, Jeffrey Milem, Alma Clayton-Pederson, and Walter Allen, *Enacting Diverse Learning Environments: Improving the Climate for Racial/Ethnic Diversity in Higher Education* (ASHE-ERIC Higher Education Report, 26/8, 1999).

24. Alberto F. Cabrera, Amaury Nora, and Patrick T. Terenzini, "Campus Racial Climate and the Adjustment of Students to College: A Comparison Between White Students and African-American Students," *Journal of Higher Education* 70 (March-April, 1999): 134-60.

25. Claude Steele, "A Threat in the Air: How Stereotypes Shape Intellectual Identity and Performance," in *Promise and Dilemma*, 94.

26. Charles Healy, "An Operational Definition of Mentoring," *Diversity in Higher Education* 1 (1997): 10.

27. Faculty mentoring programs are now common at colleges and universities. The Mellon Foundation funds programs at a number of selective institutions, and others, such as the University of Michigan, Michigan State University, the University of Minnesota, and the University of Maryland-Baltimore County, have created mentoring programs. The U.S. Department of Education funds approximately 160 Ronald McNair Scholars programs, which are designed to create faculty mentoring relationships for minority and low-income/first-generation students. Mentoring as a strategy has been recognized by the White House through creation of the Presidential Awards for Excellence in Science, Mathematics and Engineering Mentoring.

28. Bowen and Bok, *The Shape of the River.*

29. *Enhancing the Minority Presence in Graduate Education V: Summer Research Opportunity Programs, Voices and Visions of Success in Pursuit of the Ph.D.* (Washington, DC: Council of Graduate Schools, 1993); "U. of Maryland Branch is Beacon for Minorities in Math and Science," *New York Times*, 14 October 2000.

30. *Programs at a Glance: The Ronald G. McNair Postbaccalaureate Achievement* [online] available from http://www.trioprograms.org [cited 25 October 2000].

31. Miller, "Promoting High Academic Achievement," 78-79.

32. See Brent Staples, "Preaching the Gospel of Academic Excellence," *New York Times*, 5 June 2000, sec A, p. 40.

33. Terenzini and Pascarella, *How College Affects Students.*

34. Carol Kuhlthau, "The Process of Learning from Information," in *The Virtual School Library: Gateway to the Information Superhighway*, ed. Carol Collier Kuhlthau (Englewood, CO: Libraries Unlimited, 1996), 103.

35. Patricia Senn Breivik, "Education for the Information Age," in *Information Literacy: Developing Students as Independent Learners* (San Francisco: Jossey-Bass, 1992): 8.

36. As a result of their efforts, the library was asked to submit a letter of support for renewal of the Upward Bound grant proposal, highlighting their role in contributing to the information competencies of student participants.

37. Council for Equal Opportunity in Education [online] available from http://www.trioprograms.org/home.html [cited 25 October 2000].

38. *Enhancing the Minority Presence*.

39. Tom Holt, *Thinking Historically: Narrative, Imagination, and Understanding* (New York: The College Board, 1995), 54.

The New Beginnings Program: A Retention Program for Junior Faculty of Color

Camila A. Alire

SUMMARY. Retention of junior minority faculty can play an important role in the retention of students of color in higher education. This article deals with the issues minority faculty face in a mostly-white academy such as academic and social isolation, lack of support, and an uneven playing field relative to promotion and tenure. Taking these issues into account, the author describes a model program for minority faculty retention to include the program design, programming topics, costs, evaluation, and challenges. *[Article copies available for a fee from The Haworth Document Delivery Service: 1-800-HAWORTH. E-mail address: <getinfo@ haworthpressinc.com> Website: <http://www.HaworthPress.com> © 2001 by The Haworth Press, Inc. All rights reserved.]*

KEYWORDS. Academic minority faculty, minority library faculty, retention, higher education

---

Camila A. Alire is Dean, University Libraries, Colorado State University, Fort Collins, CO (E-mail: *calire@manta.colostate.edu*).

[Haworth co-indexing entry note]: "The New Beginnings Program: A Retention Program for Junior Faculty of Color." Alire, Camila A. Co-published simultaneously in *Journal of Library Administration* (The Haworth Information Press, an imprint of The Haworth Press, Inc.) Vol. 33, No. 1/2, 2001, pp. 21-30; and: *Diversity Now: People, Collections, and Services in Academic Libraries* (ed: Teresa Y. Neely, and Kuang-Hwei (Janet) Lee-Smeltzer) The Haworth Information Press, an imprint of The Haworth Press, Inc., 2001, pp. 21-30. Single or multiple copies of this article are available for a fee from The Haworth Document Delivery Service [1-800-HAWORTH, 9:00 a.m. - 5:00 p.m. (EST). E-mail address: getinfo@haworthpressinc.com].

21

INTRODUCTION AND THE PROBLEM

The ever-changing racial/ethnic demographics of our country are demonstrated by the 1990 census, which reported that one out of every four residents in the United States was a person of color. It is predicted that after 2000, one out of every three residents will be a person of color. Because of these demographics, the American higher education system is under extreme pressure to recruit, retain, and educate the emerging majority. Unfortunately, higher education has not had the best track record in recruiting minority students.

The challenge of recruiting minority students into colleges and universities has only been exacerbated by the repeal of affirmative action initiatives by many higher education institutions. This repeal, which declares that affirmative action recruitment programs are preferential treatment measures, has had a negative effect in the enrollment of students of color. Because state and federal monies had, in the past, been used to fund special initiatives and scholarships to attract minority students, these initiatives and scholarships are no longer available.

Nonetheless, if higher education institutions are successful in recruiting students of color, then the second challenge arises-retention. The attrition rate of minority students at most academic institutions is much higher than that of their white counterparts.[1] One of the reasons for this attrition rate is that there are not enough role models for the students to identify among the institutional faculty.[2] The more diverse faculty a university has, the more diverse the student body usually is. Faculty of color can offer to the students a special sensitivity and a mutual understanding of cultural differences.[3]

The issues of student recruitment and retention then become more complex when one introduces the role minority faculty play in this regard. Because of this, the challenges of recruiting faculty of color only intensify in many institutions by the high attrition rate of those minority faculty.[4]

Colorado State University (CSU), like most universities, also suffers from an unacceptable attrition rate of minority faculty. The issue of minority faculty retention also becomes a library issue because librarians at CSU have full-faculty status and are either tenure-track or tenured with faculty rank.

The Office of Budgets and Institutional Analysis (OBIA) at CSU provides, on a yearly basis, data on faculty. In the academic year of 1998-1999, OBIA reported that CSU had eighty-three (8.5% of the total faculty) faculty of color in fall of 1998. At the end of that academic year,

OBIA reported that the institution lost six faculty of color-one full professor, one associate professor, and four assistant professors. Only the full professor left due to voluntary retirement. Reasons were not given for the loss of the other five faculty of color other than they were not due to volunteer retirement.[5]

Because CSU academic departments and the Libraries invest a great deal of money in recruiting any faculty member to the University and because there was concern about losing new faculty members of color, a model program-New Beginnings-was designed and implemented to be proactive in any retention efforts of junior minority faculty. Although there are academic support units in place for the University to maintain a higher student retention rate, especially minority students, there had been no systematic support programs for faculty of color.[6]

This article includes a review of the literature relative to minority academic faculty retention and describes a model program for the retention of faculty of color at CSU. The program description includes the design, programming, costs, evaluation, and challenges.

REVIEW OF THE LITERATURE

In reviewing the literature in higher education over the past ten years, the author could find no model programs for minority faculty retention. However, there were articles that supported the issue of minority faculty recruitment and retention.[7]

CSU is no different than most academic institutions. What was found in the literature also applied at CSU. This article concentrates on the lack of supportive environment as a critical factor for minority faculty attrition.

Factors that contribute to that attrition rate include faculty of color finding themselves very isolated, working with little support, and meeting high service expectations.[8] The first two factors relate directly to a lack of a supportive environment.

Owens, Reis, and Hall wrote that the best strategy for recruiting and retaining desirable faculty was "a creation of a quality college environment that reflects attributes attractive to everyone. Minority candidates are looking for what every candidate desires: respect, warmth, genuineness, fairness, and support."[9]

Spann, in a study of all campus faculty, found that a supportive environment was the most important factor in determining successes as an academic faculty.[10] No wonder then why faculty of color have even tougher times when they arrive at an institution where the predominantly white faculty are used to selecting and supporting junior colleagues who share the same personal experiences, values, and beliefs as they do. There is usually no systematic support system in place in most academic departments. Therein lies the problem for minority faculty retention.

NEW BEGINNINGS PROGRAM

The New Beginnings (NewBs) program falls under the auspices of the CSU Minority Faculty and Staff Caucus (Minority Caucus). It is a proactive, formal, volunteer program to assist in the retention of new, tenured-track faculty of color. The program was designed to provide an academic support system for junior faculty of color (teaching and library faculty) in an effort to provide a welcoming, positive, and supporting environment as one step to retaining them successfully. The program involves senior minority faculty working and, in a sense, informally mentoring junior faculty of color. It is the first program of its kind at CSU.

The NewBs program includes programs/discussions on topics that would be very relative to and timely for the junior minority faculty's success in the reappointment, tenure, and promotion process at CSU. One of the main concerns of minority faculty is the lack of support, intentional or unintentional, from the senior faculty and/or administrators in their departments. Junior minority faculty are not privy to the informal mechanisms (e.g., tricks of the trade) in place within the institution and/or department to which tenure-track white faculty have access and which can make them successful in the tenure and promotion process. At CSU, like at many other institutions, minority faculty who achieve tenure do so in spite of neutral or non-supportive environments.

The NewBs program provides a formal mechanism to raise the level of awareness of junior faculty of color relative to tips, suggestions, and advice, thereby leveling the playing field in the tenure and promotion process. The Minority Caucus faculty thought that such proactive assistance would help in our efforts to retain minority junior faculty. CSU had to show it cares.

Program Development

Because CSU has a seven-year tenure process that involves a third-year, comprehensive midterm review and a seventh-year comprehensive review, the NewBs program is designed for first- and second-year tenure-track faculty of color to help them prepare for both reviews. However, participants in our program can continue attending especially if they were unable to attend all of the previous sessions.

The author is the designer and coordinator of the NewBs program and is assisted by a committee of three-two minority department chairs and a female associate dean. They provide the coordinator with advice, guidance, and program support.

With the assistance of the Provost Office and the deans and department chairs of all eight colleges, the author is able to identify each year new faculty of color. At the time of publication, this program had completed its second year and was beginning its third. There were fourteen participants the first year and eleven participants the second year. Participation is strictly voluntary.

The program starts each year with a Kick-Off Breakfast hosted by the CSU Provost where all of the participants are invited. Additional guests include the deans and department chairs of the colleges and departments where each minority faculty resides. All senior minority faculty are also invited. In the second semester, a reception is held for the same list of guests that is also hosted by the Provost.

NewBs Programming

NewBs programming was determined after discussions with several successful senior faculty of color and with the NewBs Advisory Committee. Additionally, members from the Provost's Office were consulted. All those consulted shared with the author the type of programs that they thought would be helpful in retention and tenure success. Based on the information gathered, the author developed a series of one-hour programs for the NewBs' participants.

One intent of the programming was to involve successful senior faculty of color as presenters and role models demonstrating to the junior minority faculty that it can be done; they can be successful at CSU. Additionally, the program utilizes white faculty and administrators who are concerned about minority faculty attrition and are committed to assist in their retention. All presenters provide nitty-gritty tips, do's and don'ts, and other tidbits of advice. Two to three programs are offered each semester. After the participants submit their schedules of availability, the date and time is set when most participants can attend.

The programming includes the following program areas:

1. *Junior Faculty Survival 101*-offered by senior minority and white faculty committed to retaining minority faculty and includes tips on accepting committee assignments, networking with senior faculty, approaching department chairs and deans, professional society/association work, et cetera.
2. *Annual Reviews ABC's*-offered by department chairs realizing that, at CSU, annual reviews are part of the tenure and promotion dossiers; consequently, how junior faculty present themselves in their self-evaluations in the areas of teaching, research/scholarly activity, and service/outreach is a very important part of the tenure and promotion process.
3. *Tenure and Promotion Basics*-offered by several department chairs and the Vice Provost of Academic Affairs, whose responsibility includes this arena.
4. *Research/Publishing Tips*-offered by senior minority faculty in various disciplines who have been very successful in maintaining an aggressive research agenda and in scholarly publishing.
5. *Successful Grantsmanship*-offered by senior minority faculty who have a successful record in securing research grants at CSU.
6. *Grantsmanship 101*-offered by program officers from the University's Research and Sponsored Programs office.
7. *Junior Faculty Career Awards Fundamentals*-offered by the staff of the Graduate School, the current chair of the Awards Committee, and a past recipient of the award. The award provides funds to support teaching, research, and/or service activities to help tenure-track faculty in their pursuit of tenure.

Social Interaction

Part of the success of any tenure-track faculty member, but more so of junior faculty of color, is to what extent that person feels a part of the culture of the institution. Opp and Smith listed one of the main predictors of minority faculty attrition as the difficulty fitting in socially at a predominantly white institution.[11] The Provost's breakfast and the receptions are part of the campus socialization of these junior faculty of color. It is the intention of the program eventually to include other smaller social events such as evening socials and family gatherings.

Costs

Because this program is entirely voluntary in regards to the program presenters and the coordinator's time, there are no costs for the program, per se. However, the Office of the Provost funds the official social events.

Evaluation

At the end of each program, participants are given evaluation forms to complete; the return rate has been 100 percent. The evaluation forms are brief and ask, "What information was most helpful, least helpful, and if there was any information that was missing?" It has always been the intent that the number of participants not determine the program's success. To be successful in retaining even one minority faculty member, in itself, would be considered a success. However, success can also be determined year-by-year by the retention of each participant as he/she continues at CSU until achieving tenure.

Limitations/Challenges

1. Although the volunteer participant system is a plus, the system can only be successful as the coordinator can keep and generate new volunteers.
2. Scheduling continues to be a challenge. Because these junior faculty of color teach and advise, their schedules are very demanding. The programs average around seven participants per program.
3. The voluntary nature of the administration of this program also has its drawbacks. If the program were institutionalized where the coordination for the program was officially included in someone's job description, then the program could be given more appropriate attention. More programs could be offered each semester and/or programs could be repeated in the same semester.
4. Social events need to be increased, as this was the primary complaint of the participants. That is, they recognized the efforts to retain them through the NewBs official program, but they continue to feel isolated socially on campus and in the community.
5. Probably the biggest challenge is the University counsel's concern that the program is preferential treatment. The Colorado State Attorney General, several years ago, declared affirmative

action as preferential treatment and declared it illegal.[12] Participants of the program believe that the dynamics of the sessions would change, and they would not be as engaging in asking questions and sharing issues alongside their non-minority peers. The Provost's Office is working on this challenge.

CONCLUSION

Whites perceive minority-group members as being treated well, while people of color often recount experiences that convince them they are still "outsiders" and that their status on campus is both marginal and vulnerable.[13]

The crux of the New Beginnings program is to provide a proactive, supportive environment for CSU's junior faculty of color, an environment which eliminates vulnerability and lends itself to the productive success of these faculty members. Minority faculty of color need "a supportive environment of collegiality . . . to create opportunities for success. Social and professional interactions are crucial to a sense of acceptance."[14]

The important conclusion to draw from such a model program is not necessarily developing such a program but the need to understand, address and resolve the issue of minority faculty retention in higher education. Supportive environments can come in various packages.

However, until mostly white institutions of higher education understand that their environmental cultures do not provide level playing fields, then they cannot begin to provide any support mechanisms for their minority junior faculty members. And, those support mechanisms must deal with the feelings of minority isolation and lack of adequate social interaction within the community, campus, individual colleges, and/or departments. Those support mechanisms must also deal with other realities that minority junior faculty face day-to-day in a predominantly white academy, such as the lack of faculty mentors, the constant need to dispel minority faculty stereotypes, and/or the pressure to represent all minorities in many campus settings.

Until there is a noticeable increase in the recruitment and retention of minority teaching and library faculty will there be a noticeable difference in the recruitment and retention of minority students. This increase in college and university minority graduates would then reflect more the changing demographics of the United States. One needs to start somewhere.

The NewBs program is an example of a model program that could serve as a spark that starts the flame of institutional support for the retention of minority faculty. If the academy is the one place from which new ideas, concepts and knowledge emanate, then it ought not to be too difficult to develop other initiatives to address minority faculty retention that fall within the confines of non-preferential treatment.

NOTES

1. Colorado State Advisory Committee to the U.S. Commission on Civil Rights, Denver, *The Retention of Minorities in Colorado Public Institutions of Higher Education: Fort Lewis and Adams State Colleges*, 1995, ERIC, ED409134.

2. Camila A. Alire, "Recruitment and Retention of Librarians of Color," in *Creating the Future*, ed. Sally Reed (Jefferson, North Carolina: McFarland & Co., 1996), 126-43.

3. Ed Wiley, "Mentor Programs Successful in Minority Retention," *Black Issues in Higher Education* 5 (22) (February 1989): 8.

4. Caroline Turner, Samuel Myers, and John Creswell, "Exploring Underrepresentation: The Case of Faculty of Color in the Midwest," *The Journal of Higher Education* 70 (1) (January/February 1999): 27-59.

5. Colorado State University. Office of Budgets and Institutional Analysis. *The Fact Book 1998-1999*, 93 [online] available from http://www.colostate.edu/Depts/OBIA/pdf/fbk/9899/fbk9899.pdf [cited 31 October 2000].

6. Colorado State University supports programs such as Asian/Pacific American Student Services, Black Student Services, El Centro Student Services (Hispanic), and Native American Student Services.

7. Turner et al., "Exploring Underrepresentation"; Helen D. Just, *Minority Retention in Predominantly White Universities and Colleges: The Importance of Creating a Good "Fit,"* 1999, ERIC, ED439641.

8. Deborah Carter, "The Status of Faculty in Community Colleges: What Do We Know?" in *Creating and Maintaining a Diverse Faculty*, eds. William B. Harvey and James Valdez (San Francisco: Jossey-Bass, 1994), 3-18; Karen S. Cockrell, Rosalita D. Mitchell, Julie N. Middleton, and N. Jo Campbell, "The Holmes Scholars Network: A Study of the Holmes Group Initiative for Recruitment and Retention of Minority Faculty," *Journal of Teacher Education* 50 (March-April 1999): 85-93; Turner et al., "Exploring Underrepresentation."

9. Jerry Sue Owens, Frank W. Reis, Kathryn M. Hall, "Bridging the Gap: Recruitment and Retention of Minority Faculty Members," in *Creating and Maintaining a Diverse Faculty*, eds. William B. Harvey and James Valdez (San Francisco: Jossey-Bass, 1994), 59.

10. Jeri Spann and Marian J. Swoboda, "Retaining and Promoting Minority Faculty Members, Problems and Possibilities: A Discussion Paper" (Madison: University of Wisconsin System, 1990).

11. Ronald D. Opp and Albert B. Smith, "Effective Strategies for Enhancing Minority Faculty Recruitment and Retention," in *Creating and Maintaining a Diverse Faculty*, eds. William B. Harvey and James Valdez (San Francisco: Jossey-Bass, 1990), 43-55.

12. There are many references to this announcement in the local media (see "Colleges told to halt Race Based Scholarships," *Denver Rocky Mountain News* 25 December 1995, 4A; "Salazar eyes Preferences," *Denver Rocky Mountain News*, 24 October 1999, 2B; Jeffrey A. Roberts, and Steve Lipsher, "Vote '96: A question of color Affirmative action 'a toe up, not a leg up'" *The Denver Post*, 19 November 1995, A-01.); however, then Attorney General Gale Norton's December 13, 1995 confidential memo was never released publicly, as it is under attorney-client-privilege from her office to the Colorado Commission on Higher Education.

13. Stephen S. Weiner, "Accrediting Bodies Must Require a Commitment to Diversity When Measuring a College's Quality," *The Chronicle of Higher Education*, 10 October 1990, 2.

14. Owens, "Bridging the Gap," 62.

Recruit, Recruit, Recruit:
Organizing Benefits for Employees with Unmarried Families

Polly Thistlethwaite

SUMMARY. This article argues that librarians should work to adopt domestic partner benefits for employees in unmarried same- and opposite-sex couples given the inequities in compensation manifest in their absence. It provides new information about the domestic partner practices of Tier 1 and Tier 2 institutions based on a spring/fall 2000 telephone survey. The article includes an outline of actions to institute domestic partner benefits in university settings. *[Article copies available for a fee from The Haworth Document Delivery Service: 1-800-HAWORTH. E-mail address: <getinfo@haworthpressinc.com> Website: <http://www.HaworthPress.com> © 2001 by The Haworth Press, Inc. All rights reserved.]*

KEYWORDS. Domestic partner benefits, domestic partners, benefits, unmarried partners, same-sex, opposite-sex, higher education, Colorado State University, gay, lesbian, homosexual, civil rights, compensation, human resources, personnel, libraries, activism

---

Polly Thistlethwaite is Coordinator of Instruction and Associate Professor, Colorado State University Libraries, Fort Collins, CO (E-mail: *pthistle@manta.colostate.edu*).

Title inspired by the popular 1990s Lesbian Avengers chant: "Ten percent is not enough-recruit, recruit, recruit!" Alfred Kinsey's 1948 estimate that 10 percent of the male population is more or less exclusively homosexual stands as a classic reference in queer politicking.

[Haworth co-indexing entry note]: "Recruit, Recruit, Recruit: Organizing Benefits for Employees with Unmarried Families." Thistlethwaite, Polly. Co-published simultaneously in *Journal of Library Administration* (The Haworth Information Press, an imprint of The Haworth Press, Inc.) Vol. 33, No. 1/2, 2001, pp. 31-44; and: *Diversity Now: People, Collections, and Services in Academic Libraries* (ed: Teresa Y. Neely, and Kuang-Hwei (Janet) Lee-Smeltzer) The Haworth Information Press, an imprint of The Haworth Press, Inc., 2001, pp. 31-44. Single or multiple copies of this article are available for a fee from The Haworth Document Delivery Service [1-800-HAWORTH, 9:00 a.m. - 5:00 p.m. (EST). E-mail address: getinfo@haworthpressinc. com].

31

I heard my girlfriend's knee pop as she stepped out the door this morning. The sound of her ligaments moving in a way they should not is dreadful enough, but it is all the more frightening in this household because she has no health insurance right now. Luckily, her knee popping sounded worse than it turned out to be. This time. We put ice on it, packed ibuprofen for later, and counted the days 'til her private medical insurance kicked in.

WHAT'S THE ISSUE?

If we were a married heterosexual couple, I could offer my Beloved terrific medical benefits through my job in the library at Colorado State University (CSU). Colorado is one of eleven states (plus the District of Columbia) recognizing common law marriage. Heterosexual couples can march into the CSU Human Resources Office anytime to sign an Affidavit of Common Law marriage immediately after which the staff smile pleasantly and offer them insurance forms to fill out. The CSU employee in that couple then receives tax-free compensation to cover "employee plus one" or "family" benefits if there are children involved. One month later, both parties in that hetero dyad plus either of their offspring are covered by CSU's generous medical and dental benefits. I can get my significant other a library card, because CSU's library "microenvironment" welcomes the partners and families of unmarried employees. But I am denied compensation from my university employer to cover the substantial and increasing costs of my family's medical benefits. The failure of academic employers to extend medical benefits to the domestic partners and families of unmarried employees constitutes disparate and unequal compensation. It is blatant, unapologetic financial discrimination.

WHY SHOULD LIBRARIANS CARE?

Everybody should care, but it is often the case that the normalized, privileged majority in any institution is sadly indifferent to practices that do not operate favorably for marginalized others. Our profession mandates that librarians advocate for equitable treatment for all library employees.[1] Following this professional guideline, librarians must logically embrace a "diversity" inclusive of sexual orientation and marital status and contribute to a professional environment that treats all employees respectfully and equally. In addition, because research is key to successful argument, librarians are in positions critical to university political efforts. Academic librarians, providing lifelines to their campus constituencies, have excellent position and authority, as well as a professional imperative to lead.

Fair, friendly employment practices are essential to fostering diversity and goodwill among employees and staff. And, as an unhappy corollary, unfair employment practices compensating only traditional nuclear families are antithetical to commonplace academic goals fostering institutional diversity. It is often the case that institutions of higher education profess intent to embrace "diversity" as it applies to sexual orientation. There may be laudable mention of sexual orientation in the official lists of discriminations prohibited by the university. Further, there may be sanctions imposed on employees who do harm or harass other employees on account of sexual orientation. Academic institutions are in large part ready to address singular, gross violations against any employee; yet they are less prepared to acknowledge and correct their own institutional role in perpetuating systemic, policy-driven discrimination against an entire class of employees. An institution must practice fair compensation in the form of benefits pay to provide meaningful substance to the assertion that it does not discriminate on the grounds of sexual orientation or marital status. Talking the talk should mean walking the walk.

M-O-N-E-Y

A friend of mine who'd lived a particularly hardscrabble life used to answer her own rhetorical question: "How do I spell 'love?' M-O-N-E-Y." She wasn't always speaking about her employer, but her sentiment is applicable to this argument. Benefits can comprise up to 40 percent of a worker's income-providing more equity percentage-wise for employees in the lower than the upper wage ranges.[2] The benefits pay for a CSU faculty member earning $31,000 annually would total an additional $2591 or 7.2 percent of the base salary-a significant amount of money that can be applied tax-free to a variety of insurance plans covering the employee and family.

Employees with families which do not fit unfortunately narrow definitions of the traditional nuclear family are compensated less (or are eligible for less compensation) than employees with married nuclear families. If any employee's family-say, an employee's significant other of any gender plus dependents of both-is denied inclusion in benefits plans, there is an inequitable compensation structure in operation favoring married heterosexuals and their offspring over unmarried and/or same-sex couples and their offspring. Clearly employers who provide the least judgement and restriction regarding an employee's family structure will be more favorably reviewed by non-traditional employees. Providing benefits only to employees with married heterosexual spouses is bad for recruitment and retention of unmarried gay, lesbian, bisexual, and heterosexual employees with families to support. The failure of academic institutions to provide benefits plans recognizing employees' domestic partners for "spousal" or "family" coverage is unfair and discriminatory, morally proscriptive, and in this day and age, also bad for business.

The number of unmarried, unrelated opposite sex couples living together has nearly tripled since 1980, comprising over 4 percent of all U.S. households.[3] Another 1.7 million households, about 1.6 percent of the U.S. total, are comprised of unrelated couples of the same sex.[4] So, nearly 6 percent of the self-identified "households" in the U.S. are comprised of unmarried, unrelated adults. All members of these households deserve medical coverage just as much as those occupying married households. Arguably, the wealthiest nation on the planet should provide every citizen, regardless of employment status, access to affordable medical care. But, as evidenced by the failure of the health care initiative in President Clinton's first term, this country is not headed immediately in that direction. In the United States during the mid-1990s, employers provided medical insurance for about 61 percent of the population.[5]

Why, in an age of rising health care costs, would some institutions of higher education condemn the families of certain employees to an increasingly costly and uncertain health care environment? The additional cost to an academic organization extending domestic partner benefits to employees is by all reports negligible, less than .5 percent.[6] Part of this low cost reflects the low participation levels in domestic partner plans. Employer-paid benefits offered to unwed and same-sex couples are counted as taxable income to the employee. Married couples are not taxed on this additional income; unmarried adults of any variety are.[7] Given the documented precedent of low cost domestic partnership plans, most universities still withholding the benefit are likely more concerned with political consequences.

University administrators often cite unfavorable or controversial political climates for gays and lesbians as reason enough to forego pursuit of necessary permission to extend domestic partner benefits. CSU administrators currently justify their refusal to pursue the benefit as a decision "good for the university," given their fear that Colorado's conservative legislators might threaten financial punishment for such activity.[8] Stanford University, in contrast, pursued equitable compensation in the early 1990s, despite speculation that there might be some budgetary fallout. Barbara Fried reported Stanford's laudable position regarding same-sex couples in 1994.

> Stanford's mission does not end with narrowly defined tasks of teaching and research. Like most colleges and universities, it has historically (and we believe commendably) perceived part of its role to be a moral force not merely in the education of its students but in society at large. Consistent with that role, it has tried to hold itself to higher ethical standards than might prevail in society in general, often at some political cost . . . Viewed in that light, the bill presents a political opportunity (indeed, some would argue a political obligation), not just a political liability. Again, we think it is instructive to keep in mind how one would view the same question with respect to other forms of discrimination. One imagines, for example, that a decision by Stanford 40 years ago to take the lead in eradicating discrimination against blacks, women, and Jews in admissions, hiring, memberships in sororities and fraternities, etc., would have been politically unpopular with many alumni, as well as with the larger political community. One also imagines that had Stanford taken such a leadership role, few in the Stanford community would look back on that decision now with anything but pride . . .[9]

Recalcitrant or fearful university administrators might alternately be persuaded to institute unmarried partner benefits if they see that they are out-of-step and therefore less competitive with institutional peers. The leaders in higher education are steadily forging ahead on this issue, leaving those failing to extend this benefit in the waning shadow of the secular majority. Assisted by Dani Holveck, an undergraduate student at CSU, the author conducted a telephone survey with personnel office representatives of Tier 1 and Tier 2 academic institutions as defined by *U.S. News & World Report* in August 1999.[10] The survey began in the spring of 2000 and was updated in the fall of 2000. As of November 2000, 72 percent of the Tier 1 institutions-the country's top fifty colleges and universities-offer benefits to the same-sex domestic partners of their employees, or plan to do so in the coming year (see Table 1). Of

TABLE 1. Tier 1 Institutions' Employee Domestic Partner Benefits

Academic Institution	Same Sex Dom. Partner	Opp. Sex Dom. Partner
*+Boston College	no	no
*Brandeis University	yes	no
*Brown University	yes	no ++
*California Institute of Technology	yes	no
*Carnegie Mellon University	yes	no ++
*Case Western Reserve University	yes	no ++
College of William and Mary	no	no
*Columbia University	yes	no
*Cornell University	yes	no
*Dartmouth	yes	no
*+Duke University	yes	no
*Emory University	yes	no
*+Georgetown University	no	no ++
Georgia Institute of Technology	no	no
*Harvard University	yes	no
*Johns Hopkins University	yes	no
*Lehigh University	no	no ++
*Massachusetts Institute of Technology	yes	no
*New York University	yes	no
*Northwestern University	yes	no
Pennsylvania State University	no	no ++
*Princeton University	yes	no
*Rice University	yes	yes ++
*Stanford University	yes	no
*Tufts University	yes	no
*Tulane University	yes	no
University of California-Berkeley	yes	no
University of California-Davis	yes	no
University of California-Irvine	yes	no
University of California-Los Angeles	yes	no
University of California-San Diego	yes	no
University of California-Santa Barbara	yes	no
*University of Chicago	yes	no
University of Florida	no	no
University of Illinois-Urbana-Champaign	no	no
University of Michigan-Ann Arbor	yes	no
Univ. of North Carolina-Chapel Hill	no	no
+University of Notre Dame	no	no
*University of Pennsylvania	yes	no ++
*University of Rochester	yes	no
University of Texas-Austin	no	no ++

Academic Institution	Same Sex Dom. Partner	Opp. Sex Dom. Partner
University of Virginia	no	no
University of Washington	yes	no
University of Wisconsin-Madison	no	no
*University of Southern California	yes	yes
*Vanderbilt University	yes	no
*+Wake Forest University	yes	no
*Washington University	yes	yes
*Yale University	yes	no
*+Yeshiva University	no	no

* Private institution; + Religious affiliation; ++ Common Law Marriage recognized for opposite sex couples. Opposite sex domestic partner benefits here refer to benefits offered to employees in unmarried relationships, without designation of marriage by common law. Eleven states and the District of Columbia recognize common law marriage.

the 14 Tier 1 schools not offering same-sex benefits, 4 have religious affiliations. Twenty-eight of the 32 Tier 1 private institutions compared to only 8 of the 18 public institutions offer same-sex benefits, suggesting that private universities might more readily implement this kind of policy. Any assumption about the relative ease or frequency with which private universities instate domestic partner benefits is challenged when examining Tier 2 institutions, the 70 colleges and universities ranked under the top 50 (see Table 2). Only 29 percent of the private Tier 2 institutions offer same-sex benefits, compared to 35 percent of the Tier 2 public universities.

This survey, summarized in Table 3, indicates that:

1. a characteristic distinguishing leading institutions of higher education from Tier 2 institutions is that they offer employee compensation for same-sex domestic partner benefits; and,
2. leading American educational institutions provide same-sex unmarried couples with partner benefits much more frequently than unmarried opposite-sex couples

Forty-nine percent of the 120 Tier 1 and Tier 2 institutions combined provide benefits compensation covering employee's same-sex partners, while only 8 percent of the Tier 1 and 2 institutions provide benefits for unmarried opposite-sex couples. Robert Anderson reported in 1997 that "the vast majority" of non-university employers providing domestic partner benefits offered them to same- and opposite-sex couples, whereas the majority of university employers offered them only to same-sex couples.[11] This trend follows the argument with most legal traction in the presence of institutional sexual orientation nondiscrimi-

TABLE 2. Tier 2 Institutions' Employee Domestic Partner Benefits

Academic Institution	Same Sex Dom. Partner	Opp. Sex Dom. Partner
*+American University	yes	no ++
Auburn University	no	no ++
*+Baylor University	no	no ++
*Boston University	no	no
*+Brigham Young University	no	no
*+Catholic University of America	no	no ++
*Clark University	yes	no
*Clarkson University	no	no
Clemson University	no	no ++
Colorado School of Mines	no	no ++
Colorado State University	no fac/staff; yes students	no ++ fac/staff; yes students
*+Duquesne University	no	no
Florida State University	no	no
*+Fordham University	no	no
George Washington University	no	no ++
*Illinois Institute of Technology	yes	no
Indiana University-Bloomington	no	no
Iowa State University	yes fac/pro; no staff	no ++
*+Loyola University	no	no
*+Marquette University	no	no
Miami University-Oxford	no	no ++
Michigan State University	yes	no
Michigan Technological University	yes	yes
North Carolina State University-Raleigh	no	no
Ohio State University-Columbus	no	no ++
*Ohio University	no	no ++
*+Pepperdine University	no	no
Purdue University	no	no
*Rensselaer Polytechnic Institute	no	no
Rutgers-New Brunswick	no	no
Rutgers-Newark	no	no
*+Southern Methodist University	no	no ++
*+St. Louis University	no	no
*Stevens Institute of Technology	no	no
SUNY-Albany	yes	yes
SUNY-Binghamton	yes	yes
SUNY-Buffalo	yes	yes
SUNY-Stony Brook	yes	yes
*Syracuse University	yes	no
Texas A&M University-College Station	no	no ++

Academic Institution	Same Sex Dom. Partner	Opp. Sex Dom. Partner
*+Texas Christian University	no	no ++
University of Alabama	no	no ++
University of Arizona	no	no
University of California-Riverside	yes	no
University of California-Santa Cruz	yes	no
University of Colorado-Boulder	no fac/staff; yes students	no ++
University of Connecticut	yes	no
University of Delaware	no	no
*+University of Denver	yes	no ++
University of Georgia	no	no
University of Iowa	yes-some unions no	no ++
University of Kansas	no	no ++
University of Kentucky	no	no
University of Maryland-College Park	no	no
University of Massachusetts-Amherst	no	no
*University of Miami	yes	no
University of Minnesota-Twin Cities	yes	no
University of Missouri-Columbia	no	no
University of Missouri-Rolla	no	no
University of Nebraska-Lincoln	no	no
University of New Hampshire	yes fac/pro; no staff	no
University of Oregon	yes	yes
University of Pittsburgh	no	no ++
*+University of San Diego	no	no ++
University of South Carolina-Columbia	no	no ++
University of Tennessee-Knoxville	no	no
University of Vermont	yes	no
Virginia Tech	no	no
Washington State University	yes	no
*Worcester Polytechnic Institute	yes	yes

* Private institution; + Religious affiliation; ++ Common Law Marriage recognized for opposite sex couples. Opposite sex domestic partner benefits here refer to benefits offered to employees in unmarried relationships, without designation of marriage by common law. Eleven states and the District of Columbia recognize common law marriage.

nation clauses: marriage is available to heterosexuals alone as evidence of a "family" relationship, and no such legitimizing state of union exists for same-sex couples. Therefore, academic employers often feel obliged to offer domestic partner benefits to same-sex couples only based on this group's denied access to the state of matrimony.

American higher education then, like a bully patriarch at a shotgun wedding, displays remarkable near consistency in granting equitable compensation and precious medical benefits to opposite-sex couples only if "properly" married. Any challenge same-sex couples might

TABLE 3. Summary

Institution type (T = Tier)	T 1	T 1 Private	T 1 Public	T 2	T 2 Private	T 2 Public	T 1 + 2	T 1 + 2 Religious Affiliation
Same Sex DP Benefits	36 of 50	28 of 32	8 of 18	23 of 70	7 of 24	16 of 46	59 of 120	4 of 20
	72%	88%	44%	33%	29%	35%	49%	25%
Opp Sex DP Benefits	3 of 50	3 of 32	0 of 18	7 of 70	1 of 24	6 of 46	10 of 120	0 of 20
	6%	10%	0%	10%	4%	13%	8%	0%

present to the legitimizing social force of marriage is near uniformly resisted by the academy in application to opposite-sex couples. This coercive institutional double standard is currently under-protested. Only 10 Tier 1 and Tier 2 institutions offer domestic partner coverage for unmarried same-sex and opposite-sex couples: four campuses of the State University of New York (SUNY), University of Oregon, Michigan Technological University, Rice University, Washington University, Worcester Polytechnic Institute, and the University of Southern California. Anderson's 1997 article predicted legal challenges to higher education's practice of offering same-sex-only domestic partner benefits given that several varieties of employment law prohibit discrimination based on sex.[12] An employee with a same-sex partner meriting compensation denied to an employee with an unmarried opposite-sex partner seems to present a situation ripe for refutation. So far, however, higher education has not been presented with significant policy precedent or legal challenge to reverse the trend towards same-sex only domestic partner benefits compensation practices.

THE ACADEMY AS MORAL ARBITER

Since the mid-1990s, several gay activist groups have focused on obtaining the right for same-sex couples to marry. Gay marriage, the argument goes, is the most direct route to a consequent legion of legal benefits the state of matrimony bestows on its citizens.[13] While it is only fair that same-sex couples should have the same set of social options available to them as opposite-sex couples, marriage is not universally embraced by heterosexuals or homosexuals as a family-forming institution of choice. With a steadily falling rate of marriage and a steadily rising rate of divorce, marriage does not necessarily signal longevity, commitment, stability, or fidelity in a relationship. But never mind that, even. Why should any employer, particularly an academic institution, dictate which employees have relationships and families deserving benefits compensation and which employees do not? Employees should not be penalized or rewarded for the composition of personal lives and families. The business of discriminating "deserving" families from "undeserving" ones is a business the academy should cease immediately, observing well-established academic principles of intellectual and personal freedom.

What might it look like for the academy, for any employer, to quit prescribing marriage as the primary qualification for benefits compensation? By eliminating marriage or a marriage-like same-sex arrangement as a necessary prerequisite for benefits compensation, employers would approach compensatory equity for employees with a diversity of family structures. To be fair within the constraints of employer-based medial insurance, every employee would be welcomed to identify one domestic partner, of married or unmarried relationship to the employee, for benefits coverage. The dependent children of both partners would be covered as well, to provide benefits equitable to married couples. Married and unmarried families of any gender combination then, would receive equal, fair benefits compensation. This type of plan, currently in place in only 10 of the above-mentioned Tier 1 and Tier 2 institutions, is simple, affordable, and fair. It delivers financial equity among married and unmarried same- and opposite-sex families, achieving equal and fair compensation for a range and variety of chosen families. Higher education will do well to widely institute fair, equal compensation practices which recognize the relationships and families of unmarried employees of all sexual orientations as well as it does married heterosexual employees.

HOW TO ORGANIZE FOR DOMESTIC PARTNER BENEFITS

Sadly, efforts to obtain domestic partner benefits at CSU have been unsuccessful so far. What follows, however, is my best sequence of action for obtaining for these benefits, based on research and experience.

1. Do your research. Essential reading includes Robert Anderson's chapter on organizing for domestic partner benefits in *Homo Economics* and the Stanford document by Fried, both cited above. The Lambda Legal Defense Fund assembles current

news relevant to domestic partner benefits.[14] The National Gay and Lesbian Task Force features a helpful manual in PDF file format with legal and strategic advice about domestic partner benefits.[15] Partner's Web site features practical advice for obtaining benefits in the workplace.[16] The Human Rights Campaign (HRC) tends to advocate for "gay marriage" but also features information about domestic partner benefits.[17] The American Association for Single People features helpful information about advocating for all unmarried people.[18] For these and other relevant links, check the author's Special Topics-Domestic Partner Benefits Web page.[19]

2. Find out the current practices at your institution, identify the roadblocks to better benefits, and know the practices at peer institutions and local businesses.

3. Find allies. Organize a group to research and strategize. It is best if all levels of university community-faculty, students, staff-work together to expand the constituency and to provide solid social and political grounding. Tap existing organizations as possible partners (e.g., unions or gay, lesbian, bisexual, transgender faculty-staff-student groups, singles rights advocates). Garner support from all on campus willing to express their support publicly.

4. Establish non-discrimination policies against sexual orientation and marital status in university by-laws. This provides precedence, argument, and legal traction.

5. Make your colleagues informed and your administration accountable. Discuss and publicize your efforts outside your group of immediate supporters. Encourage deans and directors to articulate problems of recruitment and retention to any recalcitrant administration. Indifference and ignorance means complicity with the status quo.

6. Draft and present a proposal for domestic partner benefits to administrative bodies. Publicize this effort to make administrators accountable for their actions.

7. If these do not work, the struggle begins. Publicize the issue in the local and national press. Sometimes national attention will inspire a parochial institution to meet academic standards disrespected by a conservative local polity. Garner student and faculty support. Let your community know where the roadblocks are, and who is responsible for them. Use personal stories to illustrate the inequities and hardships as a result of the lack of medi-

cal benefits. Force obstructionists to articulate and account for themselves in the press on this issue.

8. Exhaust administrative grievance procedures. Publicize the process as you go along.

9. Consider legal recourse. Many civil rights and gay/lesbian rights organizations, evidenced in the Web sites cited above, are willing to assist in these efforts pro-bono. Unions in Connecticut and New Jersey have been instrumental in reaching settlements through grievance proceedings and collective bargaining.

10. Have FUN, using the library as a springboard for activism. Throw parties.

NOTES

1. The Code of Ethics of the American Library Association states, "We treat co-workers and other colleagues with respect, fairness and good faith, and advocate conditions of employment that safeguard the rights and welfare of all employees of our institutions" (Chicago, IL: American Library Association, 1995 [online] available from http://www.ala.org/alaorg/oif/ethics.html [cited 21 November 2000].

2. American Federation of State, County and Municipal Employees, "Achieving Domestic Partner Benefits," *Collective Bargaining Reporter* no. 1 (1999), revised June 2000 [online] available from http://www.afscme.org/wrkplace/cbr199_2.htm.

3. *Statistical Abstract of the United States* (Washington, DC: GPO, 1999), 60, table 68.

4. Bureau of the Census, *Marital Status and Living Arrangements: March 1998* (Washington, DC: U.S. Dept. of Commerce, Bureau of the Census, GPO, 1994), *Current Population Reports, Population Characteristics, Series P20-514* [online] available from http://www.census.gov/prod/99pubs/p20-514u.pdf.

5. Bureau of the Census, *Health Insurance Coverage: 1995* (Washington, DC: Bureau of the Census, March 1996) [online] available from http://www.census.gov/hhes/hlthins/cover95/c95taba.html.

6. Stanford's study that costs rose only about .5% covering same-sex domestic partners. See Barbara Fried, *Domestic Partner Benefits: A Case Study* (Stanford University: College and University Personnel Association, 1994).

7. Liz Pulliam Weston, "Health Plans for Domestic Partner Can Add to Tax Bill" *Los Angeles Times*, 24 September 2000, sec. W1.

8. CSU Vice President to a group of CSU faculty, staff, and students assembled to discuss domestic partner benefits for unmarried employees 23 March 2000.

9. Fried, *Domestic Partner Benefits*.

10. "Best National Universities," *U.S. News & World Report*, 8 August 1999, 88-91.

11. Robert M. Anderson, "Domestic Partner Benefits: A Primer for Gay and Activists," in *Homo Economics: Capitalism, Community, and Lesbian and Gay Life*, eds. Amy Gluckman and Betsy Reed (New York: Routledge, 1997), 249-60.

12. Ibid.

13. Partners Task Force for Gay and Lesbian Couples, "Marriage Benefits List," 2000 [online] available from http://www.buddybuddy.com/mar-list.html [cited 21 November 2000].

14. Lambda Legal Defense Fund, 2000 [online] available from http://www.lambdalegal.org/ [cited 21 November 2000].

15. National Gay and Lesbian Task Force, 2000 [online] available from http://www.ngltf.org/ [cited 21 November 2000].

16. Partner's Task Force for Gay and Lesbian Couples, 2000 [online] available from http://www.buddybuddy.com [cited 21 November 2000].

17. Human Rights Campaign, 2000 [online] available from http://www.hrc.org [cited 21 November 2000].

18. American Association for Single People, (2000) [online] available from http://www.singlesrights.com/dp-info.html [cited 21 November 2000].

19. Gay, Lesbian, Bisexual, Transgender Studies, "Special Topic-Domestic Partner Benefits," (2000) [online] available from http://manta.library.colostate.edu/research/gnl/domparts.html [cited 21 November 2000].

Using Professional Development
as a Retention Tool
for Underrepresented Academic Librarians

Eric Kofi Acree
Sharon K. Epps
Yolanda Gilmore
Charmaine Henriques

SUMMARY. With a slow, steady rise in the number of under-represented individuals entering the profession, academic libraries are challenged to compete for and retain the talents of these individuals as are public libraries, special libraries and school media centers. Libraries that succeed in recruiting must simultaneously focus on retention and promotion. This article will discuss the use of professional development as a retention tool for entry-level, underrepresented librarians. Using the

---

Eric Kofi Acree is Library Instruction Coordinator, University at Buffalo, Oscar A. Silverman Undergraduate Library, Buffalo, NY (E-mail: *acree@acsu.buffalo.edu*).

Sharon K. Epps is Assistant Librarian and Coordinator, Circulation and Reserve, University of Delaware, University of Delaware Library, Newark, DE (E mail: *eppss@udel.edu*).

Yolanda Gilmore is Associate Academic Librarian for Library Outreach, University of Wisconsin-Madison, Memorial Library, Madison, WI (E-mail: *ygilmore@library.wisc.edu*).

Charmaine Henriques is US Federal Documents Librarian, University of Iowa, Government Publications, University of Iowa Library, Iowa City, IA (E-mail: *h-henriques@uiowa.edu*).

[Haworth co-indexing entry note]: "Using Professional Development as a Retention Tool for Underrepresented Academic Librarians." Acree, Eric Kofi et al. Co-published simultaneously in *Journal of Library Administration* (The Haworth Information Press, an imprint of The Haworth Press, Inc.) Vol. 33, No. 1/2, 2001, pp. 45-61; and: *Diversity Now: People, Collections, and Services in Academic Libraries* (ed: Teresa Y. Neely, and Kuang-Hwei (Janet) Lee-Smeltzer) The Haworth Information Press, an imprint of The Haworth Press, Inc., 2001, pp. 45-61. Single or multiple copies of this article are available for a fee from The Haworth Document Delivery Service [1-800-HAWORTH, 9:00 a.m. - 5:00 p.m. (EST). E-mail address: getinfo@haworth pressinc.com].

45

1998 University of Minnesota Training Institute for Library Science Interns and Residents as a model, attitudes, skills, training and technology necessary to foster career advancement will be identified. The article will also identify potential external barriers to advancement and suggest ways to eliminate or reduce these barriers. It does not suggest that underrepresented librarians require a different or separate standard, but rather that they must meet the professional requirements made of all librarians while also dealing with such thorny issues as race, inequality, concrete walls, and hostile environments. *[Article copies available for a fee from The Haworth Document Delivery Service: 1-800-HAWORTH. E-mail address: <getinfo@haworthpressinc.com> Website: <http://www.HaworthPress. com>* © *2001 by The Haworth Press, Inc. All rights reserved.]*

KEYWORDS. Recruitment and retention, professional development, underrepresented, minorities, diversity, multicultural, University of Minnesota Training Institute for Library Science Interns and Residents

INTRODUCTION

For most librarians, professional development is a key component in their ongoing effort to maintain employment and enhance careers. This article will address professional development as a retention tool for entry-level underrepresented librarians. It will use the 1998 University of Minnesota Training Institute (Institute) for Library Science Interns and Residents as a model, which speaks directly to the issue of professional development. The authors of this essay were among the participants in the Institute.

For many minorities in the library profession the glass ceiling or early plateauing creates a cycle of frustration. Feeling marginalized and unable to move ahead, many minorities leave the profession altogether.[1] Members from underrepresented groups take special notice of the important role professional development plays in their ongoing efforts to advance in the profession. Library literature suggests that there is a challenge in recruiting underrepresented populations into the profession.[2] In addition, evidence reveals that there is a lack of movement beyond entry-level positions, and problems exist with retaining underrepresented members once they enter the profession. In an article that appeared in the winter 1999 issue of *Library Administration & Management*, Joan Howland states: "At the heart of the issue of building a more inclusive profession, however, is the retention and promotion of librarians from diverse backgrounds."[3] She points out that for minorities, the problem does not rest at getting hired, but continues after minorities gain entrance into the profession, and their potential and skills are not fully realized. Howland concludes that this is especially true of the middle management and leadership positions.[4] In other words, there is a serious lack of diversity beyond entry-level positions.

RECRUITMENT AND RETENTION OF MINORITIES IN LIBRARIES

Literature Review

As early as the 1970s, minority recruitment was gaining momentum as a major concern for the library profession and the American Library Association (ALA). Ann Knight Randall points to the 1971 and 1988 pre-conferences on recruitment of minorities sponsored by the Office of Library Personnel Resources Advisory Committee as evidence of this gaining momentum.[5] In January 1990, at the ALA midwinter conference, the Association of College and Research Libraries (ACRL) Task Force on Recruitment of Underrepresented Minorities presented a report and action plan titled "Recruiting the Underrepresented to Academic Libraries: Opportunities and Challenges."[6] In July 2000, the ACRL committee on Racial and Ethnic Diversity sponsored a session at the ALA annual conference titled "Sharing Strategies for Achieving Diversity: Identifying and Increasing the Recruitment and Retention of Under-represented Librarians."[7] This is evidence that recruitment of minorities continues to be an issue of great importance to the library profession. However, Randall stresses that "While there has been a growing awareness of the urgency of the issues since 1971 and some successful programs of recruitment implemented, the percentages of minority professionals working in U.S. libraries and the percentages of minority students selecting librarianship as a career are insufficient."[8] Patricia Robles reports that in spite of the call for action over the years to remedy the situation, and the strides accomplished, the number of minority librarians remains low.[9]

Robles points to the ALA's Office of Library Personnel Resources (OLPR) 1995-96 report as evidence which indicates that in spite of recruitment efforts to bring people of color into the profession, it is still predominantly white. The statistics show that the library profession consists of 90.1 percent white, 3.8 percent black, 3.85 percent Asian/Pacific Islander, 2.6 percent Hispanic, and .4 percent American Indian/Alaskan Native.[10] The number is also low for minority students graduating from library school. Kathleen de la Peña McCook and Kate Lippincott,[11] in a follow-up to a previous study by McCook and Paula Geist,[12] report that new minority graduates from programs accredited by the ALA have grown from 178 (6.79% of total graduates) in 1985 to 434 (10.01%) in 1995.[13] In their report, they suggest that all minorities but Asian/Pacific Islanders remain significantly underrepresented among 1995 graduates relative to their population at large.[14] These reports suggest that despite its commitment to diversifying ranks, the library and information science profession has failed to do so.

America is bracing for the changes anticipated from the now well-chronicled demographic trends. Gregory Reese and Ernestine Hawkins provide an overview of the changing face of America and its workforce. By the year 2000, 80 percent of the U.S. workforce will be minorities, women, and immigrants from other countries. By the year 2010, white males will account for less than 40 percent of the total American workforce. Women and people of color will fill 75 percent of the 24 million new jobs created in the United States.[15]

By the year 2020, the number of U.S. residents who are Hispanic or non-white will have more than doubled to nearly 115 million. By 2058, the "average" U.S. resident will trace his or her ancestral roots to one of the present minority groups and not to white Europeans. "Educating, training, and managing this increased workforce diversity is already posing a tremendous challenge for educational institutions as well as other governmental, industrial, and major business organizations throughout the United States."[16]

Changing demographics will force more and more Americans to interact with people from backgrounds and cultures different from their own. This should signal that there is a need to increase the number of minority librarians.[17] Randall stresses, "While there are geographical differences in population growth rates among the racial and ethnic groups, the pattern of an emerging multicultural society increasingly minority in character, especially in urban areas, is apparent. The need is great for a larger number of minority teachers, librarians, and other professionals to reflect the changing demographic makeup of our society."[18] E. J. Josey points to an even more compelling reason to recruit minorities to the profession:

Since minorities will constitute a major segment of the workforce and will contribute substantially to the economic well-being of the nation, the United States government must be certain that its minority population receives a quality education and is guaranteed access to library and information resources. Further, the minorities of this country must have the knowledge and skills to use the new technologies in the workplace as well as in every aspect of their lives. The nation cannot afford to ignore the education, training and library needs of its minorities.[19]

Em Claire Knowles and Linda Jolivet reinforce this concept:

It can be surmised that since these racial and ethnic groups are growing at a faster rate than the population as a whole, these "emerging populations" will be replacing the nation's workforce. People of color need to be trained in the library and information profession, not to serve only their own communities but to serve all communities. Librarians of color are crucial to the provision of services in communities where knowledge of the language, the values, and the cultural heritage of the growing racial and ethnic minority communities is imperative.[20]

The diversity that people from underrepresented groups bring to the workplace creates a stronger workforce and better work environment.

When it comes to the recruitment and retention of underrepresented members in the workplace, some special concerns should be noted. In the book *Cultural Diversity in Libraries*, Lucy Cohen provides a solid framework which addresses what should be taking place in the recruitment and retention process for underrepresented groups in the workplace. For starters, she states that it is important for hiring supervisors to be educated about non-discrimination and affirmative action policies.[21] Supervisors and managers should understand the "big picture," which is the building of a diverse multicultural workforce. Supervisors also need to examine their own personal values and racial biases. This would include not only personal issues around racism, but institutional racism as well. In *Two Nations: Black and White, Separate, Hostile, Unequal*, Andrew Hacker points to the legacy in American society of racism, and how there are two separate and unequal Americas.[22] We can look at how Hacker defines race relations among blacks and whites as an example when looking at the way white supremacy functions. In the opening chapter Hacker writes, "America is inherently a 'White' country: in character, in structure, in culture. Needless to say, Black Americans create lives of their own. Yet, as people, they face boundaries and constrictions set by White majority."[23] So it should not be surprising that one would find racism within American libraries. Evan St. Lifer and Corinne Nelson published the results of a survey in *Library Journal*, which in part pointed out how minority librarians and white librarians in general differ in their depiction of race relations in libraries. Minority librarians surveyed reported that racism in the library profession was just as prevalent as in the larger society. On the other hand, whites by and large believed that racism in librarianship was less prevalent.[24]

Suggested Strategies

Strategies that can be used to cope with racism and the recruitment and retention of minority librarians include institutions having clear goals and objectives of how they want to pursue diversity.[25] We suggest that questions should include how much time, effort, and money is going into supporting these goals and objectives. For example, is the position description written in a way that would welcome those from diverse backgrounds? What can be done to increase minority applicants in the pool? Does the workplace climate support diversity? If not, what measures are going to be undertaken to address it? Is there staff development training which will educate staff members to the importance of having a diverse work force? When people of color are in place and excel in their jobs, are there plans and mechanisms to promote them? Is there a mentoring program for people of color? All of these issues need to be addressed when trying to achieve a diverse workplace. The University of Minnesota Libraries Training Institute for Library Science Interns and Residents directly addressed many of these questions.

THE MINNESOTA MODEL

Armed with a commitment to diversity, the University of Minnesota Libraries Human Resource Director and Assistant University Librarian set out to create a new and innovative program that would produce a community of support and give professional training to early career librarians from underrepresented groups. Under this principle the Training Institute for Library Science Interns and Residents was born.

The Institute was developed around two tracks: technology training that would familiarize early career librarians with the latest in multimedia applications to give them an edge in using modern technological advances; and a leadership skills component that would allow the librarians to develop personally and rise through the ranks of librarianship professionally. The actual planning and development of an innovative program such as this from the ground up was the most difficult aspect of this endeavor with no established model to follow. An HEA 11-B grant secured funding from the United States Department of Education. With the support of the University Librarian and the aid of staff from varying departments on campus such as the Digital Media Center, the University of Minnesota Libraries, and the Academic Distributed Computing Services (ADCS), an event that had the capability of changing the professional and personal lives of twenty individuals came to fruition.

Program Goals/Objectives

The purpose of the Institute was to:

- increase self awareness and comprehension of behavior in a large organization and furnish training in management, leadership, and decision-making skills;
- train participants in the development of multimedia projects and the use of new technologies across multiple platforms;
- develop a community of peers with similar experience where members could rely on each other for support, encouragement, and networking; and,
- give participants the opportunity to create a multimedia project, which could be implemented at their own institutions.[26]

The Institute

The Institute took place July 11 through 17, 1998. There were twenty participants from 15 different institutions in the United States and Canada. Participants were given quarters in dormitories on campus and provided with breakfast each morning. Each participant was responsible for obtaining release time from their home institutions, and initial transportation to and from the Institute was reimbursable up to $500.00. Participants were required to be from underrepresented groups. African Americans, Asians, and Hispanics made up the underrepresented groups. Participants were required to have a master's degree in library science from an ALA accredited program or foreign equivalent. Participants were also required to have no more than three years professional experience, and to have taken part in an internship or residency program at an academic institution. Finally, participants needed to bring a multimedia project that could be worked on during the Institute and submit an essay explaining why they wanted to attend the Institute.

Leadership Workshop

The leadership workshop was facilitated by staff from the Association of Research Libraries Office of Leadership and Management Services (ARL/OLMS) and ARL's Office of Diversity. The aim of the leadership component of the Institute was to give early career librarians a starting point in developing leadership skills. Participants were given reading assignments on such topics as building success through teamwork, creative problem solving, interpersonal skills and leadership's new role.

Instruments such as the *Personal Effectiveness Inventory* and the *Change Style Indicator* were used to show participants their individual strengths and weaknesses, and to make them aware of their individual preferences regarding change.[27]

Multimedia Workshop

Part of the agenda of the Institute was to introduce the participants to and increase their knowledge in the use of new technologies across multiple platforms. To achieve this goal, participants were given Zip drives and PageMill software and took part in seminars and hands-on training sessions to develop skills in copyright, Power Point and the multimedia development process, scanning and PhotoShop basics, digital audio and video basics, HTML and PageMill basics, and presentation on the Web. All sessions and seminars were taught by staff members from the Digital Media Center, a unit that provides technical assistance in the development of multimedia applications, the University of Minnesota Libraries, and the ADCS. The training sessions took place in ADCS training laboratories. The Digital Media Center and ADCS are divisions of the University of Minnesota's Office of Information Technology.

University of Minnesota Model-Reflections

The Institute kept all participants on a rapid pace each day. All participants were required to attend leadership and technology training during the day, with the evenings set aside for computer labs which were reserved for the participants to work on their individual projects. The material covered at each session was overwhelming. Ideally, if the Institute had been longer, the participants would have had the opportunity to spend more time processing the information they received. This was especially true in regards to the leadership training.

The technology training was taught at a beginner's level. This was counterproductive for the participants with advanced skills. It was difficult for the trainers to fully address the needs of the novice, intermediate, and advanced participants all in one setting. More lab time was needed to put the skills that the participants were developing into practice. It would have been more advantageous to have small multimedia group projects that could have been completed by the end of the training session. This would also have given participants the opportunity to work collaboratively together.

The multimedia and leadership training sessions did allow for the participants to bond. In fact, during the leadership training, the participants were encouraged to maintain connections after the completion of the Institute. Before the week-long training session ended, participants of the Institute realized the importance of networking, collaboration, and the need to build a community of support. During those last days of the Institute there was discussion about how to remain in contact. The Institute set up a listserv for the group to prepare for the week-long training institute, but the group decided to set up its own as a means to continue networking and collaboration. One of the participants volunteered to set up the listserv. Once all of the participants returned to their own institutions, communication started through the newly formed listserv. After much e-mail discussion, the group agreed to refer to itself as the University of Minnesota Caucus for Emerging Library Leaders or UMN-CELL.

In addition to the establishment of UMN-CELL, the Institute provided a nurturing environment of professional development, support, and encouragement which has continued long after the residents said their farewells. Since the Institute, the accomplishments of the participants can be found in the arenas of publishing, presentations, conferencing, networking, and peer support. Many of the participants contributed essays to *Diversity in Libraries: Academic Residency Programs*, which was co-edited by one of the participants.[28] Other examples of collaboration include contributing to an issue of *Leading Ideas*, an ARL publication, which highlighted the Institute;[29] presenting at the national ACRL 1999 conference; and developing and maintaining a Web site.

Another benefit that the Institute participants enjoy is networking and being able to connect professionally and socially at various conferences. For example, it is very helpful to have participants, who are now ALA committee members, nominate other participants for committee work. One tremendous benefit is having the listserv where ideas about librarianship, employment opportunities, conference information, and that much needed comic relief is shared.

University of Minnesota Model Update

Plans are underway to hold the Institute during alternate years. The 2000 University of Minnesota Libraries Institute was funded through a National Leadership Grant from the Institute of Museum and Library Service. The Institute has also changed its name to the Training Institute for Early Career Librarians. As the name suggests, it is no longer limited to just library science interns and residents, but the focus will still be on minorities.

Future Recommendations

The process of attracting people of color and bringing more minorities into the workforce must be an ongoing collaborative effort that is supported by the profession as a whole. Camila Alire points out that we are all in this together.

> Library practitioners must accept the responsibility of identifying minorities and mentoring them into the library and information science profession. Library education must assume the responsibility of recruiting minority students and retaining them throughout the degree program. Once librarians of color become practitioners, then it is the responsibility of seasoned professionals to help retain them for the profession. All of us in this profession have an important role to play in the recruitment and retention effort.[30]

Knowles and Jolivet emphasize that the relationship among librarians, library managers, and library educators must become one of trust. It is essential that mutual, respectful liaisons be constructed among these partners. Strategies for minority recruitment will not be successful unless today's librarians and library managers come to recognize the issue of minority recruitment as a common community concern.[31]

Robles stresses that early recruitment is the key. "Whether it is the ALA parent organization, library schools, librarian associations, or the individual librarian, the library profession must aggressively initiate and emphasize minority recruitment efforts earlier, specifically at elementary and high school grades, and not as college undergraduates or graduate-level students."[32]

So what can the profession do to successfully recruit minorities to the profession? Some successful recruitment strategies and models mentioned in the library literature include recruiting at the high school level,[33] having mentors for early librarians and providing funding opportunities for minorities in library school.[34]

Recruiting at the High School Level

The stereotypical image of librarians is still an obstacle to recruiting young people to the profession. Sterling confirms this fact by looking into the type of things that are important to them and comparing this with what library science has to offer. "Today's youth want to be in powerful positions that will not only garner them high salaries and prestige, but will also enable them to affect [sic] positive change in our society. The library/information science profession is not viewed as a viable means of transforming our world."[35] Reese and Hawkins contend that we need to spread the word about the library profession. "We need to target outreach programs to the full range of the population, starting with junior high and high school students. Library professionals of all ethnic backgrounds must visit high schools across the country with large minority enrollments. Many students are still impressed with visitors who represent an organization and are professionally attired."[36] We call upon ALA to sponsor a National Teen Library Association of America and recognize states that sponsor such associations. The authors suggest that the Young Adult Library Services Association (YALSA) could serve as a liaison for ALA and state teen associations. Mouton and Johnson provide two teens' perspectives as members of the Louisiana Teen-age Librarians' Association. The teens were invited to speak at the YALSA program during ALA's 1993 annual conference, where they shared their experiences participating in school and public library programs. "We are convinced that recruitment must begin at the pre-kindergarten level and continue through high school and beyond."[37]

Another important role in recruiting high school students to librarianship can be undertaken by academic libraries. Thompson and Rhodes point to the fact that academic libraries that allow access by the general public are often used extensively by high school students. These high school students are potential sources of new students for an academic institution. A positive library experience can reinforce positive opinions about the entire institution and the library profession as well.[38]

Library School

E. J. Josey contends that "recruiting students and faculty of color is not enough if the library and information science education programs are truly to embrace cultural diversity. There must be a support system that makes students of color feel that they are wanted and they are at home within the university environment."[39] Camila Alire points to the fact that in most minority groups, the family is the most important cultural characteristic. Motivation for minority students is most often rooted in the culture of their families. Library schools that can demonstrate that they have some type of support system in place for minority students are more likely to be successful in minority recruitment.[40] Khafre K. Abif reinforces this assertion: "Whatever success I have enjoyed to date in this profession is due, in part, to the development of strong and lasting mentoring relationships, which began even before I enrolled in library school."[41]

Sterling points to several successful mentorship programs which pair practicing library professionals with students entering library school. One such program is the Undergraduate Student Internship Program (USIP) at the University of California, San Diego. The California Librarians Black Caucus of Greater Los Angeles and the University of California, Los Angeles (UCLA) library school developed a recruitment and mentoring program targeting African Americans. The REFORMA/UCLA Mentor Program[42] has been very successful in increasing the number of Latinos in the professional ranks.[43]

The successful recruitment, retention, and graduation of minority students also depends on greater sums of money being identified. Randall asserts, "Perhaps the key factor in the success rate of recruiting racial and ethnic minorities into library and information science programs is the degree to which financial aid is available, including job opportunities for graduate library school students."[44]

One of the most ambitious minority recruitment programs undertaken by the ALA is the Spectrum Initiative. The association will spend

$1.3 million over three years to provide fifty annual scholarships of $5,000 each to minority students who pursue graduate library studies. The initiative also calls for an annual leadership development institute that would bring library leaders together with scholarship recipients and mid-career minority librarians. Although ALA is experiencing success with its Spectrum Initiative, the overall success of any newly instituted program is difficult to measure. It will be well worth studying the impact such programs will have on increasing diversity in the library and information science professional ranks in the coming years.

The ARL Initiative to Recruit a Diverse Workforce offers $2,500 per academic year, renewable up to two years, to exemplary master of library science students from underrepresented groups. With these stipends, ARL provides promising future librarians with an extra incentive to complete library school and join the staff of an ARL library upon graduation. Recipients are mentored by an established leader in the academic and research library community, attend a professional development institute, and upon graduation choose a position at a member library contributing to this program to begin their career as a librarian.[45]

Post-MLS

Diaz and Tellman point to strategies used by ARL libraries to insure that persons from underrepresented groups are included in candidate pools. Such methods include targeted mailings and invitation letters when positions are announced, maintaining a database of potential candidates, posting announcements on electronic lists with large minority participation, placing advertisements in publications with diverse audiences, using directories of professional ethnic caucuses, and making contacts at conferences.[46]

In September 1990, a SPEC-Kit survey of ARL libraries on minority recruitment and retention of professionals from underrepresented groups yielded several strategies and/or activities for the recruitment of minorities to professional positions. Those mentioned included targeting minority librarians for available positions, sharing position announcements with library schools that have high minority enrollment, recruiting at library schools, advertising vacant positions as entry-level positions so that extensive library experience is not a pre-requisite for hiring, removing extraneous qualifications from the job description, developing promotional materials that highlight employment opportunities within the library for minorities, establishing relationships with higher education institutions with significant minority enrollments, and establishing practicums or cooperative education programs.[47]

Post-MLS residency programs is another strategy utilized by academic libraries to recruit highly talented minority graduates from library education programs and to prepare them for accelerated careers in academic and research libraries. Brewer examines post-master's residency programs from the perspective of former residents.[48] She asserts that residency programs provide opportunities for new graduates to gain substantial professional experience and accelerated training at the beginning of their careers, which generally is not available in traditional entry-level positions. Residency programs are valuable recruitment tools that provide positive career development opportunities for new library professionals.

CONCLUSION

What is truly amazing about the University of Minnesota Libraries Training Institute for Library Science Interns and Residents is that it is a very unique program. Never before have participants of ARL minority residency programs had the opportunity to come together in one setting. Participants were able to form lasting bonds and continue to provide support and encouragement to each other as they progress in the field of librarianship. Professional development programs similar to the Training Institute are one of the weapons that can be used in the battle to retain librarians of color within the profession. The Institute provided an opportunity for new librarians in the profession to interact with others who have similar goals and ambitions. Furthermore, it gives hope that there is a way to cope in an environment which may not have an understanding of the ongoing efforts needed for minority librarians to maintain employment and enhance their careers.

NOTES

1. ACRL Task Force on Recruitment of Underrepresented Minorities, "Recruiting the Underrepresented to Academic Libraries," *College & Research Libraries News* 51, no. 11 (December 1990): 1020.

2. Joan Howland, "Beyond Recruitment: Retention and Promotion Strategies to Ensure Diversity and Success," *Library Administration & Management*, no. 1 (winter 1999): 4-13.

3. Ibid.

4. Ibid.

5. Ann Knight Randall, "Minority Recruitment in Librarianship," in *Librarians for the New Millennium*, ed. William E. Moen and Kathleen M. Heim (Chicago: American Library Association, Office for Library and Personnel Resources, 1988), 11-25.

6. Howland, "Beyond Recruitment," 4.

7. American Library Association, *Official Program ALA Annual Conference Chicago 2000: Libraries Build Community* (Chicago: American Library Association, 2000), 199.

8. Randall, "Minority Recruitment in Librarianship," 11.

9. Patricia Robles, "Recruiting the Minority Librarian," *College & Research Libraries News* 59, no. 10 (November 1998): 779-80.

10. Ibid.

11. Kathleen de la Peña McCook and Kate Lippincott, "Library Schools and Diversity: Who Makes the Grade?" *Library Journal* 122, no. 7 (15 April 1997): 30-2.

12. Kathleen de la Peña McCook and Paula Geist, "Diversity deferred: Where are the minority librarians?" *Library Journal* 118 (1 November 1993): 35-8.

13. Ibid., 30.

14. Ibid.

15. Gregory L. Reese and Ernestine L. Hawkins, *Stop Talking Start Doing! Attracting People of Color to the Library Profession* (Chicago: American Library Association, 1999).

16. Ibid., 3.

17. Joyce C. Wright, "Recruitment and Retention of Minorities in Academic Libraries: A Plan of Action for the 1990s," in *Educating Black Librarians*, ed. Benjamin F. Speller, Jr. (Jefferson, NC: McFarland & Company, Inc., 1991), 75-83.

18. Randall, "Minority Recruitment in Librarianship," 12.

19. E. J. Josey, "The Challenges of Cultural Diversity in the Recruitment of Faculty and Students from Diverse Backgrounds," *Journal of Education for Library and Information Science* 34 (fall 1993): 302-11.

20. Em Claire Knowles and Linda Jolivet, "Recruiting the Underrepresented: Collaborative Efforts Between Library Educators and Library Practitioners," *Library Administration & Management* 5 (fall 1991): 189-93.

21. Lucy R. Cohen, "Recruitment and Retention," in *Cultural Diversity in Libraries*, ed. Donald E. Riggs and Patricia A. Tarin (New York: Neal-Schuman Publishers, Inc., 1994).

22. Andrew Hacker, *Two Nations: Black and White, Separate, Hostile, Unequal* (New York: Ballantine Books, 1992).

23. Ibid.

24. Evan St. Lifer and Corinne Nelson, "Unequal Opportunities: Race Does Matter," *Library Journal* 122, no. 18 (November 1997): 42-6.

25. Wright, "Recruitment and Retention of Minorities in Academic Libraries," 76.

26. University of Minnesota, "Program Objectives," (7 December 1999) [online] available from http://www.lib.umn.edu/about/res_institute/Progobjectives.html [cited 22 December 2000].

27. W. Christopher Musselwhite and Robyn Ingram, *Change Style Indicator: Style Guide* (San Francisco: Jossey-Bass, 1998).

28. Raquel Cogell and Cindy A. Gruwell, eds., *Diversity in Libraries: Academic Residency Programs* (Westport, CT: Greenwood Publishing Group, 2001).

29. Eric Acree et al., "UMN Technology and Leadership Training Institute," *Leading Ideas: Issues and Trends in Diversity, Leadership and Career Development* 5 (December 1998) [online] available from http://www.arl.org/diversity/leading/issue5/umn.html [cited 20 December 2000].

30. Camila A. Alire, "Recruitment and Retention of Librarians of Color," in *Creating the Future*, ed. Sally Gardner Reed (Jefferson, NC: McFarland & Company, Inc., 1996), 134.

31. Knowles and Jolivet, "Recruiting the Underrepresented," 192.

32. Robles, "Recruiting the Minority Librarian," 779.

33. Reese and Hawkins, *Stop Talking Start Doing!* 61.

34. Joyce C. Wright, "Recruitment of Minorities by Academic Libraries: An Overview," in *Culture Keepers: Enlightening and Empowering Our Communities: Proceedings of the First National Conference of African American Librarians, September 4-6, 1992, Columbus, Ohio*, ed. Stanton F. Biddle and Members of the BCALA NCAAL Conference Proceedings Committee (Newark, NJ: Black Caucus of the American Library Association, 1993), 186-89.

35. Stephanie L. Sterling, "Recruiting Minorities for Librarianship: Issues and Strategies Revisited," in *Culture Keepers: Enlightening and Empowering Our Communities: Proceedings of the First National Conference of African American Librarians, September 4-6, 1992, Columbus, Ohio*, ed. Stanton F. Biddle and Members of the BCALA NCAAL Conference Proceedings Committee (Newark, NJ: Black Caucus of the American Library Association, 1993), 182-85.

36. Reese and Hawkins, *Stop Talking Start Doing!*

37. Evet Mouton and Keia Johnson, "Recruitment and the Future of Libraries: Two Teens' Perspective," *LLA Bulletin* 56 (1993): 119.

38. Ronelle K. H. Thompson and Glenda T. Rhodes, "Recruitment: A Role for the Academic Library? Creating a Good Impression for Visiting High School Students," *College & Research Libraries News* 47, no. 9 (October 1986): 575-77.

39. Josey, "The Challenges of Cultural Diversity," 308.

40. Camila Alire, "It Takes a Family to Graduate a Minority Library Professional," *American Libraries* 28 (November 1997): 41.

41. Khafre K. Abif, "A Commitment to Mentoring," *American Libraries* 30, no. 3 (March 1999): 60.

42. REFORMA, the National Association to Promote Library Services to the Spanish Speaking, was established in 1971. See Patrick Jose Dawson, "The History and Role of REFORMA," in *Latino Librarianship*, ed. Salvador Guerena (Jefferson, NC: McFarland & Company, Inc., 1990), 121.

43. Sterling, "Recruiting Minorities for Librarianship," 185. For additional background information see also Tami Echavarria, "More Minority Librarians: A Recipe for Success," *Library Personnel News* 5, no. 1 (1991): 2, 4; Tami Echavarria, "Minority Recruitment: A Success Story," *College & Research Libraries News* 51, no. 10 (November 1990): 962-64; "Recruitment and Mentoring Programs for African-Americans Developed in California," *College & Research Libraries News* 52, no. 10 (November 1991): 650; Graceanne A. DeCandido, "Mentor Program to Recruit Hispanics to Librarianship Grows at UCLA," *Library Journal* 113 (September 1988): 108.

44. Randall, "Minority Recruitment in Librarianship," 17.

45. Association of Research Libraries, "ARL Initiative to Recruit a Diverse Workforce," [online] available from http://www.arl.org/diversity/init/index.html [cited 20 February 2001].

46. Joseph R. Diaz and Jennalyn Tellman in collaboration with DeEtta Jones, "Affirmative Action in ARL Libraries," *Spec Kit* 230 (Washington: Association of Research Libraries, June 1998), 1-2.

47. Janice Burrows, Kriza A. Jennings, and C. Brigid Welch, "Minority Recruitment and Retention in ARL Libraries," *Spec Kit* 167 (Washington; Association of Research Libraries, September 1990), 1-2.

48. Julie Brewer, "Post-master's Residency Programs: Enhancing the Development of New Professionals and Minority Recruitment in Academic and Research Libraries," *College & Research Libraries* 58 (November 1997): 528-37.

Effective Retention Strategies for Diverse Employees

Linda R. Musser

SUMMARY. Retention of diverse staff is an often stated goal but frequently takes a back seat to recruitment efforts. One reason for this is a lack of understanding of the factors that influence employees to stay in an organization. Methods to determine why employees leave or stay are discussed as well as the retention tools that work best to retain diverse employees. These tools include mentoring, networking, career and learning opportunities, a balance between work and home life, a welcoming climate, and support for research. *[Article copies available for a fee from The Haworth Document Delivery Service: 1-800-HAWORTH. E-mail address: <getinfo@haworthpressinc.com> Website: <http://www.HaworthPress.com> © 2001 by The Haworth Press, Inc. All rights reserved.]*

KEYWORDS. Retention, diversity, women, minorities

INTRODUCTION

There is much concern about recruitment and retention of diverse employees but usually the focus is on the former with little or no discussion of the latter. Seventy-seven percent of organizations in a recent

Linda R. Musser is Head, Earth and Mineral Sciences Library, The Pennsylvania State University, University Park, PA (E-mail: *Lrm4@psu.edu*).

[Haworth co-indexing entry note]: "Effective Retention Strategies for Diverse Employees." Musser, Linda R. Co-published simultaneously in *Journal of Library Administration* (The Haworth Information Press, an imprint of The Haworth Press, Inc.) Vol. 33, No. 1/2, 2001, pp. 63-72; and: *Diversity Now: People, Collections, and Services in Academic Libraries* (ed: Teresa Y. Neely, and Kuang-Hwei (Janet) Lee-Smeltzer) The Haworth Information Press, an imprint of The Haworth Press, Inc., 2001, pp. 63-72. Single or multiple copies of this article are available for a fee from The Haworth Document Delivery Service [1-800-HAWORTH, 9:00 a.m. - 5:00 p.m. (EST). E-mail address: getinfo@haworthpressinc.com].

study stated that recruitment and retention of a diverse workforce was a high priority but less than ten percent had professional development or mentoring programs.[1] A survey by Winston and Li found that fifty-one percent of libraries surveyed had made no specific efforts related to retention.[2] These statistics speak for themselves. Why is retention so often overlooked? One possibility is that retention is an ongoing process requiring continuous and sustained effort rather than a periodic activity. It requires a sustained organizational commitment, not easily achieved by a task force or search committee. Commensurately, costs for retention programs are ongoing and may be harder to predict than recruitment costs. Another factor contributing to the lower profile of retention is lack of good data documenting its influence. In many organizations there is no clear understanding of the factors that influence employees to stay in an organization. This lack of understanding encourages a false sense that everything is copacetic and improvements are not needed or possible. These factors are the focus of this article.

MEASURING RETENTION

The Dean of the Pennsylvania State (Penn State) University Libraries formed a task force in 1998 to examine issues and recommend methods to improve recruitment and retention of underrepresented groups in the University Libraries workforce. Upon commencement of its investigations, the task force encountered data problems almost immediately. There was a significant lack of good data and the data available were very limited in scope, quality, and time period covered. For example, although Penn State has conducted exit interviews for faculty and staff for some time, until recently there was no systematic reporting required and little standardization for the interviews. Basic statistics on the numbers of employees categorized by ethnicity, gender and employment status were available but were scattered among different reports and contained many footnotes documenting changes in counting practices over time. Similar numbers for other academic units were difficult to obtain, reducing the opportunities for comparisons across units.

An exit survey by nature comes into play when retention efforts have failed. Nonetheless, a "well-designed" survey can provide useful information to assist in future retention efforts. Note the emphasis on well-designed. It is not enough to ask where people are going-to a promotion, to a better paying job, etc. A good survey needs to ask why the person started looking! Also key is to make certain the survey instrument is widely used across all units in the organization and, ideally, in other similar organizations as well. The availability of broad survey data across organizations would allow for benchmarking and identification of developing trends. Continuous use is also important in order to build longitudinal data. Unfortunately, according to Winston and Li's survey of liberal arts college libraries, less than three percent of these libraries make use of exit surveys.[3]

A more proactive approach is to gather data before employees leave. Find ways to determine why employees stay with an organization. Methods may include surveys to determine how satisfied employees are with their situation, or benchmarking with similar organizations. As an example, in 1996 the Penn State University Libraries performed a climate survey which strove to measure the working climate for employees within the organization.[4] This survey not only supplied valuable data on diversity issues and attitudes in the University Libraries but also provided a benchmark against which the University Libraries plans to measure its progress. Regrettably, many libraries neglect to measure or benchmark their performance on diversity retention. According to Winston and Li, sixty-seven percent of the libraries surveyed had no program in place to compare or measure their diversity employment performance against other norms or organizations and only four percent had performed a climate survey.[5] Clearly there is room for improvement in the area of assessment and data collection across libraries. Lacking good historic or comparative data to work with, the task force therefore turned to the literature of retention upon which to base its recommendations.

RETENTION STRATEGIES

The management literature is rife with articles summarizing the state-of-the-art on retention of employees. The American Management Association's survey of best retention practices, which provides a good summary of the retention strategies most widely used by organizations, lists strategies that fall into one of the following six categories (see Figure 1):

- mentoring
- networking
- career and learning opportunities

- interesting work
- good benefits
- balance between work and home life[6]

These six factors are important to all employees. It is interesting to note, however, that employees' ratings of rewards and motivators vary widely from their supervisors' perceptions of what employees value (see Table 1).[7] While there have been some slight changes in rankings over the years, decades of research on employee motivation and supervisor perceptions consistently support the conclusion that supervisors are routinely incorrect in determining their employees' motivations for remaining in a particular workplace.[8] Clearly, supervisors must become more aware of the factors that contribute to retention of all employees, not only those from traditionally under-represented groups.

It is worth noting that retention programs targeted for employees from underrepresented groups will promote the retention of employees in general. Conversely, general retention programs will promote the retention of women and minorities. In other words, when it comes to retention programs, it is a win/win scenario. That being said, certain retention tools are more effective in the retention of diverse staff than others. These specific tools will be discussed below.

TOOLS TO RETAIN DIVERSE STAFF

A 1999 study of minority faculty at Midwestern colleges and universities identified particular strategies that were effective in the retention of faculty of color.[9] These include networking, mentoring, and support for research. Improvements in climate was also mentioned as an important factor. A 1997 article cited mentoring, climate, flexible benefits and career advancement opportunities as being effective strategies for retention of diverse employees.[10] A recent article focusing on librarians of African descent found that a supportive environment was the most important factor in determining their job satisfaction.[11] This supports the results of a 1990 survey of faculty that found a supportive environment was the single most important factor in determining their success.[12] The result of an industry study on retention of women employees identified three key factors-balancing work and home life, challenging work, and access to career opportunities and networks.[13]

While there are other examples from the literature, it is clear that the best tools to retain women and minority employees include providing a

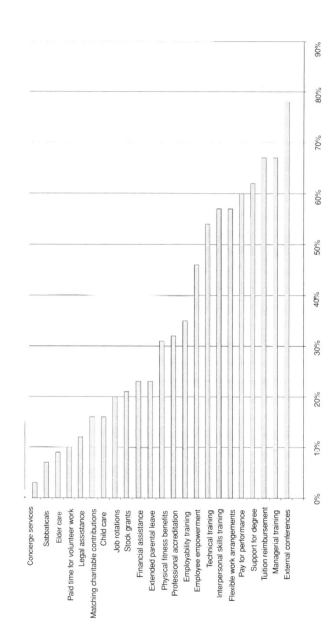

FIGURE 1. 1999 American Management Association Survey on Retention Challenges and Solutions

TABLE 1. Perceptions of Motivators for Employees

	Employee rankings	Supervisor rankings
#1	Interesting work	Pay
#2	Appreciation for job well done	Job security
#3	Being 'in' on things	Opportunity for promotion
#4	Job security	Good working conditions
#5	Good pay	Interesting work

welcoming climate, a balance between work and home life, support for research (for faculty employees), career opportunities or opportunities for professional development, plus networking and mentoring opportunities. It is worth noting that all of these strategies, with the exception of a welcoming climate, can be found on the summary of the American Management Association's list of best retention tools.[14]

Mentoring

A common misconception about mentoring is that people expect relationships simply to happen. There is a tendency among mentors to pair with someone similar to themselves.[15] For a minority employee there may be no natural match; therefore, the creation of a mentoring relationship may need some assistance. Why are mentors so important in helping to retain diverse staff? Mentors help the new employee understand the unwritten rules of the workplace and the cultural/organizational norms.[16] Issues such as the preferred organizational communication style, assertiveness, the importance of socializing, learning when it is acceptable to refuse assignments, and creating the balance between work and home are all important rules that a mentor can help employees master.

There are many examples of mentoring programs in the literature.[17] Some describe one-on-one mentoring while others illustrate ways for a single person to mentor or share advice with many employees. Certainly, mentoring is one tool that is of benefit to all employees. After all, almost everyone wants a mentor. Mentoring programs have proved cost effective as well. At Ernst & Young, the Office of Retention sponsors mentoring programs for women and others that have saved the company an estimated $13 million.[18]

Networking

It is important to create opportunities for people to get to know their co-workers. It is not always easy for new employees to meet people, and organizations should not expect these connections to be made without assistance. In academe, many networking programs are geared towards students rather than faculty or staff. Within the library, there are frequently not enough employees from underrepresented groups to create a network, therefore, it is important to look outside the library for contacts. Ways to foster networking include inviting a group of employees to lunch once a month with the library paying the tab. At Xerox, the company has established official employee networks. Dun & Bradstreet has also created employee networking groups. Among other activities, IBM hosted a symposium for employees from underrepresented groups to gather to discuss issues of importance to them. As a result of their efforts, IBM nearly doubled their minority employment numbers within three years.[19]

Career and Learning Opportunities/Work-Life Balance

The desire for interesting work, access to learning and career opportunities as well as a satisfying personal life are not unique to women or minority employees. The effect that these factors have on retention is clear and will not be discussed further in this paper.[20] Suffice it to say that organizations would do well to be attentive to these factors if they want to improve retention.

Support for Research

Minorities and women have been known to explore different avenues of research, publishing outside the mainstream and exploring interdisciplinary, gender and ethnic-based research agendas.[21] It may seem obvious but there must be support for research that is different. This implies support not only from the administration but by peers in the organization as well since tenure decisions generally involve evaluation of research by peers. An additional aspect of research support involves time to perform research. It is not uncommon for the lone woman or minority to be appointed to multiple committees in order to represent that point of view.[22] This quickly leads to disproportionate time spent in service roles, usually at the expense of research time. Avoidance of this scenario requires administrative vigilance and mentoring of the employee about the appropriate balance of research, teaching and service. A tangential benefit of such guidelines is that they can be used by all faculty in guiding their work within an organization.

Welcoming Climate

It is helpful to think of diversity as more than Equal Employment Opportunity groups. The staff in our organizations are already diverse in sundry ways. By improving employee awareness of their existing tolerance for diversity, whether illustrated by left vs. right handedness or software preferences, opportunities to discuss and improve tolerance of other types of diversity can be created. Methods to improve workplace climate through staff development include classes on cross-cultural communication, sharing stories of minority employee experiences (good and bad) via presentations, employee discussions or videos, sharing examples of the benefits and payoffs of diversity, and asking staff to work towards certain diversity goals.

The key is to keep diversity in the spotlight as an on-going organizational goal rather than a once-a-year exercise. Talk about diversity regularly. Discuss it in workplace newsletters and other forums. Measure progress-do exit surveys, etc.- and share the knowledge gained. Hire with climate in mind. Ask candidates questions designed to elicit their attitudes and communicate the organization's philosophy and commitment to diversity. Have an orientation program. We should need no reminders of the importance of making a good first impression, and a good orientation program demonstrates an organization's concern for the success of its employees.

CONCLUSION

In 1998, Penn State University began to formalize the data collection process for faculty by creating an exit survey to provide useful information to the organization. Results from the latest iteration of the *Penn State Faculty Exit Survey* indicate the primary concerns of exiting female faculty are mentoring, climate within departments, professional autonomy, support and time for research, and performance evaluation issues.[23] Respondents to the 1997/98 survey provided similar responses. There were insufficient numbers of minority faculty responses to report; however, these results support the position outlined in this paper.

If organizations are truly committed to improving the number of women and minorities in their workplace, the needs of employees for support beyond recruitment cannot be ignored. Three of the concerns mentioned in the *1998/99 Penn State Faculty Exit Survey*-mentoring, climate, and time for research-have been shown to be influential in the retention of women and minorities.[24] Other strongly influential factors for retention of these two groups include networking, career and learning opportunities, and a balance between work and home life. Improving the retention of underrepresented groups is not an impossible goal. It is an achievable goal with the additional benefit of improving the retention of quality employees of all backgrounds.

NOTES

1. Caroline Sotello Viernes Turner, Samuel L. Myers, Jr., and John W. Creswell, "Exploring Underrepresentation: The Case of Faculty of Color in the Midwest," *Journal of Higher Education* 70, no. 1 (January/February 1991): 27-59.

2. Mark D. Winston and Haipeng Li, "Managing Diversity in Liberal Arts College Libraries," *College and Research Libraries* 61, no. 3 (May 2000): 205-15.

3. Ibid.

4. Penn State University Libraries, *University Libraries Climate Survey* (University Park, PA: Penn State University Libraries, 1996 [cited 30 October 2000]); available from *http://www.libraries.psu.edu/divers/climate/appendb.htm*; Internet. Penn State University Libraries, *Climate Survey at the Penn State University Libraries* (University Park, PA: Penn State University Libraries, November 16, 1998 [cited 30 October 2000]); available from *http://www.libraries.psu.edu/divers/conf/climate.htm*; Internet. David V. Day, William E. Cross, Jr., Erika L. Ringseis, and Tamara L. Williams, "Self-Categorization and Identity Construction Associated with Managing Diversity," *Journal of Vocational Behavior* 54, no. 1 (1999): 188-95.

5. Winston and Li, "Managing Diversity," 210.

6. American Management Association, *Retention: Challenges & Solutions* (N.p.: American Management Association, 1999 [cited 1 December 2000]); available from *http://www.amanet.org/research/specials/retent.htm*; Internet.

7. Kenneth A. Kovacs, "What Motivates Employees? Workers and Supervisors Give Different Answers," *Business Horizons* 30, no. 5 (September/October 1987): 58-65.

8. Ibid.

9. Turner, Myers and Creswell, "Exploring Underrepresentation."

10. Lee Gardenswartz and Anita Rowe, "How to Overcome Retention Saboteurs," *Cultural Diversity at Work* 9, no. 6 (July 1997): 1, 14-15.

11. Joyce K. Thornton, "Job Satisfaction of Librarians of African Descent Employed in ARL Academic Libraries," *College and Research Libraries* 61, no. 3 (May 2000): 217-32.

12. Turner, Myers and Creswell, "Exploring Underrepresentation," 39.

13. Brenda Paik Sunoo, "Initiatives for Women Boost Retention," *Workforce* 77, no. 11 (November 1998): 97-100.

14. American Management Association, *Retention*.

15. Joan Howland, "Beyond Recruitment: Retention and Promotion Strategies to Ensure Diversity and Success," *Library Administration and Management* 13, no. 1 (winter 1999): 4-14. James E. Blackwell, "Mentoring: An Action Strategy for Increasing Minority Faculty," *Academe* 75, no. 5 (September/October 1989): 8-14.

16. Joe Steele, "Sharing the 'Unwritten Rules' Impacts Retention," *Cultural Diversity at Work* 9, no. 6 (July 1997): 6.

17. Blackwell, "Mentoring." Ronald B. Lieber, "Pacific Enterprises: Keeping Talent," *Fortune* 138, no. 3 (3 August 1998): 97-8. Barbara J. Wittkopf, *Mentoring Programs in ARL Libraries*. SPEC Kit, no. 239. (Washington, DC: Association of Research Libraries, 1999).

18. Hemisphere Inc., *Diversity: The Bottom Line, Part II: Strengthening the Business Case*. (N.p.: Diversity Inc., September 20, 1999 [cited 30 October 2000]); available from *http://www.diversityinc.com/Print920/print920.cfm*; Internet.

19. Ibid.

20. Lieber, "Pacific Enterprises." Sunoo, "Initiatives for Women." Hemisphere Inc., "Diversity," 12, 14. Carol Stavraka, *Retaining Diverse Talent in the Information Age* (N.p.: Diversity Inc., April 19, 2000 [cited 30 October 2000]); available from *http://www.diversityinc.com/feature.cfm*; Internet. Phyllis Shurn-Hannah, "Solving the Minority Retention Mystery," *Human Resource Professional* 13, no. 3 (May/June 2000): 22-7.

21. Howland, "Beyond Recruitment," 10. Turner, Myers and Creswell, "Exploring Underrepresentation," 30-1.

22. Mark Winston, "Promotion and Tenure: The Minority Academic Librarian," *Leading Ideas* 1 (1998 [cited 30 October 2000]); available from *http://www.arl.org/diversity/leading/issue1/promote.html*; Internet. Blackwell, "Mentoring," 13.

23. Pennsylvania State University, Vice Provost for Academic Affairs and Center for Quality and Planning. *1998-99 Faculty Exit Study, Analysis of Responses* (University Park, PA: Penn State University, September 1999 [cited 30 October 2000]); available from *http://www.psu.edu/president/cqi/assessment/reports/facultyexitsurvey/fy1 99899/index.htm*; Internet.

24. Ibid.

The Assessment of Diversity Initiatives
in Academic Libraries

Johnnieque B. (Johnnie) Love

SUMMARY. This article is a qualitative study that identifies the need
for diagnostic work before implementation of diversity initiatives. It is
also a discussion of the development of an assessment instrument used to
collect and report data from three pilot groups using the instrument. The

Johnnieque B. (Johnnie) Love is Associate Faculty Librarian III, and Coordinator
of Personnel Programs, University of Maryland Libraries, College Park, MD (E-mail:
jl345@umail.umd.edu). She was formerly Assistant Professor and Curriculum Collection Librarian, and Coordinator of the Multicultural Storytelling Project, Texas A&M
University Libraries 5000, Texas A&M University, College Station, TX.
This research study was partially funded by the Race and Ethnic Studies Institute of
Texas A&M University.

[Haworth co-indexing entry note]: "The Assessment of Diversity Initiatives in Academic Libraries."
Love, Johnnieque B. (Johnnie). Co-published simultaneously in *Journal of Library Administration* (The
Haworth Information Press, an imprint of The Haworth Press, Inc.) Vol. 33, No. 1/2, 2001, pp. 73-103; and:
Diversity Now: People, Collections, and Services in Academic Libraries (ed: Teresa Y. Neely, and Kuang-
Hwei (Janet) Lee-Smeltzer) The Haworth Information Press, an imprint of The Haworth Press, Inc., 2001,
pp. 73-103. Single or multiple copies of this article are available for a fee from The Haworth Document Deliv-
ery Service [1-800-HAWORTH, 9:00 a.m. - 5:00 p.m. (EST). E-mail address: getinfo@haworthpressinc.com].

goal of implementing diversity initiatives is to establish long-term strategies that will bring about positive change in human interaction in changing organizational culture in the workplace. To achieve this, it is
important to assess where we are, and envision how the organization
should continue to grow and change. *[Article copies available for a fee
from The Haworth Document Delivery Service: 1-800-HAWORTH. E-mail address: <getinfo@haworthpressinc.com> Website: <http://www.HaworthPress.com>
© 2001 by The Haworth Press, Inc. All rights reserved.]*

KEYWORDS. Diversity, organizational behavior, assessment, diversity initiatives, strategic planning, organizational change, work climate,
academic libraries

INTRODUCTION

Workforce diversity is one of the most widely discussed issues in our
society today. "In the next decade the work force in the United States
will clearly be far older and more heterogeneous. Nearly half of all
workers will be women, and more than 30% will more than likely be
members of minority groups, with approximately 40% of the work
force being over the age of 45."[1] The irony of this is that we are not responding appropriately to the changes in demographics. What has been
observed on the national level is that when there is a rise in acts of racial
violence, intolerance, and creation of invisible barriers, the probability
of having a productive work environment is not possible. Since the academic library is a mirror of society, a similar pattern might be found in
its ability to function as a workplace. According to Chemers, "Organizations must provide ongoing educational opportunity to develop communication skills necessary for effective collaboration and work across
cultures. Interpersonal skills needed to handle such situations of conflict do not come naturally. Volatile issues will come, and employees
will need to know how to deal with backlash, diversity, prejudice and
stereotyping."[2]

A learning organization with a climate that is responsive to the needs
of its staff is most desirable by persons working in that environment. It
is best described as a workplace with a climate and environment that is
both stimulating and supportive. The learning organization model also
makes it possible for staff to continually strive for new approaches in

acquiring knowledge and information. When an organization's culture is inclusive and responsive it creates an environment that is receptive and better able to determine the degree of success for how diversity initiatives will be received, accepted, and implemented. The author believes if no positive and agreed upon diversity strategies are integrated into the work environment, communication across cultural lines will be more difficult.

In this study diversity is defined as those attributes that make people different, having properties and characteristics of language, geography, gender, race, age, physical ability, sexual orientation, religion, skills and economics.[3] When issues of diversity are raised in the workplace, an employee's longevity within the organization becomes an additional characteristic. Understanding diversity has become very complex because it also means directing attention to conflict among and within groups. One of the key issues of diversity is the relationship between and interaction among minority groups and the dominant culture in our society.[4]

Diversity is a life work in building and developing human relationships within the workplace. Therefore, a critical need exists to determine ways in which we can identify and establish benchmarks, build upon our strengths, and improve areas that have not been developed. As we search for ways to meet the needs of the academic library staff, the question becomes how to manage this new multicultural workforce as well as maintain the value of diversity. Through reviewing the literature the author has found that other than reporting the number of new employees hired, few libraries have found ways to assess and document diversity progress.[5]

The hypothesis of this research is that diversity initiatives can be assessed, and those assessments can be used as a tool to manage and identify areas of continuous growth and development. However, we must be willing to look at all dimensions of diversity, develop new strategies that are inclusive, and work on them consistently and simultaneously. One of the goals of this research is to provide empirical support for the notion that faculty, staff, administration, and the institution pay a heavy price for intolerance in the workplace. The cost impacts productivity, work relationships among staff, and how progress in growth and development is perceived. This article also addresses issues that will impact future implementation plans of diversity initiatives. Its focus is the development and utilization of an assessment survey instrument used to collect data from three pilot survey groups. Data gathered can be used as a tool for strategic planning. Topics covered in this research are: (1) diversity assessment and its relationship to the library's mission, (2) forces that dictate change for the academic library workplace, (3) assessment of diversity in higher education and its implications for the academic library, (4) methodology and development of a diversity assessment model, and (5) development and piloting of an assessment instrument to be used for diversity documentation.

BACKGROUND

By examining the available literature it is possible to draw a correlation between the mission of the university and the mission of the academic library in assessing environmental factors, and library operations and services. The ultimate goal is to determine how diversity initiatives can be integrated into all library functions. The mission of the university is to prepare students for an economic, political, and social environment that is increasingly global and diverse. It not only has the task to provide educational experiences relevant to minority students, but also to enrich the educational experiences of majority students with an appreciation for and understanding of other cultures. Since the academic library mission supports the university functions of research, service, curriculum, and instruction, its responsibility is to provide resources in all forms, represent all perspectives, and make them accessible to students, faculty, and researchers.

Essential to providing services is having public service professionals available for interpreting the information needs of users. Skilled professionals are needed because of the rapid advances technology has made in the production of information. Since accessing and providing information is central to the responsibilities of the library profession, work becomes vulnerable to constant change.

Beginning the Assessment Process

Glaviano and Lam have stated that to change academic librarianship to meet the needs of a multicultural workforce, "attitudes must be transformed, services adapted, environments altered, openness and acceptance adopted."[6] The identified elements and proposed outcomes of diversity should be an integral part of the library's services and operations. The author contends that changes need to be made in the environment that will be facilitated through policies and procedures that reflect openness and acceptance to all staff and users. The author believes the change process should begin with self-study and careful examination of the following questions. Questions listed here are not the only ones that should be addressed. The author developed these questions based upon Glaviano and Lam's concepts, and used them as the starting point for self-study in the second and third pilot group studies in this research. The questions were also helpful in guiding the data analysis process.

1. How are we doing as colleagues and co-workers in developing positive working relationships?
2. Are there policies and procedures in place to ensure long term effectiveness of diversity initiatives?
3. How well are we serving our diverse populations that make up our user groups?
4. What can we do better to facilitate services?
5. Are our communication processes supportive at all personnel levels within the academic library?
6. Is the library environment inviting to all constituents of the university community?
7. Have we identified the benefits of diversity and know how to utilize them within our organization?

The answers and solutions to these questions may appear simple and easily obtainable, but the task of answering them proved to be complex and difficult. Gaining knowledge of diversity does not happen in a vacuum, nor does it take place overnight. The process involves interaction in numerous social systems such as family, workplace, community, and society at large. In addition, gaining the diversity advantage means acknowledging, understanding, and appreciating differences and developing a workplace that enhances their value. For years now employees in the workforce who are not part of the dominant culture have struggled with subtle demands "to adapt and fit in" with frequent not so subtle biases, discriminatory acts, and a general lack of appreciation for their points of view. Efforts to influence organizational change relating to these behaviors has been extremely slow or non-existent.[7]

Observations made by Jamieson and O'Mara provide insight as to why organizational culture and behaviors impede progress for diversity initiatives. They have observed that when an employee feels unwelcomed and disrespected [in the workplace], an adversarial climate is created between the employee and management. As a result, job satisfaction and productivity become minimal at best, and the employee frequently leaves the workplace.[8] The issues of diversity and organizational culture are as many and as varied as there are organizations and academic libraries. Evidence of basic similarities of human interaction that are essential to the operation of an organization have been identified, and help us to determine the quality of climate in the workplace.

"Within the last two decades the academic library has become an organization skilled at creating, acquiring and transferring knowledge, and at modifying its behavior to reflect new knowledge and insights."[9] Academic libraries are, by their very nature and missions, learning organizations. Change has come at such an alarming pace to every aspect of work life except diversity. Diversity initiatives must become an integral part of the organization's strategic planning process, and assessment serves as the mechanism by which these initiatives can be tailored for a particular workplace.

Demographic Changes in the Workforce Dictate Need for Diversity

Demographics changes are reflected in the general workforce which will continue to change significantly from six perspectives: age, gender, culture, education, disabilities, and values. It had been estimated that by the end of 2000, five billion of the world's population of more than six billion people will be nonwhite.[10] These demographic changes suggest that there will be a significant change within the academic library. California, Texas, and Florida are leading the nation's demographic shift. By the year 2030, the Hispanic population in the United States will nearly double from 10.7 percent to 18.9 percent. The African American population will have a small increase, from 12 percent to 13.1 percent.[11]

Another dimension to the demographic change is the aging of the academic library profession. Wilder's study of librarians finds that academic librarians are older than any other professionals in all but a handful of comparable occupations. His study examines the shape and movement of the age profile of the Association of Research Libraries (ARL) librarians and has identified factors associated with each. Wilder's study is used to reflect changes in the population into the year 2020.[12] Aging issues have implications for replacing retiring librarians, training, and competing for young people in the workforce. This will also have a direct impact on the higher education community and who will be prepared to work in the academic library.

To meet the needs of our multicultural society, diversity must be the central focus of the university community, and faculty involvement is a critical element of the process. James Anderson emphasizes that "We must be armed with good research and a good assessment plan that will back up the argument for diversity."[13] This means assessing the workplace environment, making adjustments, and integrating initiatives for improvement wherever and whenever possible.

Prior Research

The assessment of diversity allows us to analyze the impact of climate on the academic library as a workplace. We can also analyze how attitudes, behaviors, and policies (real and perceived) create barriers. Because of the lack of assessment research models in academic libraries, the research of professionals in higher education and the corporate community have proven to be beneficial in clarifying the definition of diversity, establishing guiding principles of assessment, and establishing a model for developing a sequence of steps to complete the diversity assessment process. The diversity assessment model can be found in Figure 1. Its purpose is to show how the principles of assessment and external and internal barriers impact library service and operations. It also shows how procedures, steps, and activities come together to complete the diversity assessment process.

Each of the elements in the model will be defined and correlated with other elements. Steps that identify how the assessment process should proceed will also be included. Kosseck and Lobel have pointed out the difficulty of ascribing a definition to diversity. Their premise is that diversity's definition is still unclear as to who is included in a diverse work force, and this may well be the reason why many feel diversity is still in its infancy and not sustained.[14] Moore does not view diversity as a simple concept that can be defined objectively. "As a concept, it is context dependent, selective, and relative."[15] Her research provides impetus for the research discussed here.

Thornton's research on job satisfaction has significant implications for why diversity assessment is an absolute necessity. Barriers to job satisfaction, as described by Thornton, might well be assessed by utilizing the variables identified in this study.[16] The hypotheses of research by Thornton and Moore correlates with the hypotheses presented here. They agree that there are invisible barriers in the workplace and they

FIGURE 1. Diversity Assessment Model

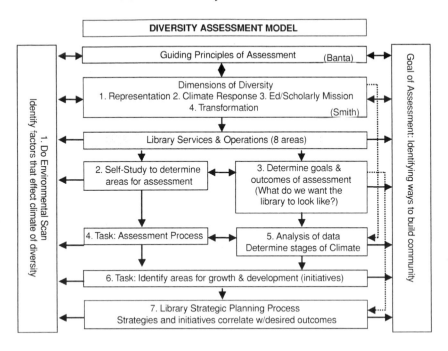

Guiding principles of assessment adapted from Banta, 1997; Dimensions of diversity adapted from Smith, 1995.

must be assessed to determine the changes that must take place in order to eradicate unhealthy work situations.

Wentling and Palma-Rivas' study has identified six crucial factors that affect diversity in the workplace: demographic changes, global marketplace, economics, comfort with being different, diverse customer base, and equal employment opportunity and affirmative action programs.[17] The six factors identified are significant indicators of external barriers that should be addressed in the environmental scan. By analyzing these factors and how they impact the institution, the factors become the basis for identification of variables to be used in the survey instrument developed for this study. This analysis will also prove to be beneficial for those who aspire to develop and tailor an instrument for their own institution. In Figure 1 the environmental scan is the first step in the diversity assessment model. An overall analysis of assessment practices in the academic library shows that there has been a consistent effort to assess collections, circulation, user trends, work procedures, job satisfaction, and management styles.[18] A logical assumption can be made that libraries want to see what works effectively for users and to provide support for them in their efforts to become independent and proficient users of information.

Research findings by Wentling and Palma-Rivas impacts data acquired from an environmental scan. The scan will identify and observe barriers that are both external and internal. Internal barriers inhibit inclusiveness in the workplace and can be categorized into two basic groups: organizational/institutional and individual barriers. For the purposes of this research only organizational/institutional barriers will be addressed. Organizational/institutional barriers that create discomfort and inhibit advancement of diverse group members include: negative attitudes, discrimination, prejudice, stereotyping, racism, and bias.[19] It can be hypothesized that these barriers can also be found within the library environment. They can be devastating to a worker as they become acclimated to the workplace. These barriers must be assessed in order to establish a starting point for implementation of diversity initiatives. Problems defined as barriers may have surfaced in the normal routine of everyday interaction and provide justification for the environmental scan step in the diversity model.

The model in Figure 2 illustrates the impact of external and internal barriers as well as Anderson's six areas of effective assessment and their impact on library services and operations as identified by Jennings.[20] The impact of all of these forces in the workplace should be regularly maintained by library administration. Figure 3 shows which external and internal/organizational barriers will be assessed by se lected variables. The goal of this process is to transform attitudes and adapt services, so that they can become highly visible and useful for users. Altering the environment means creating an atmosphere of openness and acceptance that is felt at every service point and in all activities of the library workplace.

The assessment of student achievement in higher education serves as a model for the academic library. Three nationally known scholars of assessment and diversity-Smith, Banta, and Banks-provide significant data that establish and broaden the scope of diversity and provide essential components for the diversity assessment framework. During the early 90s Daryl Smith found, in spite of the changing demographics and the proliferation of literature, a gloomy picture existed for diversity actions within higher education.[21] Her study provides the critical element

FIGURE 2. Barriers to Community Building

Adapted from Glaviano and Lam, 1990.

of the dimensions of diversity. It is clear that several processes should be taking place within the institution simultaneously in order for a comprehensive diversity plan to be effective. Smith's research documents the extent of preparedness of higher education institutions in meeting the needs of a diverse student population. Dissatisfaction with student achievement and accountability caused the academic assessment movement to go national in scope.[22]

Society is accustomed to thinking of diversity in terms of two dimensions, race and gender. These two dimensions place limitations on what is possible and what should be a holistic goal for diversity. Daryl Smith refutes the two-dimensional concept and has identified four dimensions. According to Smith, "these four dimensions of diversity must be addressed simultaneously in order for effective change to occur. All di-

FIGURE 3. External and Internal Barriers

Selected Variables	Awareness of Diversity Issues	Changing Power Dynamics	Diversity of Opinion	Lack of Empathy	Tokenism	Learning	Participation	Overcoming Inertia	Racism
External Barriers (Environmental)									
1. Demographic	X	X	X	X	X	X	X	X	X
2. Global marketplace	X	X	X			X			
3. Economics	X	X	X			X		X	
4. Comfort level	X		X		X	X	X		
5. Diverse customers	X		X	X		X		X	
6. Equal Employment	X	X	X	X	X			X	
7. Affirmative Action	X	X	X	X	X		X		X
Internal Barriers (Organizational)									
1. Negative attitudes	X		X	X	X	X	X	X	X
2. Discrimination	X	X	X	X	X	X	X	X	X
3. Prejudice	X	X	X	X	X	X	X	X	
4. Stereotyping	X	X	X	X	X	X	X	X	X
5. Racism	X	X	X	X	X	X	X	X	X
6. Bias	X	X	X	X	X	X	X	X	X

Adapted from Wentling and N. Palma-Rivas, 1994. Nine variables listed were developed by the author. *Note.* X indicates variable correlation and ability to assess external and internal barriers.

mensions are interrelated and interdependent. If they are not addressed in a comprehensive fashion, progress will be slow, sporadic, and unbalanced."[23] A brief summary of the dimensions of diversity can be found in Figure 4.

Anderson's research in areas of effective assessment includes a diversity aspect and supports Smith's findings that several dimensions of diversity are critical for a comprehensive campus diversity model. His research has identified six areas of diversity that promote a sense of community and should be maintained by ongoing assessment. The six areas are (1) frequency and focus of student-faculty non-classroom interaction, (2) nature of peer group interaction and extra-curricular activities, (3) quality of teaching, (4) extent to which institutional structures

FIGURE 4. Smith's Dimensions of Diversity

Dimensions of Diversity
1.   *Representation*-Focuses on including persons from groups previously not included. This is the most commonly understood dimension of diversity.
2.   *Climate and Response to Intolerance*-The issue of climate is referred to as the quality dimension. Its primary focus is on institutional ethos, practice, climate, and responses to intolerance.
3.   *Educational/Scholarly Mission*-Curriculum has been a part of the discussion of diversity from its inception. The institution mission is to graduate students for work in a global community. A major effort has been placed on curriculum and knowledge that has been underrepresented from an academic point of view. The educational mission must play a major role by engaging diversity on campus.
4.   *Transformation*-Requires the university to serve as the fourth and final dimension of diversity. It means changing from traditional to multiple perspectives of scholarship. This dimension requires having a diverse perspective in the decision-making process and requires the university to serve as a diverse model for effective decision-making.

Adapted from Smith, 1994.

facilitate student academic and social involvement, (5) curricular experiences and effective general education, and (6) coursework patterns.[24] Anderson's six areas of effective diversity assessment have significant implications for defining diversity and making library services and operations diverse overall. In Figure 1, Anderson's six areas of effectiveness are functioning between the external and internal barriers. They serve as a check and balance system to determine if the academic library's mission and plan for diversity is comprehensive and focuses on community.

Based upon two decades of assessment research, Trudy Banta has identified several principles for academic assessment.[25] Banta's principles, shown here in Figure 5, are holistic in concept and can be applied to assessment of diversity. The principles posit that one views the assessment process as long term and not a quick fix. The process ultimately becomes a way of life.

When assessing the quality of an inclusive work environment, we need to envision what we would like for the library workplace to look like and become. We need to establish a set of standards against which to measure performance and human interaction. The strength of this process is its ability to be continuous in light of attitudinal and behavioral changes, and it serves as a diverse model that is effective for the decision-making process.

FIGURE 5. Principles of Assessment

Principles of Assessment
■ Student learning begins with educational values.
■ Assessment is effective when it reflects understanding of learning as multi-dimensional, integrated, and revealed in performance over time.
■ Assessment works best when the program states clearly and explicitly its purposes.
■ Assessment requires that attention be relegated to outcomes but also and equally to the experiences that lead to those outcomes.
■ Assessment works when it is ongoing and not episodic with ever changing administrations.
■ Assessment fosters greater improvement when representatives from across the educational community are involved.
■ Assessment makes a difference when it begins with issues of use and illuminates questions that people really care about.
■ Assessment leads to improvement when it is part of the larger set of conditions that promote change.
■ Assessment is successful when educators meet responsibilities to students and the public.
■ Assessment is most effective when undertaken in an environment that is receptive, supportive, and enabling.

Adapted from Banta, 1997.

Developing the Diversity Assessment Model

Building the diversity assessment model means utilizing proven components that have worked well in higher education for student academic achievement. The elements as described in Smith's dimensions of diversity, Anderson's areas of effective diversity assessment, and Banta's principles of assessment, together serve as the foundation of this diversity assessment model. All elements come together to provide a cohesive framework that gives direction and establishes parameters for the implementation of diversity initiatives. The assessment model will also guide and document organizational change, initiate the research and measurement process, and strengthen ongoing education to effect change in the culture of the academic library and its management systems.

The diversity assessment process means beginning the self-study process with questions and establishing outcomes for how one envisions future working conditions of the work place. External and internal environmental factors must also be examined, and the impact they have on climate and the library's services and operations must be determined. Those services and operations as described by Jennings should include (1) administrative agenda and leadership, (2) management and supervision, (3) recruitment of a diverse workforce, (4) relationship with co-workers, (5) library services and programs, (6) interaction with library users, (7) development of collections, and (8) impact of technology on diversity.[26] As the services and operations are addressed, every effort must be made to include all levels of personnel in the assessment process to gain various perspectives and viewpoints.

The author believes that Banta's principles of academic assessment in Figure 1 are central to the diversity assessment model and confirm the need for a long-term plan for diversity strategies. Banta's principles establish credibility and support for Anderson's six areas of academic assessment that promote community building within the university. These six areas of effective assessment cover all facets of student life and interaction with faculty, staff, the library and all other organizations that make up the university community, for they provide the vision, goals and outcomes to be attained.

METHODOLOGY

General Method

The first objective of this study is to assess the climate for diversity initiative integration in the academic library as a workplace. It is a method by which data are used to document change in diversity efforts and to assist the library in its strategic planning. Compelling external and internal forces dictate change around the issue of being an information provider. Therefore, these issues must be addressed simultaneously while providing a quality workplace for those providing the services, managing the resources, and interpreting complex information as the need arises.

Diagnosis and assessment of diversity in academic libraries is critical to understanding the problems in attracting, recruiting, and retaining library professionals of diverse groups to the profession. By becoming knowledgeable of the various stages of climate for diversity, administrators in academic libraries can begin to formulate strategies for change.

Specific Procedures

This study surveyed three groups of self-selected librarians and library staff members from various academic libraries. A diversity assessment instrument was designed to collect data for nine variables. The pilot testing process involved testing the survey instrument and determining its ability to collect data that provide an accurate diagnosis of the climate for diversity in an academic library. Piloting also determined if the data provided an accurate analysis of perceptions of the library staff.

The first pilot group survey was completed in the spring of 1998. The second pilot group survey was completed in August of 1998, and the third pilot group was completed in the spring of 1999. Respondents were mailed a survey packet that included a cover letter, the diversity assessment instrument, and a form requesting that the respondents give feedback of their perceptions of the survey instrument. The respondents were asked in the survey, based upon their perceptions, if they would assess their library's preparedness for diversity initiative integration. Survey questions were developed using a four-point Likert scale with 4 indicating applies fully to their library, 3 indicating applies to a great extent, 2 indicating applies to a moderate extent, and 1 indicating applies to little or no extent. As a result of feedback from the first two pilot groups, respondents from the third pilot study were asked to use the letter "N" when the item was not applicable or they did not know. Few respondents in Pilot Group III felt the need to use the "N" as a category.

Demographics of the Pilot Groups

Respondents in the three pilot groups surveyed represented institutions at various stages of diversity initiative integration from non-existent activities and lacking vision for diversity to institutions well on their way to creating cultural awareness and other programmatic activities to enhance diversity initiative development.

Pilot Group I

In the first pilot group, participants included faculty and administrators, with a wide range of skills, experience, and tenure from colleges and universities of all sizes. These respondents were the first twenty-one participants of the Association of Research Libraries Leadership and Career Development Program of 1997. Seventeen of the librarians in this group were from ARL institutions. The group consisted of five males and sixteen females ranging in age from 25 to 55. Three librarians held doctoral degrees and one was a doctoral student. All held MLS degrees. Eighty percent of the respondents held positions in public service, 10 percent were in human resources, 5 percent were in technical services, and the remaining were in administration. Sixty-five percent of the library professionals were from academic libraries with a staff of over 100. Many of the participants expressed that they were the only minority librarians on their staff. This group was more ethnically diverse than the other two pilot groups. Participants in Pilot Groups II and III came from predominantly White public institutions with 3 to 5 percent minority library staff members and less than 12 percent minority student population.

Pilot Group II

The second pilot group consisted of ten females and four males from the same library and institution with more than 200 library staff members working in eight locations of the library. Twenty surveys were sent out and 14 returned. The second group was not as ethnically diverse as the first one, but the group represented all levels of library staff within one institution. This Pilot group represented an institution that had been involved in diversity awareness and programming for three years. The library administration had implemented the diversity program based upon data from the previous strategic planning process. Successful programming activities had been put in place. However, the diversity advisory committee was ready to move to the second phase of diversity initiative implementation-making the initiatives an integral part of the library structure. Change occurred in the composition of the committee as well as library administration. These changes in staff and administration caused the momentum for diversity initiative integration to slow down.

Pilot Group III

The third pilot group represented a large ARL library with over 300 staff members. Twenty females and five males participated in the survey. The group included all levels of library staff. Fifty-five percent of the respondents in this group were from ethnically diverse groups. This academic library also has multiple site locations, but the majority of respondents work at the main library location. Because of recommendations made in the previous two pilot phases, the instrument was revised to thirty-nine questions, and an additional variable was identified to make specific observations for invisible barriers with regard to racism.

INSTRUMENTATION

There are a few academic libraries that have committed themselves to an assessment plan and the time consuming process that is involved. Because of the lack of models for assessing diversity in the academic library, the author has drawn from resources in the corporate community. The author's major objectives for piloting the assessment instrument are to determine if there is validity in the instrument's ability to capture and report data accurately on the assessment variables, what areas of development should be addressed in order to improve the climate of the workplace, and if all questions are capable of being answered and results identified on the Intolerance Continuum based on respondents' perceptions. The piloting process made it possible for all elements of the instrument to be evaluated. Clarity of content, appropriateness of vocabulary, examination of the Likert scale used, format, and determination of balance among the variables were the criteria examined.

Through extensive reading of the literature on diversity, assessment, and learning organizations a list of nine variables have been identified to establish areas of assessment by the survey instrument. A summary of these variables can be found in Figure 6. These variables serve as key challenges that provide an intangible dimension to diversity. In many instances some are considered invisible barriers because they measure attitudinal issues. Awareness of diversity issues, lack of empathy, participation, changing power dynamics, tokenism, overcoming inertia, diversity of opinion, learning, and racism are all challenges that have been used as variables for this study. Even though these variables are viewed through one's own perceptions, concern is amplified when there is significant agreement among anonymous respondents that these barriers are "real" and that they have to deal with related issues to these barriers frequently.

Shifting power dynamics, diversity of opinion, lack of empathy, tokenism, participation, and overcoming inertia are the six variables adapted with permission from the Joplin and Daus study.[27] Awareness of Diversity Issues, Learning, and Racism are the three variables developed by the author.

FIGURE 6. Selected Variables for Diversity Assessment Survey

Selected Variables for Diversity Assessment Survey

1. <u>Awareness of diversity issues</u> assesses knowledge of diversity definitions, attitudes and understanding and of diverse people and cultures. This variable is key in identifying educational and programming needs of the library staff in regards to diversity issues. (All dimensions of diversity)

2. <u>Shifting of Power</u> identifies what happens when power is lost, and the challenges it presents. Joplin and Daus' notion is that traditional constituencies may feel an erosion of power when there is an infusion of individuals from diverse groups in the workplace. This variable will assess the volatile and delicate issue of perceived power in the work place. (Dimensions of diversity 1, 2 and 3)

3. <u>Diversity of Opinion</u> is how leadership is able to synthesize opinions, find shared ground, and reach agreement. This variable identifies one of the most time consuming and emotionally draining activities in the workplace, good communication and consensus building. (Dimensions of diversity 1, 2 and 3)

4. <u>Lack of Empathy</u> identifies those issues related to the challenge of integrating diverse viewpoints and opinions. Leadership must understand the perceived feelings, stances, and approaches to issues and be able to anticipate the varied reactions to issues. Empathy and compassion are truly important qualities needed in a workplace. (Dimensions of diversity 1, 2 and 4)

5. <u>Tokenism</u> (Real and perceived) identifies when one person has been hired over others specifically to fill a quota. In this situation library staff from diverse groups are not viewed as being qualified or skilled in a particular area and as a result, their voices are not heard. Diverse staff will experience this more where the climate is viewed as intolerant. (Dimensions of diversity 1 and 2)

6. <u>Learning</u> identifies staff needs and desires for training and educational opportunities. When staff feel that opportunities are accessible they feel that the work environment is a supportive one. Learning opportunities should be incorporated in all operations, programs and services for the library staff as well as the users. (All dimensions of diversity)

7. <u>Participation</u> variable identifies if the staff feels the work environment promotes breaking down myths of tokenism and if staffs are encouraged to take part in various activities. (All dimensions of diversity)

8. <u>Overcoming Inertia</u> is the most difficult for an organization to diagnose. Consistent communication of goals and vision for diversity must be ongoing. The leader must have exceptional, analytical, and interpersonal skills. (All dimensions of diversity)

9. <u>Racism</u> will assess the personal experiences the diverse library staff have had in regards to discrimination (real and perceived) within the library. What structures and/or policies are in place that reflect an understanding of oppression, exclusion, and knowledge of the traditional manager? (All dimensions of diversity)

Note. Variables are correlated to Smith's (1994) dimensions of diversity. See Figure 4.

Survey Instrument: Variables and Questions

The following variables were developed to assess all operations and services of the library. The objective was to assess observable and unobservable behaviors as well as attitudes. Constructing an instrument of this type is difficult because questions used to assess may appear to be subjective. However, this is one of the major hurdles in measuring attitudes, perceptions and behaviors.

The first survey instrument was designed with 52 questions and was used with Pilot Groups I and II. Respondents in the first two pilot groups felt that the instrument was too long. Revisions were made and the number of questions was reduced to 39 for Pilot Group III. In both survey instruments, variables were not equally balanced in the number of questions. Characteristics of some variables proved to be more easily recognizable and measurable than others. Definitions of variables and examples of questions used on the survey instrument follow.

> *Variable 1.* Awareness of Diversity Issues: At the onset of addressing issues of diversity, it is important to have an understanding of differences, and how our individual attitudes, prejudices, and biases impact the academic library as a workplace. Aspects of awareness include the willingness to be open to change, to participate, and to learn about other cultures.

>> 1. ____ Sexual harassment in the workplace constitutes violation of civil rights for both male and female library staff members.
>> 2. ____ Diversity issues are embraced.
>> 3. ____ There is a growing need to educate library staff on cultural differences and diversity issues.

> *Variable 2.* Changing Power Dynamics: Questions in this section will assess if there are issues regarding change in power. Struggles for power are a natural consequence of control over resources and social structures. Research shows when diversity efforts are increased in an organization, commitment and attachment decrease. As power is redistributed, doubts emerge within the mono cultured workforce as to how they will fit into the new organization.[28]

>> 4. ____ Administration uses constructive alliance building with departments and library staff.
>> 5. ____ Leadership has an identifiable vision for diversity.
>> 6. ____ There are active ongoing team building efforts and activities to facilitate the process of sharing power.

> *Variable 3.* Diversity of Opinion: Diversity of opinion means focusing on communication and using conflict resolution for ad-

dressing the challenges of working with a variety of opinions. In the best of circumstances, miscommunication will occur as change comes to an academic library. Perspectives will increase, and leaders will gather data from individuals on their unique values, cultural grounding, and behaviors.[29]

7. ____ Administration and staff actively seek opinions and perspectives.
8. ____ Minority staff members hold positions at all levels of our organization.
9. ____ Minority staff members fail to voice their opinion because they fear backlash.

Variable 4. Lack of Empathy: Administration must make it clear in words and deeds to all library staff that needs and concerns of staff members are appreciated and respected. This variable is integrally linked to diversity of opinion. When staff view library leadership as not having compassion, the environment experiences upheaval and poor morale.[30]

10. ____Contributions from minority staff members are recognized.
11. ____Administrators, supervisors, and other leaders of the library model giving empathetic expressions to staff in their communication.
12. ____My colleagues share empathetic expressions without feeling personally threatened.

Variable 5. Tokenism: "Tokenism," real or perceived, is a barrier to early stages of diversity integration. In this situation the perception is that African and/or Hispanic/Latino Americans are not viewed as being qualified or skilled in a particular area. The perception is they are selected for their positions because of pressure.[31]

13. ____ Staff members are recognized for their expertise.
14. ____Consistent effort is being made to reduce the perception that African Americans and Hispanic/Latino Americans are not viewed as "tokens."
15. ____A common practice is to acknowledge staff members for what they have accomplished in terms that make them feel recognized in their own right.

Variable 6. Learning: Technology dictates the need for continuous training and development. When library staff is trained, self-esteem, productivity, and inclusiveness increase. Since the academic library is the major information provider of the university community, it serves as the perfect model for a learning organization. This variable was developed to measure ongoing learning opportunities for all staff.

16. ____ Opportunities are dedicated to staff being coached in learning how to learn.
17. ____ There is a climate that recognizes and supports the importance of learning for all staff members.
18. ____ Managers who work hard to give honest and fair evaluations to minority staff members in a way that is sensitive yet clear and useful.

Variable 7. Participation: Ensuring everyone has a voice is a critical first step toward a full appreciation of a diverse organization. Opportunities for participation can ease the tension resulting from the issues of power sharing, changed power dynamics, the gathering of different perspectives and opinions, building of perceptions of empathy, and eliminating perceptions of tokenism.[32]

19. ____ Staff members view involvement in activities of the library as important and essential.
20. ____ I have grown and gained professionally as a result of participation in library activities.
21. ____ I have frequently served as a mentor for my colleagues.

Variable 8. Overcoming Inertia: Management of diversity in an organization takes considerably more time than what one thinks. In order for the challenge of inertia to be maintained as a focus, administration must have clearly stated and communicated organizational vision and goals.[33]

22. ____ Leaders provide guidance to staff members at all levels.
23. ____ Use of time, processes, and human resources are managed effectively so the library as an organization is empowered to move ahead with daily operations.

24. _____ Administrations takes the time to reward staff members and teams for their achievements.

Variable 9. Racism: Racism is the belief that one's own race is superior to others and the behavior exemplified, usually acted out, suppresses opportunities for those members of society felt to be inferior. It is based on the assumption that physical attributes of a racial group determine the social behavior, as well as their psychological and intellectual abilities. Racism takes place on three levels: individual, institutional and cultural. The critical issue is to understand the distinctions and similarities among the types of racism.[34]

25. _____ African and Hispanic Americans are being treated as if they are "invisible" to their departments.
26. _____ African American and Hispanic/Latino staff members have left the library because they were being discriminated against.
27. _____ Acts of discrimination and/or retaliation may take place in our library but we work through the situation using problem-solving and/or mediation methods.

The Intolerance-Appreciation Continuum Scale

A primary objective of diversity assessment is to diagnose whether the climate of the work environment is welcoming and supportive to all library staff. The scale used for diagnosing climate and stages of diversity is called the Intolerance-Appreciation Continuum. Bennett developed the scale based on the concept that individual attitudes toward diversity are not fixed, but they shift along a continuum.[35] Bennett's theory was expanded by Baldwin and Hecht when they defined the stages of the continuum as Intolerance, Tolerance/Acceptance and Appreciation for stages of diversity integration.[36] Joplin and Daus also utilized this scale for determining leadership skills and attitudes toward diversity.

Diversity assessment in academic libraries can be adapted to these same stages. In Figure 7 a description is given for each stage of the Continuum. In this study the author has adapted the scale by adding a percentage ranking to delineate where stages on the Continuum begin and end: Intolerance ranges from zero to 30 percent; Tolerance ranges from 31 percent to 49 percent; Acceptance ranges from 50 percent to 70 per-

FIGURE 7. Stages of the Intolerance-Appreciation Continuum

Stages of the Intolerance-Appreciation Continuum

Stage 1: Intolerance: At this stage the library complies at best with the legal requirements regarding the makeup of the library staff work force. Diversity issues are addressed at surface level. The library is viewed as not committed to the ideas or the benefits derived from diversity. In other words, the organization continues its daily functions as always.

Stage 2: Tolerance/Acceptance: Members of diverse groups are actively sought to become members of the library staff to participate in the daily routines of the library. However, skills and talents may not be fully utilized. Typically in a tolerant organization the leadership promotes diversity initiatives for two reasons: First, leadership believes that a diverse workforce affects the bottom line. Second, potential negative social or moral ramifications exist to justify diversity initiatives.

Stage 3: Appreciation: In the Appreciation stage the library surpasses acceptance and actively embraces diversity. Diversity is viewed as a value and a benefit. The library is fully committed and is keenly aware of the importance of inclusion of all diverse group members in all operations and services of the library.

Adapted from J. R. Baldwin and M. L. Hecht, 1995.

cent; and Appreciation ranges from 71 percent to 100 percent. These results identified a particular stage on the Continuum. The Continuum allows for each variable to be measured on its own merit. Survey questions, developed using the Likert scale format, were coded according to a rating system developed by the author. Respondents indicated to what extent a question applied to their library's climate for diversity as follows: Four-indicated applies to the library fully; three-indicated applies a greater extent to the library; two-indicated applies to a moderate extent to the library; one-indicated applies little or to no extent to the library. Percentages and average percentages were then calculated based on the total number of respondents selecting a particular rating or response to a query and the rating system. Complete findings can be found in Figure 8.

When a library has been identified as being in the Intolerance Stage, it means the library is only complying with what is legally required in regards to diversity initiatives. Advantages and benefits of diversity have not been realized. As a result, the library continues with its regular routine and does not address demographic changes taking place in the environment.

When a library has been identified in the Tolerance/Acceptance Stage, it means the library proactively seeks out and includes diverse staff in the daily routine of the organizational structure. A library in this stage may view a diverse workforce as essential to "bottom-line" issues of the library. The library is aware of the moral and social issues that ex-

FIGURE 8. Data from Three Pilot Surveys

1. Awareness of Diversity Issues	Intolerance %	Tolerance %	Acceptance %	Appreciation %
Pilot Group I	30.77%	19.66%	18.80%	30.77%
Pilot Group II	4.94%	39.51%	33.33%	22.22%
Pilot Group III	40.35%	29.82%	10.53%	19.30%
Average Percent	25.35%	29.66%	20.89%	24.10%
2. Changing Power Dynamics	Intolerance %	Tolerance %	Acceptance %	Appreciation %
Pilot Group I	31.86%	25.66%	17.70%	24.78%
Pilot Group II	16.05%	38.27%	28.40%	17.28%
Pilot Group III	36.84%	22.81%	22.81%	17.54%
Average Percent	28.25%	28.91%	22.97%	19.87%
3. Diversity of Opinion	Intolerance %	Tolerance %	Acceptance %	Appreciation %
Pilot Group I	37.36%	31.03%	20.69%	10.92%
Pilot Group II	30.25%	43.70%	19.33%	6.72%
Pilot Group III	42.76%	29.61%	16.45%	11.18%
Average Percent	36.79%	34.78%	18.82%	9.61%
4. Lack of Empathy	Intolerance %	Tolerance %	Acceptance %	Appreciation %
Pilot Group I	30.32%	27.10%	21.29%	21.29%
Pilot Group II	28.85%	31.73%	29.81%	9.62%
Pilot Group III	31.06%	23.48%	33.33%	12.12%
Average Percent	30.08%	27.44%	28.14%	14.34%
5. Tokenism (Real and Perceived)	Intolerance %	Tolerance %	Acceptance %	Appreciation %
Pilot Group I	30.77%	28.21%	25.64%	15.38%
Pilot Group II	31.65%	45.57%	20.25%	2.53%
Pilot Group III	45.61%	22.81%	15.79%	15.79%
Average Percent	36.01%	32.20%	20.56%	11.23%
6. Participation	Intolerance %	Tolerance %	Acceptance %	Appreciation %
Pilot Group I	19.30%	24.56%	35.09%	21.05%
Pilot Group II	12.82%	33.33%	38.46%	15.38%
Pilot Group III	19.30%	26.32%	38.60%	15.79%
Average Percent	17.14%	28.07%	37.38%	17.41%
7. Learning	Intolerance %	Tolerance %	Acceptance %	Appreciation %
Pilot Group I	25.36%	31.88%	26.81%	15.94%
Pilot Group II	16.13%	52.69%	21.51%	9.68%
Pilot Group III	26.32%	26.32%	30.53%	16.84%
Average Percent	22.60%	36.96%	26.28%	14.15%
8. Overcoming Inertia	Intolerance %	Tolerance %	Acceptance %	Appreciation %
Pilot Group I	33.82%	29.41%	24.26%	12.50%
Pilot Group II	28.57%	39.56%	24.18%	7.69%
Pilot Group III	28.00%	26.67%	24.00%	21.33%
Average Percent	30.13%	31.88%	24.15%	13.84%

ist in the environment and implements diversity initiatives as justification to "right the wrong."

The Appreciation Stage should be the goal of every library. When a library ranks in this stage, it embraces diversity and sees it as an essential in the normal function of the library's services and operations. This stage means that diversity benefits are realized and initiatives are seen as opportunities for growth and development in human interaction.[37]

FINDINGS

General Findings

The data from this study shows that diversity assessment is a viable tool for diagnosing the level of preparedness of academic libraries for diversity initiative integration. According to the data, academic libraries in the study are not meeting the needs of all staff members, thereby not making the workplace a welcoming environment. Figure 8 illustrates the percentage breakdown of each variable and its stages on the Intolerance-Appreciation Continuum. The following are significant findings and critical observations revealed by the data.

Figure 8 shows that all three pilot groups' ratings fell below 31 percent, thereby documenting that respondents did not feel their libraries were in the Appreciation stage of any of the variables. These data validate the author's assumptions in regards to the small percentage of respondents identifying their libraries as being in the Appreciation Stage and having a climate in which diversity initiatives might have the opportunity to flourish. The pilot group with the highest ranking for Appreciation was Pilot Group 1, scoring nearly 31 percent on the "Awareness of Diversity Issues" variable. Survey question numbers six, seven, fifteen, and thirty-five all addressed the issues of academic library leadership having a vision for diversity. Only 34.78 percent of all respondents perceived their institutions as being in the Tolerance Stage, and viewing diversity as the "morally right thing to do."

A critical concern of the author is that a significant number of the variables in all three pilot groups received percentages which placed them within the Intolerance and Tolerance Stages (zero to 49%). These percentages were high enough to hypothesize that invisible barriers exist in each of the institutions assessed by the respondents. A significant finding that needs to be addressed is that all minority library staff in all three pilot groups reported they were not getting adequate support in their libraries. Close attention was paid to survey questions that were consistently answered the same by respondents from each pilot group. When respondents answer survey questions the same, it is a clear indication that library staff perceptions are in agreement and valid.

Pilot Group I was the most ethnically diverse of the three groups surveyed, representing twenty-one different academic libraries. Rankings for 50 percent of the variables fell within the Appreciation Stage. Fifty percent of all questions were answered identically for this group. This is a clear indication that the need for diversity strategies in the libraries represented is a widely held belief.

Figure 8 shows that 5 out of 8 variables for Pilot Group II fell into the Acceptance Stage, and 6 of the variables had the lowest percentages reported in the Intolerance Stage. This group's percentage rankings also revealed the most balanced representation among all 8 variables, ranking the highest in the Tolerance Stage. Compared to the other two groups, Pilot Group II reported the lowest percentage ranking within the Intolerance Stage; however, the percentages reported in the Intolerance Stage are much higher than anticipated by the author.

In Pilot Group III, 7 out of 8 variables had the highest percentage rankings in the Intolerance Stage. This also holds true for all three groups. The data can be interpreted to mean that the respondents in this group viewed their respective institutions as barely legal in its compliance of diversity efforts. A positive highlight for this group was the finding that nearly 48 percent (47.4%) reported that "administration takes the time to reward staff and teams for achievements." While this area proved to be a strength for Pilot Group III, it was considered an area of weakness for the other two groups. Only 33 percent of all questions were answered the same for this group. Based on this data, the author concluded that respondents were not in agreement as to their perceptions of their library's climate for diversity.

Analysis of Variables

Variable #1-The Awareness of Diversity variable had the highest percentage place in the Appreciation Stage. In responding to one of the questions from this variable, respondents agreed that they "realized people of other cultures have fresh ideas and different perspectives to bring to their lives and to the library." This question made it clear that there is an understanding of diversity awareness. Eighty-four percent of the respondents were in agreement on this question.

The variable indicating the greatest concern was Variable #8-Overcoming Inertia. If issues are not addressed, this may lead to a growing amount of apathy and loss of productivity in the workplace. For this variable only 12.5 percent of the respondents perceived their institutions to be in the Appreciation Stage, while nearly 32 percent identified their institutions as being in the Intolerance Stage.

Twenty-eight percent identified their institutions as being in the Intolerance Stage of Variable #2-Changing Power Dynamics. Twenty-eight percent of responses were reported as falling in the Intolerance Stage while other stages scored less than 26 percent. In responding to specific questions in Variable #3-Diversity of Opinion-65 percent of the respondents felt that there were "no overt signs of disrespect for people of diverse groups," while 42 percent reported they "felt that people of diverse groups fail to voice opinions for fear of backlash." Forty-five percent felt there was evidence of "signs of gridlock and conflict because of the diverse opinions" in the workplace. Thirty-seven percent felt that "vigorous discussions caused conflict and threat"; and 53 percent reported they did not feel "that staff members from diverse groups were asked to be the minority voice on a committee," thus keeping them away from their responsibilities.

In Variable #4-Lack of Empathy-72 percent felt that there were "never any signs of disruptions between cultures indicating issues of acceptance." Sixty percent of those responding felt that "the people in their libraries welcomed and respected all staff regardless of their sexual orientation." In a question relating to empathetic expressions, only 5 percent reported that "library leaders practiced this skill in communicating with people." This means that the rest of responses, 95 percent, fall into the Intolerance and Acceptance Stages.

In Tokenism-Variable #5-23 percent of the respondents felt that "no efforts were being made by administration to change the perception that minority staff are not 'tokens.'" They were in the workplace because they were there on their own merit and skilled in what they do. Twenty percent felt their "libraries did not do anything to show appreciation for their work."

The Participation Variable-#6-was the most balanced in all stages. Twenty-one percent felt that their libraries were at the Appreciation Stage. The attributes of this variable are easily recognizable and did not have as many questions. Generally, academic libraries see the need for continuity in providing adequate training and staff development activities as well as professional development opportunities.

The Racism Variable-#9-was added to the survey instrument before surveying Pilot Group III, and, as a result, data collected here was not readily comparable to data from the first two pilots. However, findings do speak volumes for Pilot Group III and the need for growth and development. Percentages consistently fell in the Intolerance Stage.

A common concern expressed by all three pilot groups was that since their libraries had multiple locations, it was difficult to perceive and/or assess the overall integration of diversity initiatives. One respondent pointed out that if a library staff member had no involvement in library activities they could easily have feelings of isolation and would not feel a part of the life and activity of the library. This comment addresses the issues of the Participation Variable-#6. Overall total and average findings for all variables are represented in Figure 8.

CONCLUSION

Recommendations

Plans for future research include revisions to the assessment instrument, based on feedback from pilot respondents, and replicating the study in other public and private academic library settings. Future research will address diversity issues within the context of organizational behavior. In many instances it is difficult for library staff to distinguish the difference between an issue of climate and the direct outcomes of ineffective organizational infrastructure when the human element is taken into consideration.

Data gathered from diversity assessment have practical value in that it can be used as a tool for enhancing the strategic planning process. Many academic libraries still view diversity as a movement rather than a way of life. When diversity is viewed in such a manner it is doomed for failure. We must address all dimensions of diversity simultaneously. We can no longer look at demographic trends alone; a critical observation must be made of societal and organizational behaviors as well as individual barriers to diversity. Arredondo reinforces the concept that "diversity assessment is proactive and must precede any kind of action or intervention." In addition there are multiple benefits and positive outcomes that can accrue through the implementation of diversity assessment. Those most readily observed outcomes are (1) an open and inclusive channel for communication, (2) obtaining new information about diversity related issues, (3) validation of assumptions made about work force diversity, and (4) the development of initiatives based upon fact, and not political concerns.[38]

The assessment of diversity provides documentation of where libraries are and where they need to go with regard to actions and responses to all dimensions of diversity. Behaviors, not attitudes, create major problems in managing diversity. In order to be able to manage people effectively, we must acknowledge their experiences in the world. Individuals must feel valued for all experiences they bring to the table. It is essential for the process of assessment to be viewed as an instructional, as well as a diagnostic, tool for educating and determining the direction of cultural education within the workplace. Alire and Stielow point out that "academic libraries content on resting on the status quo are not only failing their missions, but are also likely to create a point of contention for their universities in the future."[39] Constructing and implementing diversity initiatives involves continuous experimentation, assessment, modification, and innovation. Assessment of diversity is an ongoing lifetime process of improvement.

NOTES

1. George Henderson, *Cultural Diversity in the Workplace: Issues and Strategies* (Westport, Connecticut: Quovum Books, 1994).

2. Martin Chemers, Stuart Oskamp, and Mark Costanzo, *Diversity in Organizations: New Perspectives for a Changing Workplace* (Thousand Oaks: Sage Publications, 1995).

3. Janice R. W. Joplin and C. S. Daus, "Challenges of Leading a Diverse Workforce," *Academic Management Executive* 3 (April 1997): 880-92.

4. Carlos Cortes, "Constructive Multiculturalism and Campus Community: Dealing with Diversity in Higher Education," (lecture at the Kansas Diversity Conference for Higher Education, 1995).

5. University of Pennsylvania, "Survey," (manuscript, 1993).

6. Carl Glaviano and R. E. Lam, "Academic Libraries and Affirmative Action: Approaching Cultural Diversity in the 1990's," *College and Research Libraries* 11 (1990): 513-22.

7. Elsie Cross, J. H. Katz, F. A. Miller, and E. W. Seashore, eds., *The Promise of Diversity: Over 40 Voices Discuss Strategies for Eliminating Discrimination in Organizations* (Burr Ridge, Illinois: Irwin Professional Publishing, 1994).

8. David Jameison and Julie O'Mara, *Managing Workforce 2000: Gaining the Diversity Advantage* (San Francisco: Jossey-Bass Publishers, 1991).

9. Donald Riggs and Patricia Tarins, eds., *Cultural Diversity in Libraries* (New York: Neal-Schuman, 1994).

10. United States Department of Education, *Digest of Education Statistics* (Washington, DC: National Center for Education Statistics, 1999).

11. Steve Murdock and Mitchell Rice, "Diversity, Texas A&M University and Vision 2020," (College Station: Texas A&M University: State Data Center, 1998).

12. Stanley Wilder, "The Changing Profile of Research Library Professional Staff," *ARL: A Bimonthly Report On Research Library Issues and Actions From ARL, CNI, and SPARC* (February/April 2000): 1-3.

13. James A. Anderson, *Handbook for the Assessment of Diversity* (Raleigh, NC: North Carolina State University, 1993.

14. Ellen E. Kosseck and Sharon A. Lobel, *Managing Diversity: Human Resource Strategies for Transforming the Workplace* (Cambridge, MA: Blackwell Business, 1996).

15. Sarah Moore, "Understanding and Managing Diversity Among Groups at Work: Key Issues for Organizational Training and Development," *Journal of European Industrial Training* 30 (4/5) (1999): 208-17.

16. Joyce Thornton, "Job Satisfaction of African-American Librarians in ARL Libraries," *College and Research Libraries* 60 (May 2000): 217-32.

17. R. M. Wentling and N. Palma-Rivas, *Diversity in the Workforce: A Literature Review* (Berkley, CA: National Center for Research in Vocational Education, 1994), ERIC ED 414473.

18. General consensus for the need for assessment can be found in J. S. Squire, "Job Satisfaction and the Ethnic Minority Librarian," *Library Administration and Management* 5 (1991): 194-203; Deborah Curry, "Assessing and Evaluating Diversity in the Reference Department," *College Librarian* (1992); Cynthia J. Preston, "Perceptions of Discriminatory Practices and Attitudes: A Survey of African American Librarians," *College and Research Libraries* 59 (5) (September 1998): 434-45; Patricia Robles, "Recruiting the Minority Librarian: The Secret to Increasing Numbers," *College and Research Library News* 59 (10) (November 1998): 779-80; Thornton, "Job Satisfaction of African-American Librarians in ARL Libraries."

19. Wentling and Palma-Rivas, *Diversity in the Workforce.*

20. Kriza Jennings, Association of Research Libraries (diversity forum held at the University of Kansas, Lawrence, KS, 1998).

21. Daryl G. Smith, Lisa E. Wolf, and Thomas Levitan, eds., *Studying Diversity In Higher Education*, no. 81, New Directions for Institutional Research Series (San Francisco: Jossey-Bass Publishers, 1994).

22. Daryl G. Smith, "Organizational Implications of Diversity in Higher Education," in *Diversity in Organizations: New Perspectives for a Changing Workplace*, eds. Martin Chemers, Stuart Oskamp, and Mark Costanzo (Thousand Oaks: Sage Publications, 1995), 220-44.

23. Anderson, *Handbook for the Assessment of Diversity.*

24. Ibid.

25. Trudy W. Banta, "Moving Assessment Forward: Enabling Conditions and Stumbling Blocks," *New Directions for Higher Education* 25, no. 4 (winter 1997): 79-91.

26. Jennings.

27. Joplin and Daus, "Challenges of Leading a Diverse Workforce."

28. Joplin and Daus, "Challenges of Leading a Diverse Workforce," 37.

29. Ibid., 40.

30. Ibid., 41.

31. Ibid., 41.

32. Ibid., 44.

33. Ibid., 32.

34. Henderson, *Cultural Diversity in the Workplace*.

35. Bennett, M. J., "A Developmental Approach to Training for Intercultural Sensitivity," *International Journal of Intercultural Relations* 10 (1986a): 179-96.

36. John R. Baldwin and M. L. Hecht, "The Layered Perspective of Cultural (In)Tolerance(s): The Roots of a Multidisciplinary Approach," in *Intercultural Communication Theory*, ed. Richard L. Wiseman (Thousand Oaks, CA: Sage Publications, Inc., 1995), 59-91.

37. Joplin and Daus, "Challenges of Leading a Diverse Workforce."

38. Patricia M. Arredondo, *Successful Diversity Management Initiatives: A Blueprint for Planning and Implementation* (Thousand Oaks, CA: Sage Publications, 1996).

39. Camila Alire, and S. Stielow, "Minorities and the Symbolic Potential of the Academic Library: Reinventing Tradition," *College and Research Libraries* 56 (6) (1999): 509-17.

Challenges of Working
in a Multicultural Environment

Joan S. Howland

SUMMARY. This article addresses six of the many challenges of working in a multicultural setting. As library staffs and patrons become increasingly diverse, it is critical that library administrations create environments where all individuals feel comfortable and supported. It is equally important that all individuals working in libraries are given equal opportunity to gain professional satisfaction and success, as well as demonstrate their unique strengths and skills. The six challenges addressed include: (1) fluctuating power dynamics; (2) merging a diversity of opinions and approaches; (3) overcoming perceived lack of empathy; (4) tokenism, reality or perception?; (5) accountability; and (6) transforming challenges into opportunities. *[Article copies available for a fee from The Haworth Document Delivery Service: 1-800-HAWORTH. E-mail address: <getinfo@haworthpressinc.com> Website: <http://www.HaworthPress.com> © 2001 by The Haworth Press, Inc. All rights reserved.]*

KEYWORDS. Diversity, multiculturalism, individualism, equity, accountability, library management, recruitment and retention

Joan S. Howland is Roger F. Noreen Professor of Law and Director of Information and Technology, University of Minnesota Law School, Minneapolis, MN.

The author extends deepest appreciation to Sushila Shah, 2000/01 APALA President, for her support, guidance, and editorial advice. The author also thanks April Schwartz, Business Reference Librarian at the University of Minnesota Law Library, for her expert research assistance and Paul Welling, University of Minnesota Law School ('02), for his astute editorial assistance.

This paper was presented at the Asian/Pacific American Librarians Association (APALA) Annual Meeting on July 9, 2000 in Chicago, IL.

[Haworth co-indexing entry note]: "Challenges of Working in a Multicultural Environment." Howland, Joan S. Co-published simultaneously in *Journal of Library Administration* (The Haworth Information Press, an imprint of The Haworth Press, Inc.) Vol. 33, No. 1/2, 2001, pp. 105-123; and: *Diversity Now: People, Collections, and Services in Academic Libraries* (ed: Teresa Y. Neely, and Kuang-Hwei (Janet) Lee-Smeltzer) The Haworth Information Press, an imprint of The Haworth Press, Inc., 2001, pp. 105-123. Single or multiple copies of this article are available for a fee from The Haworth Document Delivery Service [1-800-HAWORTH, 9:00 a.m. - 5:00 p.m. (EST). E-mail address: getinfo@haworthpressinc.com].

INTRODUCTION

The Civil Rights Act of 1964[1] catapulted the insidious presence of discrimination and racism in the American workplace into public and political consciousness. Statistics indicate that as our nation enters the 21st century, the population of the United States is more diverse than at any other point in history, and correspondingly our workforce, in almost all environments and at all levels, is more heterogeneous than ever before.[2] However, it is indisputable that the underlying goal of the social and legal movements of the 1960s, to ensure equal opportunity regardless of race, has not been met satisfactorily in the U.S. workplace.[3] Many companies, educational institutions, government entities, and certainly libraries, still struggle to achieve a diverse and truly integrated workforce. Most organizations continue to fall short in their efforts to recruit and effectively utilize the talents and skills of diverse individuals or to create an atmosphere that promotes the success of all ethnic groups, not just one or two that fit well defined "safe" profiles. Despite the civil rights legislation of the 1960s and its progeny, racism is still a pervasive element of many work environments, "often subtle in its manifestations, frequently not."[4]

Anyone who doubts that racism and discrimination are still alive and well in the United States needs only to refer to the fifteen part series entitled "How Race is Lived in America" that appeared on the front pages of the *New York Times* for six weeks in June and July, 2000.[5] A particularly poignant, albeit disquieting, article within the series appeared on June 16 and concerned the workforce of a slaughterhouse in Tar Heel, North Carolina. The headline of the article read, "At a Slaughterhouse Some Things Never Die: Who Kills, Who Cuts, Who Bosses Depends on Race."[6] The working conditions described were disturbingly reminiscent of the 1906 Chicago meat packing plant so graphically depicted in Upton Sinclair's *The Jungle*.[7] The blatant racism reported was tantamount to what one would expect if reading about a southern factory scene prior to the Second World War, not the year 2000. The hierarchy described in the article placed only whites in management positions with African-Americans, Latinos, and American Indians competing for the manual jobs, and if one believes the story, learning to detest one another in the process.

There has been some advancement over the past three decades in regard to achieving equal opportunity in the American workplace, even in the bastions of corporate America. Kenneth Chenault, an African-American, is currently the president and CEO of the American Express Company; Carlos Gutierrez, a Latino, is CEO of Kellogg Company; Surinder Rametra, an Asian Indian, is CEO of ATEC Group, Inc., and Charles Wang, a Chinese American, is CEO at Computer Associates International.[8] Representatives of diverse backgrounds also are leaders in higher education and government as is exemplified by individuals such as Rennard Strickland, an American Indian who is dean of the University of Oregon Law School, and Congressman J. C. Watts, Jr., an African-American who represents the state of Oklahoma.

In librarianship we have witnessed a slow, but steady, growth in the diversity of our profession with an increasing number of non-whites in upper management positions. We can be encouraged by a number of initiatives, particularly the American Library Association (ALA) Spectrum Scholarship program, which will ensure that bright, motivated individuals from diverse backgrounds are attracted to librarianship and receive the financial support to pursue the requisite graduate education. However, I agree with Teresa Y. Neely, assistant professor at Colorado State University Libraries, when she contends that librarians must be careful not to be lulled by persuasive rhetoric stressing how much better the situation is for people of color and diverse cultures than it was ten years ago.[9] One needs to only reference the sub-set of the profession that I represent-law librarianship-to find support for Dr. Neely's statement. There is only one person of color who is the director of the law library in a first quartile law school. And there are only a handful of law library directors of color among the other approximately 140 accredited law schools. Law librarianship is traditionally one of the most lucrative areas of librarianship, and yet less than an estimated 10 percent of law librarians in America are from diverse ethnic backgrounds.[10]

It is worthwhile to reflect on the rationale behind the need to ensure a diverse workforce in our libraries and to create environments where individuals from all backgrounds feel comfortable and supported. The American Council on Education recently released a statement that includes a credible list of reasons why multiculturalism should be supported in any environment: (1) it enriches the educational experience and learning environment; (2) it promotes personal growth-and a healthy society; (3) it strengthens communities and the workplace; and (4) it enhances economic competitiveness.[11] There are equally laudable, albeit practical and economically advantageous, reasons to promote multiculturalism and diversity in the workplace: (1) discrimination is both legally and morally wrong; and (2) a diverse workforce increases organizational effectiveness through improvement in morale, greater access to new segments in the marketplace, and enhanced productivity.[12]

In addition, with the continuing ethnic and cultural diversification of American society, the consumers of products in all environments, including libraries, have become more diverse. As service providers, librarians and their administrations obviously need to be able to respond effectively and sensitively to the changing demographics of our primary and secondary clienteles by employing a workforce, at all levels, that reflects this diversification. The more diverse an organization becomes, the more receptive it will find its clientele to the organization itself and the services it provides. John Deere, president of John Deere and Associates, says that human resources professionals have been arguing about diversity initiatives for years, and continually ask the question, "Is it the moral imperative or the legal compliance piece that drives support of multiculturalism in the workplace?" According to Mr. Deere, the best driver is pure business sense. He contends that, "as our consumers become more diverse, it is imperative that our managers, sale forces, executives, and service personnel become more diverse in order to adequately respond to the needs and concerns of those buying the products."[13]

The shift in labor market demographics is the leading reason that businesses support diversity. The U.S. Census Bureau predicts population growth through 2025, and the resulting statistics indicate that in many areas of the country non-whites will far outnumber whites in terms of both pure numbers and consumption.[14] Mr. Deere argues that these Census Bureau figures connote that ". . . in the majority of cases, the person knocking on our doors for employment is not going to be a white male. So we had better have the culture and systems ready [in the workplace] for the diversity of talent that will come in."[15]

Lost revenue due to turnover is another reason to support multiculturalism and diversity. Each employee who leaves because she feels unsupported or who fails, despite apparent talent and skills, costs an organization money. A recent survey indicates that the turnover of people of color is significantly greater than for whites, particularly greater than for white males. The study reports that in corporate America the overall turnover rate for non-whites is 40 percent higher than for whites. As reported, the primary reason for turnover is that the employees from diverse backgrounds have the perception that there will be a lack of career growth or a general dissatisfaction with the rate of professional progress.[16]

CHALLENGES OF WORKING
IN A MULTICULTURAL ENVIRONMENT

Organizations differ in their ability to capitalize on the diverse characteristics of a multicultural workforce and to utilize this diversity to create a richer, more productive environment. Many entities cannot get past entrenched attitudes and practices.[17] In some draconian organizations, legal requirements regarding the composition of the workforce are followed, but little other effort is expended to recruit or retain a multicultural workforce. The organization's routines and employment continue in much the same manner as they have for decades. In other organizations, marginally more committed to diversity, individuals from multicultural backgrounds are actively recruited and included in the daily practices and routines of the organization, but the skills and talents of these individuals are still never fully utilized. Conformity and the attitude of "go along to get along" and "don't rock the boat" are the tickets to even a modicum of success in such organizations. There are some organizations, unfortunately not the majority, that embrace the concept of multiculturalism and exploit the diversity of its employees to develop a non-conforming, creative, dynamic, and audacious, in the most positive sense of the word, environment. These also are environments in which differences are not just tolerated, but enthusiastically encouraged.

The challenges of working in a multicultural environment are as countless as the varied demographics and dynamics of work environments themselves. However, there are six common challenges which merit discussion.

Challenge One: Fluctuating Power Dynamics[18]

In any work environment, the infusion of new, diverse individuals, who may not mirror the traditions of an organization, may cause long-term or traditional staff members to fear an erosion of their personal institutional power and/or to fear power shifts throughout the organization that may have a negative impact upon them. As diversity and the pace of change increase within an organization, the commitment and attachment of long-term employees frequently decrease.[19] According to Janice Joplin and Catherine Daus in their definitive article "Challenges of Leading a Diverse Workforce":

> As power is redistributed, doubts may emerge within the veteran constituencies about how they will fit into the new organization.

An uneasiness about how to navigate what was once familiar territory may arise among these long term employees, and with it, an increasing tension may pervade the environment. Power struggles are natural consequences of competition for scarce resources and control over social structures. Diversity dynamics interact with unstable power structures and can result in lowered individual and organizational performance. Potential negative outcomes from this instability include poor work attitudes, withdrawal behaviors such as absenteeism and turnover, and perceptions of procedural injustice. In the worst scenario, long term employees will take the defensive and sabotage efforts that support a multicultural environment.[20]

Instances of these sorts of power struggles are replete in libraries. For example, when long honored dress codes are amended to accommodate individuals from diverse cultures, many veteran employees feel either that the standards of the organization are being eroded or that the administration is bending to the interests of one particular group. Another example arises when an administration broadens the decision-making processes to include a wider range of employees and viewpoints; employees, especially supervisors, who are accustomed to a more hierarchical, top down decision-making process may feel threatened or undermined. In other situations employees who have been raised to believe that tardiness to meetings is rude may need to recognize that arriving five minutes late to a meeting is not the cardinal sin in some societies that it is in the Anglo culture. A final example arises in the academic environment when an administration amends tenure requirements to recognize the wide range of contributions that individuals from diverse backgrounds can bring to the workplace in addition to traditional activities such as leadership positions in professional organizations and scholarship within a relatively narrow band of appropriate subject matters. Criticisms, including declarations of the lowering of academic standards and pandering to minority librarians, are invariably lobbed at the administration from librarians who have a stake in maintaining the status quo.

Uneasiness and increasing tensions can occur when individuals from a variety of cultures gain a significant voice in an organization and openly express their concerns. Veteran constituencies with large blocks of power, such as senior management or department heads, may be uncomfortable with accepting diverse viewpoints that are likely to challenge the old guard's power, either explicitly or implicitly. Also, if top management in an organization supports the concerns of an emerging voice, the old guard will often cry favoritism or capitulation.

Libraries that experience a rapid expansion of multiculturalism in their workforce or clientele frequently send all employees to the obligatory diversity training workshop. However, if employees are forced to attend training sessions when they do not believe in the basic tenets of racial equality and universal opportunity in the workplace, the training actually makes the situation worse.[21] "Employees who are required to attend diversity training against their will, and who already hold negative attitudes and stereotypes about other groups, are likely to become even more negative, rather than more positive and accepting."[22] I have attended many diversity training sessions throughout my career and have learned a great deal, but I have always approached these programs with the belief that diversity is a positive component of any organization. However, I have never attended a diversity training program, including those offered by the ALA, where the speaker was so charismatic or persuasive that I think she/he would have converted me had I been a non-believer.

An alternative to traditional diversity training sessions, utilized with great success in the business world, is an approach that strategically integrates veteran power holders in an organization with new hires from diverse backgrounds through committee work, teams, and project pairings. This approach provides an avenue for individuals from different backgrounds to become better acquainted and to learn to respect one another. This tactic has been employed with great success in environments such as the traditional corporate law firm where attorneys generally do not care who they work with as long everyone carries a fair share of the workload and contributes to the winning effort for the client.

In regard to this proposed tactic, library managers must learn to acknowledge the potential benefits of instigating the creative tension of randomly mixing individuals from diverse backgrounds without overemphasizing the process of diversity integration, which can create skeptics among employees and can be destructive rather than productive for the organization.[23] However, this strategy is no more obvious or contrived than summoning everyone to a diversity training program.[24]

Challenge Two: Merging a Diversity of Opinions and Approaches

Janice Joplin and Catherine Daus identify the need to integrate varied and often diametrically opposed opinions as one of the primary challenges in managing a diverse workforce:

As the face of an organization changes and its workforce becomes more diverse, the number and range of perspectives will increase exponentially, and the institution must synthesize a diversity of opinions driven by unique values, experiences, and cultural groundings. Two people can view the same event with very different interpretations and formulate opinions on the basis of those perceptions and interpretations. Getting to the crux of critical issues, while respecting and maintaining the core integrity and dignity of participants, is essential to creating an accepting and productive multicultural environment. Even in the best of circumstances, miscommunication will inevitably occur, because we all have unique frames of reference. The challenge . . . is to identify and recognize these different frames of reference and to extract common denominators that may serve as a foundation for issue resolution. Synthesizing diverse opinions, finding shared ground, and reaching at least some modicum of agreement may be one of the most time-consuming, emotionally-wrenching, and energy-draining activities any of us can undertake. Each differing perspective is likely to reflect the emotional attachments of the bearer. The critical exercise is to separate substance from rhetoric and to determine the essential content of the message, rather than get lost in the manner of delivery or the particular characteristics of the person expressing the opinion.[25]

There are still libraries where there is a relatively low tolerance for diversity, not only of races and cultures but also of viewpoints. In these libraries, lack of tolerance is reflected in visible disdain for non-conformity in opinions, communication patterns, dress, work styles, or personal habits. In such environments, staff members from diverse backgrounds may choose not to engage in conflict or not to voice non-conforming views for fear of sanctions. This results in less confrontation and in the illusion of agreement and cooperation, although it does not usually result in the best decision making processes nor the most creative management practices. I have frequently witnessed this type of dynamic at law school faculty meetings where assistant professors, with vastly divergent viewpoints from the senior faculty, have chosen not to confront the old guard for fear of retaliation when they come up for tenure in the foreseeable future. I also have witnessed similar interactions in libraries where newer librarians with diverse viewpoints are reluctant to contradict veteran library administrators who are wedded to mainstream conventions.

Most organizations today, including libraries, pay at least lip service to the concept of valuing the broad diversity of opinions and experiences that a multicultural workforce brings to the environment. This perceived or actual lip service can be seen in documents, "emanating from the administration, that tout the benefits of capitalizing on diverse opinions to both internal operations and external stakeholders,"[26] such as library patrons. However, far too frequently varied perspectives are actively sought and theoretically integrated into the decision-making process, but in reality these diverse views are dismissed without any real consideration.[27] I have witnessed this phenomenon countless times during discussions of cataloging rules and procedures. In a typical scenario, a staff member questions the appropriateness of a subject classification or suggests that a subject heading be altered to make it more intuitive to a larger segment of the patron population. The standard response by senior librarians (and I regret some librarians fresh out of graduate school) is a vague reference to that mammoth beast known as the Library of Congress Classification system. These strident librarians fail to focus on the obvious fact that the Library of Congress schedules represent the perspective and values of white America during the 1950s and 1960s, rather than the patron populations served by libraries in the 21st century.

In most management situations, dismissing non-traditional ideas and perspectives is the easiest, least time-consuming strategy; yet it reflects a considerable loss of effort and resources, particularly when an organization is theoretically committed to inclusion and tolerance. The challenge for an organization is to act upon and implement the ideas of diverse members of the organization, while respecting those traditional policies and standards that are still appropriate for the evolving environment. It also should be noted that not every innovative idea is a good idea, no matter what its source. The response to this second challenge should include the creation of an organization where appreciation of diverse perceptions and ideas is the standard, and conflict takes on a constructive and collaborative tone.

Challenge Three: Overcoming Perceived Lack of Empathy

The challenge of integrating diverse viewpoints and opinions into the culture of an organization is integrally linked with the third challenge-overcoming perceived lack of empathy.[28] Perceptions that an organization does not truly care about the distinct concerns of individual groups can be disruptive to an organization and impede its ability to advance in any number of directions. This challenge is complicated by the fact that often one unique group within the broader spectrum of diverse populations does not perceive that they are supported or understood by other diverse populations.

Perceptions of lack of empathy are often rampant throughout an organization. Just as staff members, supervisors, and managers frequently believe that top level administrators do not truly understand the issues associated with multiculturalism, top level administrators often believe that staff members with diversity concerns have no idea how hard it is to balance all the competing issues that need to be resolved. For example, I once served as an administrator in a library where a staff member from a diverse background had a variety of problems with her supervisor, who was not particularly sensitive to the dynamics of working in a multicultural environment. The staff member asked to be reassigned to another supervisor. I was reluctant to do so because I thought this was an avoidance strategy rather than a tactic that would lead to a positive solution. Also, a transfer made no sense organizationally. At the time my perception was that the staff member felt that I was being insensitive and unsupportive. However, the answer to this problem was clearly not a transfer, but rather improved communication and openness about the many dimensions of the issue at hand. The best response to this type of situation is "to listen, with empathy, in a way that inspires openness and trust, while attempting to understand where others are coming from, what they have been through, and where they are going."[29]

Part of the dynamic of addressing this challenge is the reality that claims of favoritism and lack of empathy arise in even the most supportive and inclusive environments. Some members of one diverse group may feel that an organization that espouses concerns about another diverse group and diverts resources to that group is not concerned about them.[30] The competition between factions can place administrators, as well as co-workers, in the middle of political and emotional battles. Often dissimilar groups, with common goals and concerns, are reluctant to work together and, in reality, show very little empathy toward one another. There is sometimes a fear that by working together the gains for any one group will be diluted (and this certainly is an issue we see throughout society, not just in the work environment). The response to this part of the challenge is for library managers to foster an environment that encourages diverse groups to work together to identify commonalities, as well as learn to understand culturally specific needs, concerns, and attitudes.

Challenge Four: Tokenism, Reality or Perception?

A disturbing but very real challenge in any environment attempting to create a positive multicultural environment is the issue of dealing with real or perceived tokenism. "Real tokenism occurs when an employee is hired over other clearly more qualified candidates in an effort to address stakeholder concerns or simply to fulfill numbers. Quota systems, which often communicate blatant tokenism, are rarely in the best interests of an organization."[31] Historically, quota systems have been utilized in some situations when it was the only way to ensure that diverse individuals would be recruited and given fair consideration in the selection process. In other situations, quotas have been an ill-conceived method to achieve racial integration.[32]

While true tokenism can, and in my opinion should, be avoided by not using any sort of quota system, perceived tokenism can still arise. Perceived tokenism occurs when an individual is hired based purely on experience, credentials, and ability, but is perceived by others to have been hired based on ethnic background, gender, or some similar criteria.[33] Where tokenism is presumed, there is a tendency to attribute failures to a person's race, lack of intelligence, laziness, and similarly biased observations, and to attribute success to pure luck, "the benevolence of the organization,"[34] or to a lowering of standards. These beliefs are not only falsehoods, but can damage an employee's self-esteem and self-identity.[35]

This challenge needs to be addressed from an institutional perspective. Pursuant to fair and balanced hiring procedures that look to diversity as just one of many factors in determining the development of the strongest workforce possible. Evaluation and promotion policies must respect diverse backgrounds but not show preference to any one group over others. As part of addressing this challenge, it is critical that all individuals are given the same chance to succeed and therefore have the same opportunity to receive the desirable assignments, serve on the important task forces, chair critical committees, and to work with senior professionals who may serve as mentors. An important component of this concept is maintaining the same rules for everyone-this includes both rewards and matters involving discipline.[36]

Institutionally, it is critical to utilize the skills and talents of staff from diverse backgrounds and clearly communicate that these individuals are fully participating, valued members of the organization. It is equally important for an administration to aggressively dispel rumors of tokenism as soon as they rise to the surface. These rumors must be directly countered with hard facts regarding selection and promotion decisions before these distortions become accepted truths.[37] One must always remember that no matter how wrong the perception, if the falsehood is repeated enough times it becomes, for all intents and purposes, reality.

Before leaving the discussion of this challenge, one must be cognizant that tokenism is a critical and disturbing concern not only from an institutional perspective but also from a personal perspective. As mentioned above, in a situation where an employee is aware that others perceive her as a token hire and thereby communicate the message that she is not as worthy as other staff members, the employee can't help but feel disadvantaged in the workplace.

Challenge Five: Holding Everyone Throughout the Organization Accountable for Achieving a Positive Multicultural Environment

Talk is cheap. Rhetoric, especially about sensitive issues such as diversity, can roll easily off the tongue. However, the real challenge is to implement strategies to achieve a diverse, universally supportive environment, and to withstand diatribes from the naysayers who contend that the possibility of equality in the workplace is a fairytale left over from the 1960s. And at the heart of this challenge is the reality that to successfully meet this challenge everyone throughout an organization must be held accountable for ensuring a positive multicultural environment.

Few diversity initiatives in any organization succeed unless there is unconditional support from top level management. Therefore, when discussing accountability, the logical place to start is administration. Roger Wheeler, the Chief Tax Officer at General Motors and a strong proponent of incorporating multiculturalism into all aspects of corporate management, has stated, "To put it bluntly, we should get rid of, fix, or not hire in the first place any leaders who cannot manage diversity-if a corporate leader can't create a healthy climate at all levels of the organization for all groups within the organization, then he should not be in a position of responsibility."[38]

Leaders who voice a commitment to multiculturalism "must be passionately dedicated to the vision of diversity and fanatically committed"[39] to carrying out the necessary vision and goals. There is always the danger that, after a great deal of grandstanding about the importance of diversity and inclusion, inertia will set in and the administration will move on to the next challenge or crisis, leaving a series of unfinished (and frequently underfunded) initiatives in their wake. Administrative leaders must be committed to supporting multiculturalism for the long term if the creation of an inclusive environment is to be assured. The challenge is to ensure that leaders keep diversity on their "radar screens" at all times and as a priority within all organizational initiatives.

Holding middle management accountable is an equally critical component of addressing this challenge because these individuals are invariably critical to the implementation and success of programs designed to ensure equality and to promote awareness of diversity concerns. Frequently, middle managers are the strongest advocates of the promotion of diversity in the workplace because they are close enough to the "front lines" to perceive the manner in which diversity will strengthen the organization and create an environment that is more sensitive to the concerns of the varied patron populations. As part of their annual evaluation process, it may be advisable to require middle managers to demonstrate how they have supported and furthered the organization's commitment to developing a work climate that supports diversity and multiculturalism.

The third part of this challenge concerns the need for the cooperation and participation of representatives of the multicultural groups themselves. All staff members must assume responsibility for helping to build a universally supportive environment and to make adjustments to their own behaviors as appropriate. In addition, everyone within the organization must learn patience-it may take months or even years to break down the psychological barriers that have been in place for decades. There must be considerable give and take on all sides, along with the acceptance of diverse viewpoints. There also needs to be an acceptance that reasonable minds can disagree on even the most fundamental issues.

Challenge Six: Turning Challenges into Opportunities

Perhaps the most critical challenge is that of transforming the challenges of working in a multicultural environment into opportunities. Although at times the challenges cited above may seem intimidating or even insurmountable, there is no point in: (1) bemoaning the situation; (2) criticizing the actions of institutions or individuals; or (3) dissecting the work environment and its leadership ad nauseam, if one makes no effort to help rectify the situation and/or elicit either a lesson or an opportunity from the situation. As mentioned earlier, talk is cheap and complaining about others is the cheapest rhetoric of all.

Although I am rarely a Pollyanna, I firmly believe that there are tremendous gains to be realized by forcefully addressing the issues and concerns encountered when working in multicultural environments. However, opportunities will be realized only by those individuals who discipline themselves to be focused, astute, creative, non-judgmental, and action-oriented. By confronting challenges head on-regardless of whether these challenges are driven by miscommunication, intolerance, ignorance, insecurity, callousness, irresponsibility, or lethargy-we can utilize the knowledge gained to create strategic advantages for ourselves and those constituencies that we wish to support. If we have learned one lesson in our careers as librarians, it is that we cannot rely on our institutions, professional associations, the law, or any other entity to defend us. If we fail to protect our own interests, no one else is going to champion our concerns and needs.

The first challenge mentioned in this article was the fluctuating dynamics of power in today's libraries. These power struggles are the natural consequence of introducing new people, ideas, values, processes, and concerns into a traditionally stable environment. Veteran power holders are often tremendously threatened by any perceived erosion of the status quo. Difficulties can arise for those who bring diversity to an otherwise homogenous environment, but they should take advantage of the changing dynamics of power and aggressively assert themselves. While I hesitate to use the word "grasp" which may have negative connotations, I would definitely encourage individuals from diverse backgrounds to reach for power by openly voicing concerns, stepping up to help solve the problems that confront the institution, holding the institution and its leadership accountable for ensuring equality in the workplace, and, at the same time, continually proving their own ability to further the overall goals of the organization.

Rosabeth Kanter is often quoted as saying, "Power is the last dirty word in the American vocabulary. It is easier to talk about money-and much easier to talk about sex-than it is to talk about power."[40] Yet power is basically what we all need to achieve our objectives. In libraries, power is access to the personnel or material resources "to make things happen." We are all acutely sensitive to the fact that in many cultures aggressive behavior or assertiveness is not considered appropriate, especially when such behavior means questioning one's superiors. However, "there is more than one way to skin a cat," there is more than one way to obtain power, and often the more circumspect ways are the most effective. Two exceptionally powerful librarians in my organization-and, once again, I define power as having the ability to acquire resources and to achieve one's institutional goals-are the most quiet and most unassertive. They rarely speak up in meetings and have never publicly contradicted their supervisors. However, they both quietly communicate with their supervisors and other colleagues through detailed and well reasoned memos and by forwarding information relevant to their concerns. They both almost always get what they want, not so much by being aggressive, but by being rational and relentless. These librarians are achieving power and acquiring institutional respect through educating their colleagues, including the leaders in the library, to the real facts. Both of these individuals are very perceptive about power shifts in the organization and are taking the appropriate steps to ensure that they end up with "a piece of the pie."

The second challenge noted above stems from the issue that as working environments become more diverse, a variety of opinions, values, experiences, and cultural groundings need to be synthesized and incorporated into the dynamics of the organization. Obviously, it can be exceptionally difficult to effectively merge and process divergent points of view to resolve problems and address institutional concerns. The opportunities this challenge offers are equally obvious. The integration of all that can be learned from a multitude of cultures into the decision making processes will undoubtedly make everyone involved more productive, insightful, and reflective. This process also may very well result in individuals taking greater pride in their own cultures as they gain respect for other ethnic and cultural groups.

In addition, this second challenge provides the opportunity for individuals to hone their communication skills when dealing with others who have dissimilar ways of expressing themselves or approaching issues. This does not mean that we need to learn to express ourselves in the same way as those around us; we only need to learn to express ourselves in a way that they understand. Sushila Shah of the DeWitt Wallace Library at Macalester College in St. Paul, Minnesota shared with me the story of how in the early years of her career, due to her upbringing and culture, she did not feel comfortable disagreeing or asserting her rights in the workplace. Verbal conflict was very difficult for her because confrontation made her feel uncomfortable. However, over time, Sushila realized that she could communicate in a way that she found comfortable and appropriate, and still assert her position. In her situation, written memorandums proved the most effectual and beneficial method of communication.

The third challenge presented involves the need to overcome actual or perceived lack of empathy. This challenge arises when an organization fails to demonstrate any true commitment to addressing the diverse concerns of employees and to promoting an integrated working environment. This challenge can become even more complicated when distinct groups within a multicultural environment fail to support one another. The most effective response to this challenge is to create an environment driven by effectual communication and at least a modicum of trust-not only between the staff and the administration, but also different interest groups. The obvious opportunity created by addressing this challenge and building effectual avenues of communication is the identification of commonalties between the groups as well as unique needs, concerns, and attitudes. This knowledge can subsequently be used to push the organization forward. We can seize this type of opportunity not only in institutional situations but also within our professional organizations. ALA's Diversity Council is a perfect example. Those involved in the work of the Council have seen that pulling different interest groups together-APALA, CALA, AILA, BCALA, REFORMA, and others-is not always an easy process, and there is often considerable dissent. However, the opportunities derived from this initiative in terms of information sharing, coalition building, programming, and just good fun have been tremendous.

Combating tokenism is the challenge I personally find the most troublesome and disturbing. True inclusion is driven by a desire to address the needs of varied groups, a desire for the participation and input of these groups, and a desire to provide equality for all groups. However, we are all acutely aware of situations where inclusion is tainted by other motives and agendas. In addition to working towards a future where individuals are valued solely by the unique skills, knowledge, perspective, and sensitivities that they bring to any situation, this challenge includes the need to develop a climate where no one questions the inclusion of any one group or individual. The inherent opportunity to be found in this challenge is the possibility to educate the naysayers and skeptics to the strengths of every group.

The fifth challenge-holding everyone throughout the organization accountable for achieving a positive multicultural organization-stems from the concept that an institution needs to back up its rhetoric about the creation of an inclusive and diverse environment by rewarding those individuals throughout the organization who actively support this goal and sanction those who fail to do so. The flip side of this concept is that staff must hold the library's leaders accountable if the organization fails to fulfill its promises. This challenge provides individuals from diverse backgrounds with the opportunity to educate others by working together, and while pushing forward on individual agendas, devoting an equal amount of energy towards those concerns that support the common good. In addition, this challenge allows us to hone our communication and resolution skills, as well as those skills associated with patience and perseverance.

CONCLUSION

The mere presence of a multicultural workforce in an institution and the identification of the challenges associated with working in a multicultural environment do not ensure that a library will automatically deal with the issues surrounding this situation in an effective manner. The staffs of most organizations spend a great deal of time talking and not acting because individuals are constantly revisiting the same issues.[41] To respond effectively to these challenges, we must bring talented and committed people together-individuals who can question one another's thinking, who can collectively approach problems from multiple points of view, and who can develop sound solutions to complex problems. However, aggressive action must be taken, results must be delivered, and staff at all levels throughout the organization must be held accountable. There will no doubt be some casualties along the way and staff who fail to respond to the changing world around them may find themselves left behind or even discarded. Also, as the face of our multicultural environments continue to evolve with the change in the demographics of our country, we must continually reevaluate our perspectives and action plans to make certain that they are still appropriate. In addition, we need to constantly look beyond the walls of not just our libraries, but our profession, to find methods to create inclusive environments and to develop responses to the challenges identified above. Librarians spend too much time talking to one another. Most professions are dealing with issues associated with the increasing multiculturalism in our country. We should adapt whatever successful strategies that we find elsewhere to our own environments.

NOTES

1. *Civil Rights Act of 1964. U. S. Code*, vol. 42, sec. 2000 (1999).
2. David A. Thomas and Suzy Wetlaufer, "A Question of Color: A Debate on Race in the U.S. Workplace," *Harvard Business Review* 75 (September/October 1997): 118-132.
3. Ibid.
4. Ibid.

5. New York Times Writers, *How Race Is Lived in America: Pulling Together, Pulling Apart* (New York: Henry Holt & Company, Inc., 2001).

6. Charlie LeDuff, "At a Slaughterhouse, Some Things Never Die: Who Kills, Who Cuts, Who Bosses Can Depend on Race," *The New York Times*, 16 June 2000, A1, A22-A23.

7. Upton Sinclair, *The Jungle* (New York: The Jungle Publishing Co., 1906).

8. Patricia Kitchen, "A White Man's World: Diversity in Management," *Newsday*, 10 April 2000, A07.

9. As referenced in Martin Goldberg and Susan Hamburger, "The Challenge to Change: Creating Diversity in Libraries," *College & Research Libraries News* 59 (December 1998): 841-43.

10. Yvonne Chandler, "Why Is Diversity Important for Law Librarianship," *Law Library Journal* 90 (fall 1998): 545-60.

11. "ACE Adopts Diversity Statement," *Black Issues in Higher Education*, 19 February 1998, 32-3.

12. David A. Thomas and Robin J. Ely, "Making Difference Matter: A New Paradigm for Managing Diversity," *Harvard Business Review* 77 (September-October 1999): 79-90.

13. Jean-Marie Martino, *Diversity: An Imperative for Business Success* (The Conference Board, 1999), 7.

14. U.S. Bureau of the Census, *Current Population Reports* (Washington, DC: 1998), 25-1130.

15. Martino, *Diversity.*

16. Taylor H. Cox and Stacy Blake, "Managing Cultural Diversity: Implications for Organizational Competitiveness," *The Executive* 5 (August 1991): 45-6.

17. Janice R. W. Joplin and Catherine S. Daus, "Challenges of Leading a Diverse Workforce," *The Executive* 11 (August 1997): 32-47.

18. Ibid. The first four challenges listed in this article are very similar to those identified and discussed by Janice Joplin and Catherine Daus in the cited article.

19. Ibid.

20. Ibid.

21. Ibid., 35.

22. Ibid.

23. Ibid.

24. The author does not intend to convey the position that the typical diversity training session is an inappropriate strategy in all situations; however, there are credible alternative strategies that should be considered.

25. Joplin and Daus, "Challenges of Leading a Diverse Workforce."

26. Ibid.

27. Ibid.

28. Ibid.

29. Ibid.

30. Ibid.

31. Ibid., 41.

32. Ibid.

33. Joplin and Daus, "Challenges of Leading a Diverse Workforce," 42.

34. Ibid.

35. Ibid.

36. Howland, "Beyond recruitment," 9.

37. Joplin and Daus, "Challenges of Leading a Diverse Workforce," 43.

38. Patricia Digh, "The Next Challenge: Holding People Accountable," *HR Magazine* 43 (October 1998): 63-9.

39. Rosabeth Moss Kanter, *When Giants Learn to Dance: Mastering the Challenge of Strategy, Management, and Careers in the 1990s* (New York: Simon and Schuster, 1989).

40. Rosabeth Moss Kanter, "Power Failure in Management Circuits," *Harvard Business Review* 57 (July-August 1979): 65.

41. U.S. Bureau of the Census, *Current Population Reports*, 11.

Cultural Diversity and Gender Role Spillover: A Working Perspective

Bertie Greer
Denise Stephens
Vicki Coleman

SUMMARY. One of the more sensitive topics within the diversity literature concerns gender issues. This paper explores the effect of gender role spillover in the workplace and examines the relationship of men and women in library administration. Most gender issues are based primarily upon cultural influences. These influences can bring rise to work-related conflicts pertaining to stereotypes, differences in leadership styles, occupational segregation, sexual harassment, and discrimination. Organizations must be proactive and create environments conducive to the success of both male and female workers. *[Article copies available for a fee from The Haworth Document Delivery Service: 1-800-HAWORTH. E-mail address: <getinfo@haworthpressinc.com> Website: <http://www.HaworthPress.com> © 2001 by The Haworth Press, Inc. All rights reserved.]*

KEYWORDS. Gender, gender role, females, spillover, discrimination, sexual harassment, stereotypes, leadership, diversity

---

Bertie Greer, PhD, is affiliated with Northern Kentucky University, Highland Heights, KY (E-mail: bmgreer@exchange.nku.edu).

Denise Stephens is Director, Anschutz Library, University of Kansas, Lawrence, KS (E-mail: dstephens@ukans.edu).

Vicki Coleman is Director, Clemons Library, University of Virginia, Charlottesville, VA (E-mail: vc4n@virginia.edu).

[Haworth co-indexing entry note]: "Cultural Diversity and Gender Role Spillover: A Working Perspective." Greer, Bertie, Denise Stephens, and Vicki Coleman. Co-published simultaneously in *Journal of Library Administration* (The Haworth Information Press, an imprint of The Haworth Press, Inc.) Vol. 33, No. 1/2, 2001, pp. 125-140; and: *Diversity Now: People, Collections, and Services in Academic Libraries* (ed: Teresa Y. Neely, and Kuang-Hwei (Janet) Lee-Smeltzer) The Haworth Information Press, an imprint of The Haworth Press, Inc., 2001, pp. 125-140. Single or multiple copies of this article are available for a fee from The Haworth Document Delivery Service [1-800-HAWORTH, 9:00 a.m. - 5:00 p.m. (EST). E-mail address: getinfo@haworthpressinc.com].

125

BACKGROUND

The challenges addressed in this paper pertain to the effect of gender-related cultural influences in the workplace. Cultural influences can create different expectations and perceptions about the role of men and women in the workplace.[1] Globalization and other business initiatives are driving most organizations to venture into new endeavors that are a part of a culture that is different from their own. While some organizations have been successful in their new environment, others are finding that cultural differences present obstacles to success.[2] Issues such as stereotyping, leadership styles, discrimination, and sexual harassment all complicate an otherwise effective business environment.

This study focuses on the effects of increased cultural diversity in an unbalanced gender workforce. Researchers have found in many cases that gender role spillover does not occur in gender-balanced work forces.[3] It is our goal to assess this concept in a female-dominated profession, librarianship. There are many cases where sexual harassment and other gender-related conflicts are demonstrated in male-dominated work environments.[4] But how do these conflicts reveal themselves in librarianship? Librarianship is a field that is over 80 percent female; yet, women are still underrepresented at the top.[5] This article will explore the relationship between men and women in library administration and analyze how cultural diversity impacts co-worker relationships by assessing gender role issues and conflicts. It also discusses methods that library management can use to reduce dysfunctional conflicts caused by cultural, societal, and gender differences.

INTRODUCTION

Gender Role Spillover Defined

Gender role spillover refers to the carryover of gender-based expectations into the workplace. The expectations associated with social roles are determined primarily by culture. Women are often characterized as passive, loyal, emotional, and nurturing. On the other hand, traits typically associated with men include rational, analytical, assertive, tough, and competitive.[6] Spillover may occur for several reasons. First, gender is the most noticeable social attribute. Second, studies show that people feel comfortable reacting to work colleagues of the opposite sex in the same manner as they react to the opposite sex in their personal lives.

Third, the characteristics of work and sex roles may make possible the carryover of gender roles into the workplace. Gender roles remain stable throughout our lives and are learned earlier than work roles. Thus, there is a strong likelihood that gender roles will permeate all other domains of our lives.[7]

Negative Impact of Spillover

It is important to heighten awareness of the negative consequences of gender role spillover in the workplace. Negative consequences comprise, but are not limited to, gender bias, gender stereotypes, sexual harassment, and barriers to career growth.[8]

Although librarianship is a female-dominated profession, both males and females within the profession endure work-related pressures based on the practices of gender bias. In a study conducted on the job satisfaction of male librarians, some men complained that because of their gender, quite often they were relegated to performing "scout jobs" such as lifting and moving large items; others were asked to work nights and weekend hours because security was assumed to be "no problem."[9] With regard to females, this profession became "feminized" due to gender bias in the mainstream workforce. Librarianship has become a refuge for educated women barred from entering other professions. "The movement from home into librarianship was seen as a genteel calling and an extension of women's traditional role because it involved service, transmittal of societal values and culture, focus on the individual and attention to detail."[10]

Overall, men in female-dominated professions report lower levels of negative cultural pressure than women in female-dominated professions. An explanation may be that men only perceive themselves in the numerical minority in the workplace but not less powerful than women. In contrast, women in male-dominated professions report similar levels of pressure from tokenism as women in female-dominated professions. It is suspected that regardless of gender dominance, all women managers face the same general pressures.[11]

Much of the pressure placed on each gender derives from stereotypes associated with males and females in a female-dominated profession. Men moving into female-dominated jobs are perceived as stepping down in status while women entering traditionally male professions are viewed as stepping up.[12] This perception could explain why men who might show aptitude for a particular type of job, e.g., teaching, librarianship, or nursing are possibly discouraged from pursuing it because of the stigma associated with working in a female-dominated profession. Female sex stereotypes place women into a double bind situation. Women who adopt stereotypically masculine leadership techniques are sometimes depicted as abrasive and maladjusted. Those who use stereotypically feminine styles, e.g., showing emotion, yielding, nurturing, etc., are often seen as ineffective and incompetent as managers.[13]

The majority of librarians are female; however, they do not comprise the majority of senior level positions within libraries. Perceived spillover from personal life to work has been attributed as the rationale for the low representation. Spillover stereotypes of females suggest that women are so active outside of work that their personal lives may pose conflicts within the work domain and that their capacity to perform at work will be reduced.[14] A recent article dispelling this myth contends that employers' concerns need not be how active professional women are in nonwork domains, but rather how well both men and women manage their multiple domains.[15]

In addition to strictly gender-related issues, there are also issues that result from the combination of gender roles and cultural influences. In the next section, we will discuss the issues that have resulted from the interaction of cultural diversity and gender role spillover.

INTERACTION OF CULTURAL DIVERSITY AND GENDER ROLE SPILLOVER

Self-Concept

Self-concept, "an individual's most complete description of himself or herself, including internal and external attributes,"[16] is influenced by many factors. When gender role spillover in the workplace is considered, two factors are of particular significance, namely, socialization and stereotyping. As more women enter the professional ranks, the question of how their gender role socialization impacts individual professional placement and achievement is of importance in all fields. Dodd-McCue and Wright note that women face professional and personal tension with regard to organizational commitment and home-life responsibilities, ". . . men appeared to identify with their organizations and to value their organizational roles as a central life interest. This suggests that men are more likely than women to associate their identity with their work environment."[17] The socialization of women in western culture places higher value on family roles (nurturer and conciliator) than on affinity with the professional work environment. Males are generally socialized to value competition and professional achievement. Consequently, gender role expectations create an ongoing source of role conflict for professional women, while the socialization of men is more likely to promote consistency in personal and professional role expectations.[18]

The belief that men and women exhibit attitudes and behaviors in organizations as a consequence of gender role socialization describes the Gender-Centered Model, an often-studied explanation for the influence of innate and learned gender-based tendencies among leaders. This theoretical approach has been the focus of considerable research in gender studies, particularly in the area of leadership behaviors.[19] The Gender-Centered Model serves as a useful context for discussing the second major factor related to gender role spillover at work-stereotyping. The Model suggests that stereotypes about male and female attitudes, behaviors, and competence may be closely linked to their perceived compliance with widely held gender role expectations. We live and work in environments governed by cultural norms. These norms include expected behaviors and attitudes that influence our experiences at home and work.

Gender roles that are norms for one environment may produce role conflict in another. Stereotypes about how men and women are perceived to be, their attributes and limitations, combined with role conflict, produce real consequences at work. Reskin posits that the gender roles commonly associated with women promote perceptions that hinder the placement of women in positions or occupations that are inconsistent with their perceived desires or organizational commitment. "Employers' reservations about women may be based on presumed differences in strength of tolerance for adverse working conditions or the belief that women's domestic roles will lead to excessive absences and turnover rates."[20] Perceived tendencies toward absenteeism and the presumption that women are intolerant of adversity are stereotypical barriers to employment in non-gender role consistent occupations.

Organizational Life and Work

Gender roles play a part in the nature of life and work in organizations. The work life of staff in the organizational culture is reflected in their job assignments, compensation, and co-worker relationships. As previously noted, sex segregation persists in American work life. This separateness of work experiences for men and women is found even in female-dominated organizations, such as libraries. Stanley Wilder observes a growing trend toward male-concentrated and female-concentrated job categories among Association of Research Libraries (ARL) institutions. Of particular interest is the growth of males in higher-paying "functional specialist" positions and the continued high affiliation of females in lower-paying reference positions. Wilder notes,

> The distribution of men and women in these job categories also points to sex segregation. A disproportionate number of men are reported as working in the functional specialist position (17.4% of all men are reported as functional specialists and only 11.4% women) . . . Functional specialists often tend to be those professionals with increased technological sophistication whereas reference librarians have a strong service orientation.[21]

This trend is significant due to the current and historical low participation of men in the library profession. Among ARL libraries, the rate of male participation has held steady at approximately 35 percent since 1980.[22] Although a predominantly female profession, research libraries may, in fact, see positions that are consistent with gender role expectations less valued in terms of compensation. Since the extent to which women and men self-select professional job categories is unclear, further research on this topic would prove useful in determining the potential impact of gender role stereotyping on job assignment and position redeployment in these rapidly changing organizations.

Research by Sharon Lovell and her colleagues suggests that the interaction of organizational performance values and even widely desired behaviors and attitudes in organizations may not prove professionally beneficial for women. They report that the practice of Organizational Citizenship Behavior (OCB) is consistent with female gender role attributes (helpfulness, supportiveness, and willingness to make personal sacrifices for the organizational good). In studying OCB orientation and performance evaluation, they find that women practice significantly higher OCB than men. However, no positive relationship is found between the practice of OCB and women's performance evaluations. "The more members of either group engaged in OCB, the more highly they tended to be rated by their supervisor. The discrimination was that, overall, women engaged more highly in OCB than men yet were not evaluated more highly than men were."[23] Thus, while OCB may be beneficial to an organization, the behaviors earn less performance value when practiced by women. This is consistent with what Lovell and other researchers describe as a devaluation of attributes stereotypically associated with women, such as those affiliated with OCB. Co-worker relationships and training appear to be linked to organizational satisfaction for both men and women. Both sexes tend to report more positive work experiences when they have supportive same-sex relationships with managers. These same-sex relationships may have added positive effects for women as well as other minorities. Assessment of small group leadership training indicates that women report a more positive learning experience when the training leader is female. Further, women managers report feeling better understood by women leaders who can share private and professional insights and advice.[24]

Leadership

Leadership, specifically gender-based differences in leadership styles, and perceptions by others of leader's attributes and effectiveness, are also explored in this study. The topic is of substantial relevance in research libraries, as this predominantly female profession struggles with constant organizational change and a rapidly aging professional workforce. In 1998, nearly 40 percent of librarians in the United States were between 45 and 54 years of age. This is compared to 25 percent of comparable professionals in the same age group.[25]

While the existence of stereotypes about gender and leadership expectations is evident, empirical distinctions in the actual leadership behaviors practiced by men and women are limited. Eagly and Johnson determine that women and men practice leadership differently. Their 1990 study indicates a greater tendency among women leaders to practice a democratic style-participatory decision-making and bi-directional communication. Men in leadership positions tend to practice a more autocratic style-sole decision-making and greater use of directive communication.[26] These leadership behaviors may be associated with the cultural foundations of gender roles-socialization. Stereotypes of male and female leaders are identifiable as expectations about how men and women will behave in positions of power. These stereotypes are consistent with the male and female leadership styles described, respectively, as autocratic and democratic.

Gardiner and Tiggemann posit that leadership style and gender stereotypes are intimately connected, "There are definite gender stereotypes of leadership style."[27] A correlation exists between two predominant models of leadership and male and female leadership styles. Transformational leaders operate by ". . . inspiring others to excel, giving individual consideration to others, and stimulating people to think in new ways. Transactional leaders, on the other hand, tend to maintain a steady-state situation and generally get performance from others by offering rewards."[28] While neither sex is found to practice either of these leadership styles exclusively, women tend to practice transformational more than men. "Female managers are more likely than male managers to report that they take an interest in the personal needs of their staff, encourage self-development, use participative decision-making, give feedback and publicly recognize team achievements."[29]

The intersection of gender role and leadership presents an unclear picture of how others in organizations perceive and evaluate men and women leaders. The gender role expectations (stereotypes) we have about men and women influence the way we interpret and evaluate their behaviors. In his study of gender and hierarchical echelon implications on organizational perceptions, Adam Nir finds that, ". . . both men and women direct plans and planning processes toward shorter or longer perspectives when holding positions in lower or higher level echelons of the system's power hierarchy. It is evident that a direct correlation exists between the hierarchical position of an echelon and the perspectives that echelon's members use."[30] Nir further argues that gender plays less of a role than hierarchical position in perceptions about the leadership of men and women who lead planning processes. "Our study does not support the gender-centered perspective that argues for differences in behavior strategies between men and women . . . our study reinforces the position-centered perspective: men and women are equally oriented at comparable future perspectives when attaining and performing roles in similar hierarchical levels."[31] While some disagreement exists in the above research regarding the weight of gender role expectations in perceptions about leaders' behaviors, the research itself is arguably a confirmation of the existence and persistence of gender role stereotypes.

Libraries have witnessed a major surge in the appointment of women to top leadership positions. In 1990, women comprised 37 percent of ARL libraries' directors. That percentage has risen dramatically to 47 percent of total non-law institutions.[32] As more women ascend to leadership of these large and complex institutions, their ability to effectively lead is critical. Their numbers in libraries, as well as in other female-dominated professions, warrant consideration about their preparation and impact on organizations. They are potential leaders.

The attributes associated with feminine leadership (encouragement of self-development, focus on relationships, participatory decision-making, and recognition of group achievement) are highly consistent with the leadership requirements of the modern library. Richard Sweeny describes the "post-hierarchical" library as an organizational structure representing institutional flexibility and focusing on the information needs of its users. It is a ". . . flattened organization, unlimited by the traditional hierarchy, anti-bureaucratic, with empowered cross-functional teams, fewer people, constant learning, and redefined and re-engineered work processes focused on customer service." Sweeny's depiction of the emerging library institution requires a distinctly transformational leader: "The post-hierarchical library leader is a planner, coordinator, motivator, negotiator, innovator, communicator, listener, recruiter, risk-taker, problem solver, and evaluator."[33] The apparent predisposition of women toward democratic leadership practices, combined with the imperative that libraries transform as organizations, present an encouraging future for women seeking to participate in library leadership.

The potentially bright outlook for women in library leadership does not eliminate the continuing burden of gender role stereotypes. In both male- and female-dominated fields, women leaders are identified throughout the hierarchy as generally practicing democratic or feminine leadership. However, supervisors do not necessarily value that style of leadership equally for men and women. Gardiner and Tiggemann comment, ". . . if women utilize stereotypically feminine styles, they are considered less capable and their performance may not be attributed to competence."[34] While librarianship is a predominantly female field, masculine leadership attributes may still hold high value in supervisors' assessment of performance.

Women seeking to participate in top-level library leadership may face frustrating institutional limitations. Janice Kirkland argues that many women in libraries suffer from a deprivation of inside information, challenging (growth-producing) assignments, and recognition in their organizations. These are critical experiences for anyone seeking promotion to leadership.[35] It is unclear whether gender role stereotypes have directly limited women's access to library leadership. However, like male-dominated professions, the top leadership roles are largely held by males. The occupational benefits enjoyed by men as a consequence of their achievement orientation and gender role expectations are likely to play a part in the continued prevalence of male leadership in libraries. Thus, the promise of opportunity for advancement in libraries is still contingent upon experiences that create visibility and contribute to an image of competence within the institution and in the profession.

Sexual Harassment

When discussing the topic of sexual harassment, many researchers have identified a relationship between societal gender roles and co-worker relationships. Stringer et al. suggest that individuals can behave inappropriately at work because of the confusion created by having to relate to the opposite gender in various roles in the workplace. For example, men who come from cultures that view women only as dating partners may have difficulty working with women because of sexual issues.[36] Gutek and Cohen have identified the spillover of societal gender roles as a primary contributor to sexual harassment.[37]

If organizations wish to retain the best employees, regardless of gender or other characteristics, harassment and bias must be addressed. A recent study indicates that 65 percent of women of color have left their jobs because of subtle gender bias.[38] Sexual harassment has become a major issue for most organizations. The results of another recent survey suggest that 31 percent of women reported that they had been sexually harassed at work.[39] These types of statistics reflect the need for organizations to address sexual harassment and its derivations.

Many think only women are victims of sexual harassment. However, men report an increasing number of complaints.[40] In 1995, a federal judge awarded a man $237,257 for being sexually harassed by a female supervisor at a Domino's Pizza restaurant.[41] The results from a survey of male librarians conducted by Carmichael show that 18 percent of respondents have had experiences of sexual discrimination and harassment.[42] Sexual harassment and its derivations are a continuing challenge that organizations will face as both gender and cultural diversity increase.

The interaction of cultural influences and gender role spillover creates unique and challenging issues. As diversity increases, organizations will be faced with new benefits and new conflicts. But these obstacles can be conquered. In the next section, we will discuss best practices to manage diversity issues. We will also offer recommendations to minimize gender and cultural conflicts (see Figure 1).

FIGURE 1. Four Cornerstones of the Work Environment

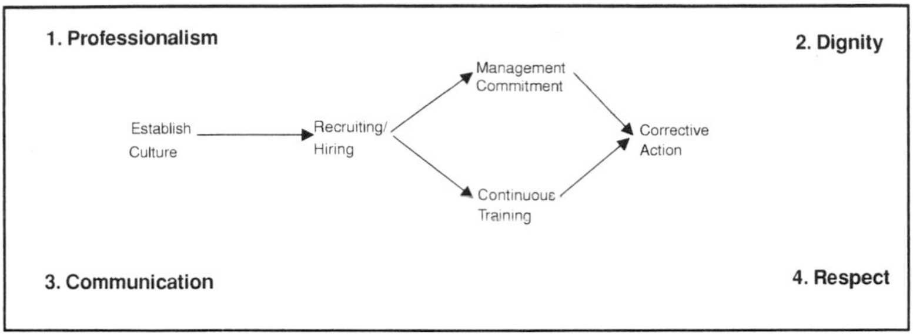

MINIMIZING NEGATIVE SPILLOVER

Work Environment

Successful diverse work environments are based upon four cornerstones: (1) professionalism, (2) dignity, (3) communication, and (4) respect. These cornerstones serve as the basis for creating work environments that enhance an employee's chances for success. The proposed model in Figure 1 conveys how organizations can minimize the negative impacts of gender spillover in the work environment.

Establish the Culture

In order to manage the diversity within an organization, there must be clear guiding principles. This starts with the establishment of the organization's culture.[43] Each organization must ask itself: Who are we? What do we value? How do we wish to achieve our goals? These questions help formulate the mission, prevailing philosophy, and values of the organization. These statements allow an organization to make it clear that it values differences and that it intends to practice cultural inclusion. This is where the commitment to diversity begins.

Recruiting/Hiring

Once an organization is clear about its culture, it can focus on hiring employees that fit within that prevailing value system. This does not mean hiring the perfect employee. Rather, it means one who, with proper training and orientation, can successfully operate within the culture. The organization must also be clear about the skill sets needed to perform the work. Establishing clear job descriptions and selection criteria will minimize the likelihood of bias in hiring. Typical skills necessary to minimize conflicts are teambuilding, problem solving, negotiation, and interpersonal communication skills. It is also important that employees are able to cope with ambiguity.[44] Organizations must identify and assess the behaviors that facilitate success.

Management Commitment

Commitment starts at the top. For any organizational change to be effective there must be commitment and agreement among the leadership in the organization. It is the leadership ranks that must clarify the vision, motivation, and focus of diversity.[45] It is also management who promotes knowledge and acceptance. Management has the power to appraise, reward, and punish acceptable and unacceptable behavior. Therefore, it is critical that managers have the core competencies necessary to communicate and implement policies, procedures, and practices of inclusion. Managers must be held accountable for diversity goals and policy change.[46] Good leaders lead by example. It is important that management practices are consistent and that managers demonstrate desired behaviors. People in management positions must know how to manage and motivate a diverse workforce. Therefore, effective management and leadership development will always be a necessary factor in organizations. Finally, fundamental understanding by men and women in management/leadership positions about gender and cultural roles as well as the influence of sex role expectations on career-impacting decisions in the workplace is vital.

Continuous Training

Many organizations are finding it necessary to implement effective diversity training.[47] Effective training should cover the effects of cohesiveness, communication, conflict, and morale. It should also cover issues that relate to prejudice such as racism, stereotyping, and ethnocentrism. Effective training should address cultural awareness and gender issues such as sexual harassment, sexism, work family conflicts, and cultural differences. The main objective of any diversity training should be to minimize dysfunctional conflicts. Minimizing conflicts requires understanding, education, valuing differences, and developing effective communication skills. Organizations must also

provide training that disseminates knowledge about policies, procedures, and practices. Employees should have a clear understanding
about the organization that employs them and why diversity matters.
Staff should be informed about the culture, prevailing value system, behavioral expectations, grievance and disciplinary procedures, as well as
potential consequences for noncompliance.

Corrective Action

When rules are broken, corrective action should follow. Management must maintain accurate and complete documentation on inappropriate employee actions and avoid basing disciplinary measures on
speculation.[48] It is the discretion of the organization to determine the se-
verity of discipline. The potentially detrimental consequences an organization could suffer due to sexual harassment and discrimination are
substantial. Thus, it is imperative that policies reflecting zero tolerance
and associated penalties are clearly communicated throughout the organization and that the penalties for violation are discouragingly costly.

Corrective action could take the form of sensitivity training, cultural
mentoring, or, in some cases, demotions and/or transfer. Disciplining
employees is a difficult responsibility. If ineffectively done, the results
can be chaotic. The failure to act when required would further aggravate
difficult organizational problems in need of decisive resolution.[49]

CONCLUSION

As cultural diversity in organizations increases, the conflict that is
created by the interaction of gender and cultural influences can also increase. Gender roles can "spillover" into the workplace and create conflict. Conflict can manifest itself as sexual harassment, dysfunctional
co-worker relations, stereotyping, discrimination, and other detrimental
manifestations such as violent acts. As organizations become more diverse, leaders cannot passively assume that the cultural and gender role
perceptions and expectations of the workforce will harmlessly settle
into balance. Organizations must be proactive to create an environment
that increases the likelihood of success for all members.

The four cornerstone model for minimizing organizational cultural
and gender conflict suggests that organizations must control the work
environment, establish the organizational culture, be proactive in hir-
ing/recruiting, demand effective leadership, institute effective and on-

going training, and demonstrate corrective action when necessary. Cultural and gender diversity can contribute positively to the organization. However, deliberate intent and action are required to ensure the inclusive environment necessary to make it a reality.

NOTES

1. Geert Hofstede, "Motivation, Leadership and Organization: Do American Theories Apply Abroad?" *Organizational Dynamics* 9 (1980): 43-62.

2. Jack Gordon, "Rethinking Diversity," *Training* 29 (1992): 24.

3. Barbara A. Gutek and Aaron G. Cohen, "Sex Ratios, Sex Role Spillover, and Sex at Work: A Comparison of Men's and Women's Experiences," *Human Relations* 40, no. 2 (1987): 97-15.

4. Alan Deutschman, "Dealing with Sexual Harassment," *Fortune*, 4 November 1991, 145-48.

5. Suzanne Hildenbrand, "Still Not Equal: Closing the Library Gender Gap," *Library Journal* 122 (March 1997): 44-6.

6. Barbara A. Gutek and Vera Dunwoody, "Sex Object and Worker: Incompatible Images of Women," *ISSR Working Paper* 3, no. 13 (1987) [online] available from www.sscnet.ucla.edu/issr/paper/issr3-13.txt.

7. Ibid.

8. Taylor Cox, Jr., *Cultural Diversity in Organizations: Theory, Research & Practice* (San Francisco: Berrett-Koehler Publishers, 1994).

9. James V. Carmichael, "Gender Issues in the Workplace: Male Librarians Tell Their Side," *American Libraries* 25, no. 3 (1994): 227-30.

10. Glenda Northey, "New Zealand Library Association 1910-1970: Its Role in the Demise of a Feminized Profession," *New Zealand Libraries* 48, no. 2 (1995): 25-30.

11. Maria Gardiner and Marika Tiggemann, "Gender Differences in Leadership Style, Job Stress and Mental Health in Male- and Female-Dominated Industries," *Journal of Occupational and Organizational Psychology* 72, no. 3 (1999): 301-15.

12. Cynthia J. B. DeCorse and Stephen Vogtle, "In a Complex Voice: The Contradictions of Male Elementary Teachers' Career Choice and Professional Identity," *Journal of Teacher Education* 48, no. 1 (1997): 37.

13. Ibid., 5.

14. Diana Burgess and Eugene Borgida, "Sexual Harassment: An Experimental Test of Sex-Role Spillover Theory," *Personality and Social Psychology Bulletin* 23, no. 1 (1997): 63.

15. Catherine Kirchmeyer, "Nonwork-to-Work Spillover: A More Balanced View of the Experiences and Coping of Professional Women and Men," *Sex Roles* 28 (1987): 531-52.

16. *Dictionary of Science and Technology*, s.v. "self concept."

17. Diane Dodd-McCue and Gail B. Wright, "Men, Women, and Attitudinal Commitment: The Effects of Workplace Experiences and Socialization," *Human Relations* 49, no. 8 (1996): 1089.

18. Karen C. McClusky, "Gender at Work," *Public Management* 79, no. 5 (1997): 5-9.

19. For extended discussion see Ellen A. Fagenson, "Perceived Masculine and Feminine Attributes Examined as a Function of Individuals' Sex and Level in the Organizational Power Hierarchy: A Test of Four Theoretical Perspectives," *Journal of Applied Psychology* 75 (1990): 267-74; Alice H. Eagly and Blair T. Johnson, "Gender and Leadership Style: A Meta-analysis," *Psychological Bulletin* 108 (1990): 233-56.

20. Barbara Reskin, "Sex Segregation in the Workplace," *Annual Review of Sociology* 19 (1993): 248.

21. Stanley Wilder, "The Changing Profile of Research Library Professional Staff," *ARL: A Bimonthly Report on Research Library Issues and Actions from ARL, CNI, and SPARC* 208-209 (February 2000): 10.

22. Ibid., 9.

23. Sharon E. Lovell et al., "Does Gender Affect the Link Between Organizational Citizenship Behavior and Performance Evaluation?" *Sex Roles* 40 (1999): 474.

24. Edward Klein, Ellen Kossek, and Joseph Astrachan, "Affective Reactions to Leadership Education: An Exploration of the Same-Gender Effect," *Journal of Applied Behavioral Science* 28, no. 1 (1992): 102-17.

25. Wilder, "Changing Profile," 1.

26. Eagly and Johnson, "Gender and Leadership Styles."

27. Maria Gardiner and Marika Tiggemann, "Gender Differences in Leadership," 301.

28. James M. Kouzes and Barry Z. Posner, *The Leadership Challenge* (San Francisco: Jossey-Bass Publishers, 1995), 321.

29. Sally A. Carless, "Gender Differences in Transformational Leadership: An Examination of Superior, Leaders, and Subordinate Perspectives," *Sex Roles* 39 (1998): 892.

30. Adam E. Nir, "Time Perspectives of Strategic Planning Processes and Plans as a Function of Gender and Echelon Socialization," *Sex Roles* 40 (1999): 741.

31. Ibid., 742.

32. Wilder, "Changing Profile," 3.

33. Richard T. Sweeney, "Leadership in the Post-hierarchical Library," *Library Trends* 43, no. 1 (1994): 33.

34. Gardiner and Tiggemann, "Gender Differences in Leadership" 302.

35. Janice J. Kirkland, "The Missing Women Library Directors: Deprivation versus Mentoring," *College and Research Libraries* 58 (1997): 376-84.

36. Donna M. Stringer, Helen Remick, and Jan Salisbury, "The Power and Reasons Behind Sexual Harassment: An Employer's Guide to Solutions," *Public Personnel Management* 19 (1990): 45-52.

37. Shelley Taylor et al., "Categorical and Contextual Bases of Person Memory and Stereotyping," *Journal of Personality and Social Psychology* 36, no. 7 (1978): 778-93.

38. B. Grey, "Diversity in the New Millennium," *Working Woman* 25 (September 2000): 76-87.

39. *BNA's Employee Relations Weekly* 12 (April 1994): 367.

40. Elizabeth Kadetsky, "Million-Dollar Man," *Working Woman* 18 (October 1993): 45-53.

41. Paula Dwyer and Alice Z. Cuneo, "The 'Other Minorities' Demand Their Due," *Business Week*, 8 July 1991, 62.

42. Carmichael, "Gender Issues in the Workplace."

43. Lin Grensing-Pophal, "Hiring to Fit Your Corporate Culture," *HR Magazine* 44, no. 8 (1999): 50-4.

44. Ibid., 50.

45. Jaqueline A. Gilbert and John M. Ivancevich, "Valuing Diversity: A Tale of Two Organizations," *Academy of Management Executive* (February 2000): 98.

46. Ibid., 103.

47. "Diversity-related training session gain popularity" *HR Focus* 70, no. 11 (November 1993): 12.

48. Rebecca K. Spar, "Keeping Internal Investigations Confidential," *HRMagazine* 41, no. 1 (January 1996): 33-6.

49. Dave Day, "Help for Discipline Dodgers," *Training and Development* 47, no. 5 (May 1993): 19-22.

African American Female Librarians: A Study of Job Satisfaction

Joyce K. Thornton

SUMMARY. This article examines the responses of ninety-eight female respondents to a survey on job satisfaction of librarians of African descent employed in seventy-nine Association of Research Libraries (ARL) academic libraries in relation to other gender studies on job satisfaction of librarians. Dependent variables are race, age, years of experience and years at present institution. This article also provides information about the perceptions of the survey respondents regarding isolation in the workplace, racial discrimination in the workplace and diversity programs and how these factors affect their job satisfaction. *[Article copies available for a fee from The Haworth Document Delivery Service: 1-800-HAWORTH. E-mail address: <getinfo@haworthpressinc.com> Website: <http://www.HaworthPress.com> © 2001 by The Haworth Press, Inc. All rights reserved.]*

KEYWORDS. Job satisfaction, female librarians, African American librarians

INTRODUCTION

The labor force of the 21st century will change significantly. The workforce will be more diverse due to changes in gender, race, and age

Joyce K. Thornton is Associate Professor, Director for Specialized and Distance Library Services, Texas A&M University Libraries, College Station, TX (E-mail: *jkthorn@tamu.edu*).

[Haworth co-indexing entry note]: "African American Female Librarians: A Study of Job Statisfaction." Thornton, Joyce K. Co-published simultaneously in *Journal of Library Administration* (The Haworth Information Press, an imprint of The Haworth Press, Inc.) Vol. 33, No. 1/2, 2001, pp. 141-164; and: *Diversity Now: People, Collections, and Services in Academic Libraries* (ed: Teresa Y. Neely, and Kuang-Hwei (Janet) Lee-Smeltzer) The Haworth Information Press, an imprint of The Haworth Press, Inc., 2001, pp. 141-164. Single or multiple copies of this article are available for a fee from The Haworth Document Delivery Service [1-800-HAWORTH, 9:00 a.m. - 5:00 p.m. (EST). E-mail address: getinfo@haworthpressinc.com].

141

composition, with women and minorities growing at a fast rate. Increased participation of women will be the most dramatic.[1] In 1920, 8.25 million women sixteen years old and older were in the labor force. By 1980 the number increased to forty million, and by 1997, women numbered fifty-six million or forty-five percent of the nation's civilian workforce.[2] It is projected that by the year 2008 women will make up forty-eight to fifty percent of the labor force.[3] The majority will be concentrated in female intensive occupations such as librarianship where currently eighty-seven percent of all librarians are women.[4] In higher education women accounted for nearly thirty-nine percent of all American higher education faculty positions in 1992 and constituted more than sixty percent of the academic librarians.[5]

Immigration accounted for over fifty percent of the workforce increase in the 1990s, and will also drive the change in the racial composition of the future workforce. Hispanics in the labor force will rise to fourteen percent, Asians to six percent, while African American workers will remain steady at eleven percent.[6] African American women made an accelerated entry into the workforce in the 1960s, and in the 1970s the expansion of the services economy and the restructuring of occupational and work systems contributed to their increase in numbers.[7] In 1996 the number of African American women in the labor force reached 7.9 million, the highest ever labor force participation rate of sixty percent. The Bureau of Labor Statistics has projected that nine million African American women will be labor force participants in 2005.[8] The predictions of demographers that the workforce will be increasingly female and minority have renewed interests in academe in the recruitment of women and minorities. This in turn has focused more attention on the determinants of job satisfaction for women and minorities.

Historically, librarianship is a women's profession. Carmichael stated that the demographics of occupational entry indicate that the mix of students entering the profession has changed little over the past twenty-five years.[9] With women and minorities comprising a larger segment of the future labor entrants, libraries must find ways to recruit and retain these groups by confronting all obstacles that hinder them from becoming productive and satisfied employees.

As the gender and racial demographics change the face of the workforce, libraries sound an alarm regarding the number of African American librarians currently employed and the fewer that will be employed in the future library workforce.[10] Squire attributed the underrepresentation of ethnic groups in the library workforce in part to the lack of African American graduate students in library and information science programs, lack of recruitment and affirmative action policies in libraries, and the inability to retain African Americans in the profession.[11] The recruitment, retention and advancement of librarians of color are critical to the long-term future of libraries. Indications are that race and gender are very real issues in the profession. Butler and DeSole stated that race and gender are very real issues in our culture, and suggested that libraries that do not have librarians that reflect the diversity of this nation will be hard pressed to serve the needs of their clientele.[12]

Libraries must move from being philosophically committed to increasing, retaining and advancing the number of minorities, especially African Americans, into the profession. An examination of the job satisfaction of African American women and the identification of factors that contribute significantly to or hinder the job satisfaction of these individuals is critical to the accomplishment of this goal.

This study will examine library job satisfaction research and compare those findings with the findings of this study in relation to gender, race, age, years of experience in the profession and years at present institution. The study will also provide information about the respondents' perception of isolation, racial discrimination, and diversity programs and how these factors affect their job satisfaction. This type of study can provide information to help library managers develop programs and strategies to ensure that library positions attract women, especially African American women. The information obtained from this study can also help library managers improve recruitment and retention strategies for underrepresented groups, improve on the factors that positively influence job satisfaction and eliminate those contributing to job dissatisfaction.

METHODOLOGY

This study examines a subset of the data collected in a previous study, "Job Satisfaction of Librarians of African Descent Employed in the Association of Research Libraries Academic Libraries."[13] Data was collected from ninety-eight female (73%) respondents in the previous study and is compared to previous library job satisfaction studies in relation to gender, race, age, years of experience as a professional librarian and years at present institution. Perceptions of isolation, racial discrimination, and diversity programs in the workplace were also analyzed. General data on respondents is listed in Appendix A.

JOB SATISFACTION

Job satisfaction, as defined by Vaughn and Dunn, is "the feeling an employee has about his pay, work, promotion opportunities, coworkers, and supervisors."[14] A review of the literature revealed that there is broad research on job satisfaction. The job satisfaction of academic librarians has generated a number of studies. However, little research has connected job satisfaction with people of color in libraries. Library job satisfaction studies, according to Leckie and Brett, produced conflicting or confusing results because: (1) much of the research used different variables and different instruments to assess satisfaction, (2) the work of academic libraries varied considerably with institution type making it difficult to conduct comprehensive surveys that were meaningful, and (3) very few studies were ever replicated using another population of academic libraries for direct comparison.[15] Job satisfaction studies as they related to academic libraries began around the 1970s and covered broad issues of job satisfaction. The early studies were instrumental in citing reasons for job dissatisfaction. The studies included research about general job satisfaction, job satisfaction in specific types of libraries, job satisfaction within library units and occupational groups, job satisfaction and work schedules, job satisfaction and management style, job satisfaction and attitude, job satisfaction and age and tenure, and job satisfaction and gender.[16] More recent studies of job satisfaction in librarianship included job satisfaction and various interventions including faculty status, technology, performance, unionization and job responsibilities.[17]

Studies on the job satisfaction of minority librarians are still relatively few; most address recruitment and retention. Very little was found in the literature addressing job satisfaction and African American librarians. Two studies that addressed job satisfaction and African American librarians will be discussed in other sections of this paper.

FINDINGS OF PREVIOUS AND CURRENT STUDIES

Gender and Job Satisfaction

The state of disarray for research on gender-related issues occurred primarily because researchers differed in opinion on the fundamental areas of methodology. Smith, Smits, and Hoy suggested that scholars differed for many reasons including: gender differences were not accurately understood and thus were not reported completely and accurately; studies with insignificant results were not reported; and the absence of checking for significant variables may have confounded the integrity of reported data.[18]

Several studies on job satisfaction in libraries included the gender issue; however, disagreement existed within this body of literature. Several researchers concluded that women were more dissatisfied than men, including Wahba, who concentrated on comparing the job satisfaction of 202 librarians from twenty-three college and university libraries from the New York City area. Wahba compared the perceived degree of need fulfillment and need deficiencies of men and women librarians. The study also contrasted the importance of these needs as viewed by men and women. She found that women were more dissatisfied than men in three of the four need categories.[19] Roberts, in a study of sixty-two male and fifty-six female postgraduates of Sheffield University, hinted that a greater proportion of men achieve greater satisfaction than women.[20] Other researchers disagreed and found that women were more satisfied. Nzotta's study of eighty male and eighty female librarians in Nigeria found that, in a developing country where male librarians outnumbered female librarians, women were more satisfied than men.[21] Some researchers indicated that there were no significant differences in job satisfaction based on gender. D'Elia surveyed 228 beginning librarians, 185 of whom were female, to identify factors which were highly related to librarians' job satisfaction. He concluded that job satisfaction was not related to the gender of the respondents.[22] In 1983, Lynch and Verdin explored the relationship between sex, occupational group, age and length of service on the job with job satisfaction of library employees in three university libraries. The responses of the 320 females and sixty-four males indicated that job satisfaction was not related to gender. The 1987 replication involved three of the Association of Research Libraries (ARL) twenty-five largest libraries. The 213 female and seventy male respondents again indicated that job satisfaction was not related to gender.[23] Mirfakhrai studied job satisfaction in small and medium-sized academic libraries, and found no significant relationship between the sex of forty-eight male and seventy-one female academic librarians and their overall job satisfaction.[24] Ilene Rockman randomly surveyed tenure-track faculty and librarians employed by the California State University System. Of the 220 respondents, fifty-nine were male librarians and fifty-three were female librarians. She found that there was a positive relationship between job satisfaction and gender, but that gender alone could not be viewed as a predictor of job satisfaction.[25]

Thornton identified sources of satisfaction and dissatisfaction for 136 librarians of African descent.[26] The data collected from the ninety-nine female and thirty males regarding satisfaction in twenty-three aspects of their jobs indicated that men were more satisfied than women. Although the findings tend to support Wahba's conclusion that women are more dissatisfied than men are, the differences may not be very significant.[27]

Race and Job Satisfaction

The small number of African American librarians has become an issue for academic libraries generally and more so for the ARL, as indicated in Table 1, because the number of African American librarians has increased very little in the last ten years. In the realm of academic libraries, African American librarians were often in a unique situation. Many times they were in libraries where they had additional pressures on them. They may have encountered attitudes about their abilities to perform a job well and endure other stresses and anxieties solely based on race, all of which could negatively affect job satisfaction. Very little was found in the literature on job satisfaction and race, while practically nothing was found regarding African American women and job satisfaction. Martha Tack and Carol Paitu, in *Faculty Job Satisfaction: Women and Minorities in Peril*, suggested that job satisfaction played

TABLE 1. Minority Librarians at U.S. ARL Academic Libraries

Year	Total Filled Positions	No. of Minority Librarians	No. in Academic Libraries	Total No. of Librarians of African Descent
1990/1991	7,654	818	699	272
1991/1992	7,520	804	689	248
1992/1993	7,484	802	687	272
1993/1994	7,318	830	710	276
1994/1995	7,411	841	724	274
1995/1996	7,435	842	723	262
1996/1997	7,561	853	721	279
1997/1998	7,682	848	706	275
1998/1999	7,671	854	715	281
1999/2000	7,858	893	743	321

Source: ARL Annual Salary Survey, 1990/1991-1999/2000

an important role in nurturing, developing and retaining a racially diverse faculty. They found that a number of factors, including salary, advancement, promotion and tenure caused women and people of color to be less satisfied than their male and white faculty counterparts.[28]

A study conducted by Estabrook, Bird and Gilmore, to determine whether automation made a difference in job satisfaction of professional and support staff, found that among professional librarians race was the second largest factor in explaining job satisfaction; white librarians were more satisfied than black librarians. "This finding is disturbing, for it suggests that libraries do not treat minority workers equally."[29] In a study on the job satisfaction of librarians of African descent, Thornton found that as a race, librarians were generally satisfied but race was a contributing factor to dissatisfaction.[30] Patrick Hall related that he was constantly reminded that as a black librarian, he is subjected to biases about his intellectual capacity because of his race. Performing frequent placatory acrobatics, being snubbed or ignored, dealing with negative attitudes, having his credibility questioned, and trying to make people comfortable when trying to perform his job left him emotionally drained.[31] How can these experiences not affect one's job satisfaction?

Age and Job Satisfaction

The library profession is unusually old and is aging at a fast rate. According to Stanley Wilder, in 1998, nearly fifty-seven percent of librarians were forty-five years of age and older. For the ARL university librarians, sixty-six percent were forty-five years old and older. Additionally, Wilder stated that while African American librarians are significantly younger than white librarians, they are aging rapidly as well. In 1998, fifty-one percent of African American librarians in the ARL were forty-five years old and older.[32]

The minority youth population will double from 1995-2050.[33] This indicates a change in the composition of the workforce. Libraries should step up efforts to recruit young minorities, especially African Americans and Hispanics, and should be concerned about the job satisfaction of these potentially young recruits to the profession.

Relevant literature regarding age and job satisfaction suggested that there was some association between employee age and job satisfaction. One of the earliest library studies which focused on age and job satisfaction was conducted by Scamell and Stead. They analyzed, in a small sample survey of special librarians, the relationship between age and tenure as it pertained job satisfaction. They hypothesized that a librarian's job satisfaction was positively related to his/her age, and that there was a significant difference between librarians in the thirty and under age category and the thirty-one to forty and the forty-one and older categories with respect to overall job satisfaction and the individual dimensions that influenced job satisfaction. While the hypotheses were not confirmed, the study suggested a negative relationship between the age of special librarians and their overall job satisfaction.[34] In their 1983 study, Lynch and Verdin believed that there was no difference between the age of the library employee and job satisfaction. They discovered that the 119 respondents who were less than twenty-five years old were the least satisfied group. They differed significantly from the thirty to thirty-four, the thirty-five to thirty-nine, the forty to forty-four, the forty-five to forty-nine, the fifty to fifty-four, and the over sixty year old age groups. They differed little from the twenty-five to twenty-nine and the fifty-five to fifty-nine year old groups. Thus younger librarians were less satisfied than their older counterparts.[35] The 1987 replication included three university libraries and 292 respondents using the same age groups as in the 1983 study. The replication found that older employees showed higher levels of satisfaction, but not to any significant degree.[36] Mirfakhrai randomly sampled 119 full time academic librarians in small and medium-sized libraries and found a negative correlation between age and overall job satisfaction in both sized libraries.[37]

Job satisfaction by age groups for the current study is shown in Table 2. More than fifty percent of the twelve respondents in the twenty-five to thirty-four year old group were satisfied with fifteen of the twenty-three aspects of their jobs. More than fifty percent of the thirty-seven respondents in the thirty-five to forty-four age group recorded satisfaction with thirteen of the twenty-three aspects of their jobs.

Of the forty-two respondents in the forty-five to fifty-four age group, fifty percent and more were satisfied with nineteen of the twenty-three aspects of their jobs. The seven respondents who were fifty-five years old and older were most satisfied with only seven areas of their jobs. Surprisingly, the oldest group was the least satisfied of the four groups. Some of the additional comments from this group indicated a sense of apathy to their jobs. Even though the oldest group reported satisfaction in fewer aspects of their jobs, when combined with the forty-five to fifty-four age group, findings support studies, which indicated that older librarians are more satisfied than younger librarians.

TABLE 2. Age and Job Satisfaction

	Dissatisfied & Very Dissatisfied				Satisfied & Very Satisfied			
	25-34	35-44	45-54	55 & Over	25-34	35-44	45-54	55 & Over
Job Duties	1	6	2	0	8	29	39	7
Working Conditions	1	4	4	1	9	26	34	6
Autonomy on the job	1	2	3	0	10	32	37	6
Challenges of the job	2	5	4	0	8	30	36	2
Variety of occupational tasks	2	5	5	0	9	29	37	6
Work assignment and workload	3	12	7	0	7	21	27	5
Job security	4	4	6	1	4	24	32	6
Interaction with peers	1	3	6	1	6	24	31	5
Interaction with patrons	0	2	0	1	8	24	28	6
Status of librarians at your institution	3	7	5	1	9	28	36	4
Salary	3	22	10	4	6	15	31	3
Fringe benefits	3	11	6	5	7	19	25	2
Opportunities for advancement	2	15	6	4	8	18	32	3
Opportunities for collegial interaction within your department	4	11	5	4	3	12	23	1
Opportunities for collegial interaction with faculty in other departments	5	11	4	3	5	14	29	3
Opportunities for professional development	5	11	4	3	6	15	27	2
Interest of department colleagues in your work	4	10	6	4	7	22	34	2
Opportunities to pursue research	5	6	9	4	6	14	20	0
Proportion of faculty of African descent at the university	10	24	31	6	2	8	25	0
Proportion of faculty of African descent in the library	10	30	29	6	1	4	1	0
Manner in which administration handles faculty problems	4	18	9	6	1	4	3	0
Lines of communication	5	18	9	4	1	4	13	1
Serving as role model for students of African descent	7	5	7	4	4	23	22	2

Note: number of respondents
25-34   =   12
35-44   =   37
45-54   =   42
55 & Over   =   7

Years of Experience and Job Satisfaction

According to a *Library Journal* exclusive report, a seasoned professional woman has been in the profession for 16 years.[38] Does tenure in the profession relate positively to job satisfaction? Norman Roberts, in a study of the postgraduates of Sheffield University, collected data that suggested that overall job satisfaction increased as librarians settled into their work and gained experience and confidence.[39] Jones, in an early study of job satisfaction, agreed that job satisfaction tended to increase with experience.[40] In 1983, Lynch and Verdin found that people with more years of experience reported higher job satisfaction than less experienced groups.[41] However, in the 1987 replication, no significant differences emerged on tenure as measured by any of the tenure variables used.[42] Scamell and Stead analyzed tenure and satisfaction of librarians with three or less years of full-time work experience in libraries, those with four to ten years of experience and those with eleven or more years of experience. Among the three groups, they found no significant difference between tenure and job satisfaction.[43] Phillips, Carson and Carson investigated how attitudes toward the profession evolved as librarians aged and passed through the progressive stages of their careers. They found that newcomers reported lower levels of satisfaction because they entered the field with naïve and unrealistic expectations about the world of work, they were overly ambitious and idealistic about their abilities to influence the functioning of the library, and the "reality shock" associated with the initial expectations being unrealized brought about high levels of disappointment. They concluded that, as librarians become more experienced, they become more pleased with their profession or in some cases, they were bound to the profession because of the accumulated investments and decreased career options.[44]

The current study (Table 3) shows that respondents with more than fifteen years of experience recorded higher satisfaction levels than the 0-3.9, the 4-9.9 and the ten to fifteen years of experience groups. The ten to fifteen years of experience group recorded higher satisfaction levels than the two younger groups. Age and tenure are closely intertwined. One would expect that if older librarians were more satisfied than younger librarians, then the same would be true for tenure in the profession. This study supports the conclusions of five of the six previous studies that found that years of experience positively affects job satisfaction.

Years at Present Institution and Job Satisfaction

If librarians are satisfied with their jobs, do they tend to remain at the same institution for long periods of time or indefinitely? Does remaining at the same institution for a long period of time or indefinitely indicate job satisfaction?

Some of the same studies that addressed years of experience and job satisfaction also addressed years at present institution and job satisfaction. Roberts reported that the length of time a person worked in a particular library might influence the level of job satisfaction.[45] In Lynch and Verdin's 1983 study, they reported that people who worked in a particular library relatively short periods of time (1-4 years) were less satisfied than those who had worked for longer periods of time (11-14 or 15-24 years) in that same library.[46] In the replication, no significant differences emerged.[47] Mirfakhrai found that length of employment with present institution was negatively correlated with overall job satisfaction of academic librarians in small and medium-sized libraries.[48]

Table 4 shows the satisfaction of respondents based on years at the present institution. The group that had been at the same institution 4-9.9 years was satisfied in more aspects of their jobs than any of the other groups. All groups reported high levels of dissatisfaction for proportion of faculty of African descent at the university and in the library, salary and lines of communication. When comparing the number of respondents in each group with the number satisfied with each aspect of their job, the findings indicate that there is no significant correlation between years at present library and job satisfaction.

Isolation and Job Satisfaction

Isolation, the feeling of being alone, can affect a person's morale. Some isolated individuals feel they have no support system, and certainly no one to whom they can express their feelings of disappointment or frustration. In higher education, studies on the implications of isolation found that (1) African Americans leave predominately white institutions because they frequently found themselves small in numbers and isolated; (2) when there was only one or a very small number of black faculty members in a given institution, the burden of institutional and individual racism weighed heavily; (3) when isolated, a person might not be psychologically supported, because understanding, warmth, and empathy were not always part of the environment, and (4) scholarly

TABLE 3. Years of Experience and Job Satisfaction

	Very Dissatisfied				Dissatisfied			
	0-3.9 yrs	4-9.9 yrs	10-15 yrs	over 15 yrs	0-3.9 yrs	4-9.9 yrs	10-15 yrs	over 15 yrs
Job Duties	0	2	0	1	2	1	3	1
Working Conditions	2	2	0	0	0	0	2	3
Autonomy on the job	0	0	0	3	2	1	0	2
Challenges of the job	3	0	0	0	2	1	4	1
Variety of occupational tasks	0	0	0	0	3	2	2	2
Work assignment and workload	1	2	2	2	5	3	5	4
Job security	1	0	0	1	2	3	0	2
Interaction with peers	1	0	0	0	5	1	3	3
Interaction with patrons	0	0	0	0	0	1	1	2
Status of librarians at your institution	2	2	0	0	7	2	3	5
Salary	4	3	2	5	10	3	14	7
Fringe benefits	2	1	0	2	6	0	3	3
Opportunities for advancement	3	2	3	4	7	3	9	5
Opportunities for collegial interaction within your department	1	1	1	1	4	1	2	3
Opportunities for collegial interaction with faculty in other departments	3	1	1	4	8	2	4	0
Opportunities for professional development	1	0	1	0	4	4	2	4
Interest of department colleagues in your work	1	0	0	5	6	5	5	2
Opportunities to pursue research	1	1	4	0	6	1	6	4
Proportion of faculty of African descent at the university	9	7	9	12	9	6	10	18
Proportion of faculty of African descent in the library	10	7	13	11	9	6	7	16
Manner in which administration handles faculty problems	1	2	2	6	5	4	4	4
Lines of communication	4	3	2	4	7	3	6	5
Serving as role model for students of African descent	0	0	0	1	2	1	4	3

Note: number of respondents

0-3.9	=	21
4-9.9	=	15
10-15	=	26
Over 15	=	34

Can't Decide or Neutral				Satisfied				Very Satisfied			
0-3.9 yrs	4-9.9 yrs	10-15 yrs	over 15 yrs	0-3.9 yrs	4-9.9 yrs	10-15 yrs	over 15 yrs	0-3.9 yrs	4-9.9 yrs	10-15 yrs	over 15 yrs
3	1	0	1	10	6	15	22	6	6	8	10
3	3	4	2	8	8	17	20	8	3	3	10
3	1	3	3	10	7	13	20	6	6	10	8
1	3	1	6	9	5	11	14	8	6	10	13
2	1	1	4	9	7	13	17	7	6	10	12
3	0	5	5	9	9	12	18	3	2	2	6
7	2	7	4	7	8	13	15	4	2	6	12
7	1	6	4	6	10	11	20	3	3	6	8
3	0	5	7	14	9	14	17	3	6	7	9
4	6	7	7	7	4	14	14	1	3	2	8
1	5	1	3	6	3	8	14	0	1	2	6
4	4	3	6	7	8	12	12	3	2	8	12
8	5	5	13	2	4	6	7	1	1	3	7
2	5	8	7	13	5	13	17	1	3	2	8
4	4	10	12	6	8	9	11	0	0	2	9
3	0	5	4	4	7	13	15	9	4	5	13
7	6	8	13	5	3	13	12	1	1	0	5
2	4	11	10	7	5	7	10	3	4	4	8
3	2	5	5	0	0	2	1	0	0	0	0
0	0	5	9	2	1	1	1	0	0	0	0
14	7	18	16	1	2	1	7	0	0	1	3
4	1	6	11	6	7	11	13	1	1	1	2
13	8	10	9	3	4	8	16	3	3	3	7

TABLE 4. Years at Present Institution and Job Satisfaction

	Very Dissatisfied					Dissatisfied				
	less 1 yr	1-3.9 yrs	4-9.9 yrs	10-15 yrs	over 15 yrs	less 1 yr	1-3.9 yrs	4-9.9 yrs	10-15 yrs	over 15 yrs
Job Duties	0	1	1	0	0	0	3	3	2	0
Working Conditions	0	2	1	0	0	0	2	2	0	1
Autonomy on the job	0	0	2	0	0	0	2	2	0	0
Challenges of the job	0	1	0	0	0	0	3	3	1	0
Variety of occupational tasks	0	0	0	0	0	0	3	3	0	0
Work assignment and workload	1	2	0	2	0	2	5	8	0	3
Job security	0	1	1	0	0	1	3	2	0	1
Interaction with peers	0	0	1	0	0	1	4	3	3	1
Interaction with patrons	0	0	0	0	0	0	0	0	0	1
Status of librarians at your institution	1	1	1	0	0	1	5	1	4	5
Salary	1	3	5	0	2	2	9	8	10	6
Fringe benefits	1	2	0	0	0	0	5	2	3	3
Opportunities for advancement	1	2	3	1	0	1	8	7	6	5
Opportunities for collegial interaction within your department	0	1	2	0	0	2	4	2	1	2
Opportunities for collegial interaction with faculty in other departments	2	1	0	0	0	3	8	2	2	2
Opportunities for professional development	0	2	0	0	0	1	3	5	2	0
Interest of department colleagues in your work	0	1	1	0	1	4	5	5	2	2
Opportunities to pursue research	0	1	1	0	0	1	6	2	3	3
Proportion of faculty of African descent at the university	4	10	10	4	3	3	12	13	7	12
Proportion of faculty of African descent in the library	6	14	9	7	3	2	6	12	4	14
Manner in which administration handles faculty problems	1	1	3	2	1	1	3	5	1	2
Lines of communication	0	5	2	1	1	4	6	7	5	5
Serving as role model for students of African descent	0	1	1	0	1	1	1	1	1	1

Note: number of respondents

less 1	=	9
1-3.9	=	25
4-9.9	=	28
10-15	=	17
over 15	=	19

Can't Decide or Neutral					Satisfied					Very Satisfied				
less 1 yr	1-3.9 yrs	4-9.9 yrs	10-15 yrs	over 15 yrs	less 1 yr	1-3.9 yrs	4-9.9 yrs	10-15 yrs	over 15 yrs	less 1 yr	1-3.9 yrs	4-9.9 yrs	10-15 yrs	over 15 yrs
1	3	1	0	0	6	12	16	9	14	2	6	7	6	5
2	3	6	1	1	4	13	15	12	13	3	5	4	4	4
0	1	4	1	2	6	18	12	9	14	3	4	8	7	3
2	1	5	2	3	5	11	12	8	9	3	9	8	6	7
1	2	2	2	2	5	13	13	9	12	3	7	10	6	5
1	4	3	1	3	4	11	12	10	11	1	3	5	4	2
2	6	8	2	2	6	8	14	9	10	0	6	3	6	6
3	5	5	2	2	4	13	14	7	11	1	3	5	5	5
3	3	2	4	1	5	15	19	9	11	1	7	7	4	6
2	6	12	3	2	5	9	11	6	7	0	4	3	4	5
0	2	5	1	2	5	8	8	1	7	1	3	2	5	2
2	2	7	1	6	5	10	14	4	5	0	6	5	9	5
4	8	9	3	7	2	5	6	4	5	1	3	3	3	2
1	3	9	6	2	5	14	11	5	11	1	3	4	5	5
3	8	9	3	6	1	7	13	8	6	0	1	4	4	5
2	3	4	3	3	1	10	13	9	9	5	7	6	3	7
2	9	11	6	6	2	8	9	4	6	1	2	2	5	4
3	8	10	5	6	2	7	10	7	6	3	3	5	2	4
2	3	4	3	3	0	0	1	3	1	0	0	0	0	0
1	3	6	3	2	0	2	1	2	0	0	0	0	1	0
6	19	15	9	14	1	2	4	4	2	0	0	1	1	1
2	5	6	2	7	3	9	11	7	8	0	0	2	2	0
3	15	15	3	5	2	6	8	10	10	3	2	3	3	3

productivity could be negatively affected in this type of organizational environment.[49]

Being the only one is a situation in which many African American librarians find themselves at several predominately white institutions. The library literature does not directly address the effects of isolation and job satisfaction. This is an area where more research is needed.

Twenty-eight of the current survey respondents felt isolated at the institution to a moderate degree and eighteen felt isolated to a high degree. In the library, twenty-three respondents felt isolated to a moderate degree and fourteen felt isolated to a high degree. More than a third (37%) of the respondents felt isolated in the library.

Of the twenty-three respondents who felt a moderate degree of isolation in the library, high areas of dissatisfaction included forty-three percent dissatisfied to very dissatisfied with work assignment and workload, and with opportunities for advancement; forty-seven percent with salary; 100 percent with proportion of faculty of African descent at the university; ninety-one percent with proportion of faculty of African descent at the library; and thirty-nine percent with interest of colleagues in their work. Of the fourteen respondents who felt a high degree of isolation in the library, high areas of dissatisfaction were with the number of faculty of African descent at the university and the library (78%), fringe benefits (71%), opportunities for collegial interaction with colleagues within their departments (57%), interest of colleagues in their work, lines of communication and manner in which administration handles problems (50%), interaction with patrons (42%) and interaction with peers and opportunities for professional development (35%). These findings indicate that isolation, by itself, does not negatively affect job satisfaction of librarians of African descent to a great extent. It is, however, a source of dissatisfaction that must be addressed.

Racial Discrimination and Job Satisfaction

Racial discrimination takes place when individuals are unfairly or wrongly treated compared to others because of their race, color, national or ethnic origin. It may come about because people have unfair, stereotypical, prejudicial ideas or beliefs about individuals of other races. Racial discrimination, even in the most subtle form in the workplace, can affect the job satisfaction of those persons discriminated against. In a survey by Curry and Johnson-Cooper to determine the "fit" of African American academic librarians, they found that 101 of the 173 respondents acknowledged that they had been discriminated against because of race.[50] In 1998 Cynthia Preston addressed the issue of discriminatory practices and attitudes in the workplace and their influence on job satisfaction. Preston's survey focused on African American librarians' relationships with supervisors, patrons, coworkers, and management in all types of libraries. She found that most of the respondents (67%) were generally satisfied with their job and that the most significant factor that influenced overall job satisfaction was related to the librarian's individual feeling of accomplishment. While relationships with supervisors, coworkers and management were satisfactory, fifty-one percent of 123 respondents observed racial discrimination in their work environment.[51] Thornton's study revealed that forty-seven percent of 136 respondents experienced incidences of racial discrimination and racial discrimination negatively affected the job satisfaction of thirty-two respondents.[52] Curry suggested that the impact of racism, prejudice and discrimination often resulted in early burn out for African Americans. This burn out impacted the recruitment and retention of African American librarians. She also asserted that libraries must work to eliminate "everyday racism" and examine its effect on job satisfaction.[53] These studies support the fact that racial discrimination must be acknowledged as a factor affecting job satisfaction.

Of the ninety-eight respondents in this survey, only twenty-eight reported no incidences of racial discrimination in the workplace. Thirty-six respondents reported little (at least one) incidence while twenty respondents reported incidences of racial discrimination to a moderate degree and eight to a high degree. Sixty-four incidences of racial discrimination are too many, and the numbers suggest that racism is alive and flourishing in academic libraries. It is interesting to note that of the twenty-three respondents who felt moderately isolated, nineteen reported incidences of racial discrimination. Of the fourteen who felt isolated to a high degree, nine reported incidences of racial discrimination.

Of the twenty-eight respondents feeling a moderate to a high degree of racial discrimination, Table 5 shows their dissatisfaction in the twenty-three aspects of job satisfaction. Twenty-one of these twenty-eight respondents had considered leaving their present position. Opportunities for advancement was listed by more of the respondents as the number one reason for leaving and better salary was the second most frequently expressed reason for leaving. Five respondents listed experiencing racial discrimination as their first reason for considering leaving their present positions.

These statistics should alert library administrators to the presence of racial discrimination in the workplace and the need for it to be eradi-

TABLE 5. Respondents Experiencing Moderate to High Degree of Racial Discrimination (Number of Respondents = 28)

	Very Dissatisfied	Dissatisfied	Can't Decide or Neutral	Satisfied	Very Satisfied
Job Duties	1	4	3	15	5
Working Conditions	1	1	6	16	4
Autonomy on the job	1	1	2	17	7
Challenges of the job	1	4	4	9	10
Variety of occupational tasks	0	3	3	12	10
Work assignment and workload	1	8	2	12	5
Job security	1	3	6	11	7
Interaction with peers	1	6	8	9	4
Interaction with patrons	0	1	4	14	9
Status of librarians at your institution	1	10	5	10	2
Salary	7	12	2	6	1
Fringe benefits	2	5	6	10	5
Opportunities for advancement	6	12	5	5	0
Opportunities for collegial interaction within your department	1	3	8	14	2
Opportunities for collegial interaction with faculty in other departments	1	6	7	11	3
Opportunities for professional development	1	7	2	11	7
Interest of department colleagues in your work	2	9	9	8	0
Opportunities to pursue research	1	4	8	10	5
Proportion of faculty of African descent at the university	15	11	1	1	0
Proportion of faculty of African descent in the library	19	8	1	0	0
Manner in which administration handles faculty problems	6	8	10	3	1
Lines of communication	2	13	3	9	1
Serving as role model for students of African descent	1	3	9	10	5

cated before it negatively affects morale and retention. New entrants into the profession will certainly not tolerate racial discrimination.

Diversity and Job Satisfaction

Diversity has been and will continue to be an issue in higher education and in the library profession. While the library literature on diversity is extensive, no studies addressed diversity and job satisfaction.

Marcus proposed that managers should understand the ways diversity influences employees and that leaders should create work climates that promote the potential of diversity.[54] Most libraries sponsor or participate in some type of diversity program or initiative. Some programs are limited to diversity plans.[55] Such plans/programs are designed to increase diversity in the workplace and to encourage staff to welcome and value diverse views. They often focus on recruitment and retention of members of underrepresented groups, increasing diversity awareness in the workplace, building multicultural collections, and designing and providing library services for users from diverse cultural backgrounds.[56] Diversity within a library's workforce should be viewed as a source of strength and richness. Librarians of color can bring unique insights and perspectives to the development of programs, services, and collections for the populations served.[57] Diversity programs, if properly implemented, encourage an environment that is welcoming and fosters the success of people of color.

This survey revealed that forty-nine percent of the respondents believed that the library administration had a high commitment to diversity, and forty-eight percent felt that the library welcomed and valued diversity; however, sixty-seven percent perceived the diversity programs to be inadequate.

Eight of the respondents cited the library's non-commitment to diversity as one of the top reasons for leaving their positions. These findings indicate that what is proclaimed may not be practiced in regards to diversity programs.

CONCLUSION

Although females dominate the library profession, African American women have a minor presence in librarianship. Predictions of changes in the composition of the workforce, based on gender, race and age should impel library administrators to closely examine factors that affect recruitment, retention and advancement of ethnic minorities, especially African Americans, Hispanics, and young employees to the profession.

This study indicated that the determinants of job satisfaction for African American female librarians were similar to those that affected their white counterparts, but included other determinants based on skin tones. The combination of gender and race made African American women the least satisfied librarians. Other relevant findings were:

(1) older librarians were more satisfied than younger librarians, (2) tenure in the professions increased job satisfaction, (3) there was no significant correlation between years at present library and job satisfaction, (4) isolation affected job satisfaction, but more research is needed in the area, (5) racial discrimination negatively influenced job satisfaction, and (6) diversity programs were merely "window dressing" in most institutions. From the sources of dissatisfaction identified, steps should be taken to eliminate the barriers perceived by African American librarians. If more minority and young librarians are to be attracted to the profession, and if those who are currently employed are to remain and advance, library administrators must take steps to enhance job satisfaction. Administrators must act now to achieve their goals of increasing the number of minority librarians in the profession.

NOTES

1. Employment Policy Foundation, "The American Workplace, A Century of Progress . . . A Century of Change," 1999, [online] available from http://www.epf.org/labor99/tcentury.htm [cited 19 December 2000].

2. U.S. Department of Labor, *Milestones: The Women's Bureau Celebrate 70 Years of Women's Labor History* (U.S. Government Printing Office, 1990).

3. "Women's Share of Labor Force to Edge Higher by 2008," *Monthly Labor Review Online* (14 February 2000) [online] available from http://Stats.bls.gov/opub/ted/2000/Feb/wk3/art01.htm.

4. Research Division, Defense Equal Opportunity Management, *Review of Data on Women in the United States* (Washington, DC: The Institute) (21 February 1986).

5. "More Good News, So Why the Blues? The Annual Report on the Economic Status of the Profession 1999-2000," *Academe* 86, no. 2 (March/April 2000): 33-5.

6. Employment Policy Foundation, "The American Workplace."

7. Betty Woody, *Black Women in the Workplace: Impact of Structural Change in the Economy* (New York: Greenwood Press, 1992).

8. U.S. Department of Labor, "Facts on Working Women, 97-1," 1997 [online] available from http://www.dol.gov/dol/wb/public/wb_pubs/bwlf97.htm [cited 25 August 1999].

9. James V. Carmichael, Jr., "Gender Issues in the Workplace: Male Librarians Tell Their Side," *American Libraries* 25, no. 2 (March 1994): 228-30.

10. Joyce K. Thornton, "Job Satisfaction of Librarians of African Descent Employed in the Association of Research Libraries Academic Libraries," *College and Research Libraries* 60 (May 2000): 217-32.

11. Jan S. Squire, "Job Satisfaction and the Ethnic Minority Librarian," *Library Administration and Management* 5, no. 4 (fall 1991): 194-203.

12. Meredith A. Butler and Gloria DeSole, "Creating the Multicultural Organization-A Call to Action," in *Libraries as User-Centered Organizations: Imperatives for Organizational Change*, ed., Meredith A. Butler (New York: The Haworth Press, Inc., 1993), 156-74.

13. Thornton, "Job Satisfaction," 225-29.

14. William J. Vaughn and J. D. Dunn, "A Study of Job Satisfaction in Six University Libraries," *College and Research Libraries* 35 (May 1974): 163-77.

15. Gloria J. Leckie and Jim Brett, "Job Satisfaction of Canadian University Librarians. A National Survey," *College and Research Libraries* 58 (January 1997): 32-47.

16. Kenneth Plate and Elizabeth Stone, "Factors Affecting Librarians' Job Satisfaction: A Report of Two Studies," *Library Quarterly* 44 (April 1974): 97-110; Kamala Chopra, "Job Satisfaction among the Librarians of Lucknow City," *Herald of Library Science* 23 (July 1984): 156-61; Vaughn and Dunn, "A Study of Job Satisfaction"; Beverly Lynch and Jo Ann Verdin, "Job Satisfaction in Libraries: Relationships of the Work Itself, Age, Occupational Group, Tenure, Supervisory Level, Career Commitment, and Library Department," *Library Quarterly* 53 (October 1983): 434-47; Norman Roberts, "Graduates in Academic Libraries: A Survey of Past Students of the Post-Graduate School of Librarianship and Information Science, Sheffield University, 1964/65-1970/71," *Journal of Librarianship* 5 (April 1973): 97-115; Suzanne P. Wahba, "Job Satisfaction of Librarians: A Comparison between Men and Women," *College and Research Libraries* 36 (January 1975): 45-51; Noragh Jones, *Continuing Education for Librarians* (Leeds: Leeds Polytechnic School of Librarianship, 1977), 132-51; Steven Chwe, "A Comparative Study of Job Satisfaction: Catalogers and Reference Librarians in University Libraries," *Journal of Academic Librarianship* 4 (July 1978): 139-43; Richard Scamell and Bette Stead, "A Study of Age and Tenure as it Pertains to Job Satisfaction," *Journal of Library Administration* 1, no. 1 (spring 1980): 13-18; Lynch and Verdin, "Job Satisfaction in Libraries: A Replication," *Library Quarterly* 57 (April 1987): 190-202; Carol Saunders and Russell Saunders, "Effects of Flextime on Sick Leave, Vacation Leave, Anxiety, Performance, and Satisfaction in a Library Setting," *Library Quarterly* 55 (January 1985): 71-88; Dale Susan Bengston and Dorothy Shields, "A Test of Marchant's Predictive Formulas Involving Job Satisfaction," *Journal of Academic Librarianship* 11 (May 1985): 88-92; Edet Nkereuwem, "The Correlation Between Job Satisfaction, Job Attitudes and Work Behaviour Among the Staff in Academic Libraries in Nigeria," *Information Science* 12 (1992): 252-61.

17. Bonnie Horeinstein, "Job Satisfaction of Academic Libraries: An Examination of the Relationship Between Satisfaction, Faculty Status, and Participation," *College and Research Libraries* 54 (May 1993): 255-69; David Waters, "New Technology and Job Satisfaction in University Libraries," *LASIE* 18 (January/February 1988): 103-8; Leigh Estabrook, Chloe Bird, and Frederick Gilmore, "Job Satisfaction: Does Automation Make a Difference?" *Journal of Library Automation* 13, no. 1/2 (1990): 175-79; Jo Bell Whitlach, "Automation and Job Satisfaction Among Reference Librarians," *Computers in Libraries* 11 (September 1991): 32-4; Jack A. Siggins, "Job Satisfaction and Performance in a Changing Environment," *Library Trends* 41 (fall 1992): 299-315; Tina Hovecamp, "Unionization and Job Satisfaction Among Professional Library Employees in Academic Research Institutions," *College and Research Libraries* 56 (July 1995): 341-50; Patricia Kreitz and Annegret Ogden, "Job Responsibilities and Job Satisfaction in the University of California Libraries," *College and Research Libraries* 51 (July 1990): 297-312.

18. Patricia L. Smith, Stanley J. Smits, and Frank Hoy, "Employee Work Attitudes: The Subtle Influence of Gender," *Human Relations* 51, no. 5 (May 1988): 649-50.

19. Wahba, "Job Satisfaction of Librarians," 45-6.

20. Roberts, "Graduates in Academic Libraries," 100.

21. Brigg Nzotta, "Factors Associated with the Job Satisfaction of Male and Female Librarians in Nigeria," *Library and Information Science Research* 7 (January/March 1985): 75-84.

22. George P. D'Elia, "The Determinants of Job Satisfaction Among Beginning Librarians," *Library Quarterly* 49 (July 1979): 283-302.

23. Lynch and Verdin, "Job Satisfaction in Libraries," 660; Lynch and Verdin, "Job Satisfaction in Libraries: A Replication," 195.

24. Mohammad H. Mirfakhrai, "Correlates of Job Satisfaction Among Academic Libraries in the United States," *Journal of Library Administration* 14 (1991): 117-31.

25. Ilene F. Rockman, "Job Satisfaction Among Faculty and Librarians: A Study of Gender, Autonomy, and Decision-Making Opportunities," *Journal of Library Administration* 53 (fall 1984): 43-56.

26. Thornton, "Job Satisfaction of Librarians," 226.

27. Wahba, "Job Satisfaction of Librarians," 45.

28. Martha Tack and Carol Paitu, *Faculty Job Satisfaction: Women and Minorities in Peril.* ASHE-ERIC Higher Education Report No. 4 (Washington, DC: The George Washington University, School of Education and Human Development, 1992).

29. Estabrook, Bird, and Gilmore, "Job Satisfaction: Does Automation Make a Difference?" 183.

30. Thornton, "Job Satisfaction of Librarians," 229.

31. Patrick A. Hall, "Yassuh! I's the Reference Librarian!" *American Libraries* 19, no. 10 (November 1988): 900-1.

32. Stanley Wilder, "The Changing Profile of Research Library Professional Staff," *ARL: A Bimonthly Newsletter on Research Library Issues and Actions from ARL, CNI, and SPARC* 208/209 (February/April 2000): 1-5.

33. Wan He and Frank Hobbs, "Minority Population Growth: 1995-2050," *The Emerging Minority Marketplace* (Washington: US Department of Commerce, Minority Business Development Agency, 1999).

34. Scamell and Stead, "A Study of Age and Tenure," 9, 12-14.

35. Lynch and Verdin, "Job Satisfaction in Libraries," 445.

36. Lynch and Verdin, "Job Satisfaction in Libraries: A Replication," 194-95.

37. Mirfakhrai, "Correlates of Job Satisfaction," 128.

38. Evan St. Lifer, "Are You Happy in Your Job? LJ's Exclusive Report," *Library Journal* 119, no. 18 (November 1994): 44-9.

39. Roberts, "Graduates in Academic Libraries," 99.

40. Noragh Jones, *Continuing Education for Librarians.*

41. Lynch and Verdin, "Job Satisfaction in Libraries," 445.

42. Lynch and Verdin, "Job Satisfaction in Libraries: A Replication," 195.

43. Scamell and Stead, "A Study of Age and Tenure," 14.

44. Joyce S. Phillips, Kerry D. Carson, and Paula P. Carson, "Evolution of Affective Career Outcome: A Field Study of Academic Libraries," *College and Research Libraries* 55 (November 1994): 541-49.

45. Roberts, "Graduates in Academic Libraries," 105.

46. Lynch and Verdin, "Job Satisfaction in Libraries," 446.

47. Lynch and Verdin, "Job Satisfaction in Libraries: A Replication," 195.

48. Mirfakhrai, "Correlates of Job Satisfaction," 128-29.

49. Dennis Andrulis, Melvin Sikes, Ira Iscoe, and Thomas Friedman, *Journal of Negro Education* 44 (1975): 6-11; Tack and Paitu, *Faculty Job Satisfaction*, 72.

50. Deborah A. Curry and Glendora Johnson-Cooper, "African American Academic Librarians and the Profession: An Uncomfortable Fit?" (1993).

51. Cynthia Preston, "Perceptions of Discriminatory Practices and Attitude: A Survey of African American Librarians," *College and Research Libraries* 59 (September 1998): 434-45.

52. Thornton, "Job Satisfaction," 229.

53. Deborah A. Curry, "Your Worries Ain't Like Mine: African American Librarians and the Pervasiveness of Racism, Prejudice and Discrimination in Academe," *The Reference Librarian* 45/46 (1994): 299-311.

54. Laurence R. Marcus, "Staff Diversity and the Leadership Challenge," *Equity and Excellence in Education* 33, no. 2 (September 2000): 61-7.

55. Marilyn Shaver, "Cultural Diversity Programming in ARL Libraries," *SPEC Kit No. 165* (Washington, DC: Association of Research Libraries, Office of Management Studies, 1990).

56. Mark D. Winston and Haipeng Li, "Managing Diversity in Liberal Arts College Libraries," *College Research Libraries* 61 (May 2000): 205-15.

57. Theo S. Jones-Quartey and Kit S. Byunn, "Ethnic Minorities in Librarianship: A Selected Bibliography," *Special Libraries* 84 (spring 1993): 104-11.

APPENDIX A. General Characteristics of Respondents

Age	N
25-34	12
35-44	37
45-54	42
Over 55	7

Faculty Rank	N
Asst. Professor	13
Instructor	6
Assoc. Professor	4
Professor	1
Other	27
Not Applicable	47

Area of Service	N
Reference	28
Administration	17
Combination of 2+ areas	13
Cataloging	8
Archives	4
Circulation	4
Government Documents	4
Automated Systems	3
Technical Services	3
Acquisitions	2
Collection Management	2
ILL	2
Instruction	2
Special Collections	1
Other	5

Eligible for Tenure	N
Yes	33
No	5

Tenured	N
Yes	15
No	5

Education	N
MLS/MA	94
Additional Master's	21
PhD	2
Other	3
No Responses	1
Yes	15
No	18
No Responses	5

Years as a Professional Librarian	N
0-3.9	21
4-9.9	16
10-15	26
Over 15	35

Years at Present Institution	N
Less than a year	9
1-3.9	25
4-9.9	28
10-15	17
Over 15	19

Salary	N
Under $25,000	4
$25,001-$30,000	9
$30,001-$40,000	38
$40,001-$45,000	15
Over $45,000	31

Stories Told But Yet Unfinished: Challenges Facing African-American Libraries and Special Collections in Historically Black Colleges and Universities

Irene Owens

SUMMARY. Practices of discrimination based on race forced the creation of "separate and unequal" colleges and universities with similarly separate and unequal libraries. Even the Morrill Land Grant Acts of 1860 and 1890, which were not intended to discriminate based on race, did in fact discriminate, leading to the creation of separate and unequal land-grant institutions. It was *Brown vs. Board of Education* that challenged successfully this "separate and unequal" custom and prompted the first major change in the composition of dominant institutions. By that time, however, many of the predominantly African-American institutions, although weak in library resources as a whole, had established outstanding collections on the history, literature, and art of persons of African descent.

Irene Owens is affiliated with The Graduate School of Library and Information Science, The University of Texas at Austin, Austin, TX (E-mail: *iowens@gslis.utexas.edu*).

[Haworth co-indexing entry note]: "Stories Told But Yet Unfinished: Challenges Facing African-American Libraries and Special Collections in Historically Black Colleges and Universities." Owens, Irene. Co-published simultaneously in *Journal of Library Administration* (The Haworth Information Press, an imprint of The Haworth Press, Inc.) Vol. 33, No. 3/4, 2001, pp. 165-181; and: *Diversity Now: People, Collections, and Services in Academic Libraries* (ed: Teresa Y. Neely, and Kuang-Hwei (Janet) Lee-Smeltzer) The Haworth Information Press, an imprint of The Haworth Press, Inc., 2001, pp. 165-181. Single or multiple copies of this article are available for a fee from The Haworth Document Delivery Service [1-800-HAWORTH, 9:00 a.m. - 5:00 p.m. (EST). E-mail address: getinfo@haworthpressinc.com].

165

This article examines the historical context of these issues, and makes clear that, despite inadequate resources, many of these libraries had created significant collections for education, research, and services. But there is still much work to be done. *[Article copies available for a fee from The Haworth Document Delivery Service: 1-800-HAWORTH. E-mail address: <getinfo@haworthpressinc.com> Website: <http://www.HaworthPress.com> © 2001 by The Haworth Press, Inc. All rights reserved.]*

KEYWORDS. African-American university and college libraries, African-American library resources, Historically Black Colleges and Universities

INTRODUCTION

The idea for this article, which discusses the past and future development of Black colleges and their libraries, appeared when I was asked to write a review of the book *Untold Stories: Civil Rights, Libraries, and Black Librarianship* edited by John Mark Tucker.[1] It documents an era not usually remembered or studied for its contributions to libraries-the Civil Rights era of the 1960s. Tucker's book, however, is not limited to the contributions of libraries during the Civil Rights era, but develops two other topics, "Legacies of Black Librarianship" and "Resources for Library Personnel, Services and Collections." Each section has at least one essay that contains information appropriate to the collections and services of academic libraries in Historically Black Colleges and Universities (HBCUs).

Of particular significance in the study of the development of the collections of HBCUs is Rosie L. Albritton's 1998 essay.[2] Albritton documents the founding of these societies and libraries, explains why they existed (to promote self-improvement and to share useful knowledge), maps the distribution of these libraries and societies in the United States (located mostly in the Northeast), and points out the many contributions they made.[3]

More important is Albritton's description of the contributions of these libraries and societies to the building of many of today's major collections of Black literature, history, and art. Early bibliophiles associated with the collection of Black history, literature, and art were drawn together by a cause and shared passion for searching out and documenting evidence of the accomplishments of African-Americans. Their collections became the core of the development of modern collections on African-American history, literature, and art. For example,

Howard University benefited from the donation of the Jesse E. Moorland Library, and Atlanta University from the Henry Proctor Slaughter Collection. The Library of Congress benefited as well since the Daniel A. Murray Collection helped to form the core of its collection of African-American resources.[4] The story of Black education and librarianship would be incomplete without noting the work of these early societies and libraries.

James E. Hooper, in "Private Dominance in Black Academic Libraries, 1916-1938," shows how White philanthropy, especially the gifts of John D. Rockefeller, Jr., of Standard Oil and Julius Rosenwald of Sears, Roebuck and Company, enabled some HBCUs to experience remarkable growth during the decades of the 1920s and 1930s. In addition, the Rosenwald Fund, which began in 1929, provided matching funds for the purchase of books for selected HBCUs. Later, in the 1940s and 1950s, some HBCUs began to make important strides thanks to the contributions of the General Education Board (GEB).[5]

Another reason for improvement in some of the libraries during these periods was the presence of larger numbers of trained library personnel, due largely to the creation in the late 1920s of the Hampton Library School, and later the library school at Atlanta University, which was created at a time when most library schools followed discriminatory admissions policies based on race.[6]

It was the practice of segregation that prompted the creation of HBCUs as a way to provide a college education to former slaves and offer them the opportunity for a productive role in American society. The Higher Education Act of 1965, as amended, defines an HBCU as "any historically Black college or university that was established prior to 1964, whose principal mission was, and is, the education of Black Americans, and that is accredited by a nationally accrediting agency or association determined by the Secretary [of Education] to be a reliable authority as to the quality of training offered or is, according to such an agency or association, making reasonable progress toward accreditation."[7]

There are 107 HBCUs in nineteen states located mostly in the south. The eldest of these schools is Cheyney State in Pennsylvania (1849), while the youngest is Valley State College in Mississippi (1950). Sixteen of these colleges were founded in the nineteenth century as land grant colleges or were later given this status to conform with federal requirements that benefits of land grant programs be available to both Blacks and Whites.

A newer group of Black colleges was described by Ploski and Williams as schools receiving this HBCU designation due to their location in major urban areas.[8] These were mostly two-year colleges, as opposed to the four-year and graduate institutions comprising the earlier HBCUs. At least one HBCU (Howard) has true university status in that it offers advanced degrees (including the PhD in several areas), as well as professional degrees in such areas as pharmacy, divinity, law, dentistry and medicine. One of the challenges of the newer Black colleges is that they must keep constantly before them the task of ensuring that their mission fits consistently into the overall goal of providing equality for Blacks in higher education.

One of the challenges that increased the complexity of sustaining all the Black colleges was declining enrollment in the 1970s.[9] The HBCUs that had served for such a long time as the primary provider of higher education for Blacks were now being challenged by the perception that higher education was now more accessible to Blacks than in earlier decades; therefore, the unique role of HBCUs had diminished. Federal government support continued to decline in the 1980s, placing a greater responsibility on the HBCUs to garner private support.[10]

Another group of HBCUs, founded as state colleges as a result of Black leadership, is significant. Elizabeth City State University, for example, was created in 1891 by a bill introduced into the North Carolina legislature by Hugh Cale, a Black legislator from Pasquatank County. In 1871, when Alcorn A&M University was officially opened for Mississippi Black citizens, Hiram R. Revels, the first Black elected to the United States Senate, resigned his seat to become the college's first president.[11]

Other HBCUs started as private institutions with gifts from Black and White individuals and groups. For example, the soldiers and officers of the sixty-second United States Colored Infantry gave $5,000 to fund Lincoln University's incorporation in Missouri, and are credited with the College's founding.[12] Fort Valley State College was established in 1895 by the altruism of local Black and White citizens, with a dominant role being played by Anna T. Jeanes of Philadelphia.[13]

The boards of northern religious denominations also succeeded in developing institutions of higher learning in the south. The Presbyterian Church founded two such schools, Scotia Seminary (now Barber-Scotia College), and Biddle Memorial Institute (now Johnson C. Smith University), located respectively in Concord and in Charlotte, North Carolina. Other religious denominations that founded historically Black colleges include the Catholic church (Xavier University in New

Orleans), and the United Christian Missionary Society of the Disciples of Christ (Jarvis Christian College in Hawkins, Texas).[14]

The Black church, long providing leadership to the Black community, contributed immensely in the establishment of Black colleges. These institutions, like most other HBCUs, offered curricula aimed at preparing persons for the ministry, as well as training teachers to help educate a struggling Black society. Jessie Carney Smith cites several examples of these institutions that were founded before the Civil War but were more fully developed after the war's end. Some of these institutions include Wilberforce University in Tawana Spring, Ohio, founded by the Cincinnati Conference of the Methodist Episcopal Church; Paul Quinn College in Waco, Texas, Edward Waters College in Jacksonville, Florida, and Morris Brown College in Atlanta Georgia, all founded by the African Methodist Episcopal Church; Livingstone College in Salisbury, North Carolina, founded by the African Methodist Episcopal Zion Church; and Lane College in Jackson, Tennessee, Paine College in Augusta, Georgia, Texas College in Tyler, Texas, and Miles College in Birmingham, Alabama, founded by the Colored Methodist Episcopal Church.[15]

The Freedmen's Bureau, a federally funded agency which had power over the affairs of newly freed slaves, was responsible, in part, for the founding of Howard University in the District of Columbia, and St. Augustine's College in West Virginia (now merged into Virginia Union University in Richmond, Virginia).[16]

There are several histories of these Black colleges and universities.[17] Unfortunately, however, some of these histories make no mention of the history of the library in these institutions, creating a need for further research: (1) to understand more fully the histories of all libraries in the United States; (2) to document the significance of these libraries alongside those of non-HBCU institutions; (3) to document inequities, as well as strengths as a basis for improved funding for services and collections; and, (4) to identify cooperative efforts needed among HBCUs and non-HBCUs.

REVIEW OF THE LITERATURE

Studies and surveys on the libraries of the HBCUs can be divided into three periods: 1917 to 1952, 1965 to 1970, and 1971 to the present. Jessie Carney Smith's work is easily the most thorough.[18] These studies demonstrate that even though these schools were founded before the turn of the century, they did not receive much attention regarding their status until decades later. Of the existing studies, there are several challenges. There were few studies that include all of the HBCUs, some are studies of only the public ones, others of the private ones, and still others, representing only the private United Negro College Fund (UNCF) members (Table 1). The UNCF has made substantial contributions to improving the quality of higher education for Blacks.

The UNCF was formed on April 25, 1944 under the leadership of Frederick D. Patterson (president of Tuskegee Institute, now Tuskegee University) as an appeal to presidents of the private Black colleges urging them to "pool their small monies and make a united appeal to the national conscience."[19] Herman L. Totten cites a further reason for the founding of the UNCF: "They dreamed that their colleges-all of them predominantly Black-soon would be able to offer education comparable to the best in the nation."[20]

Since that time, the UNCF has grown from its original twenty-seven members to include thirty-nine members and has become the nation's oldest and most successful African-American higher education assistance program. In its fifty-six year history, UNCF has raised more than $1.6 billion toward the operation of HBCUs. It currently serves as the administrator of the Bill Gates Millennium Scholars Program, a $20 billion scholarship program for minority students.[21]

TABLE 1. Studies Conducted on HBCU Libraries

Researcher/Agency	Year	Number of Schools in Study
USOE	1917	All types and grades
USOE	1928	All types and grades
USOE	1942	All types and grades
Marshall, A. P.	1952	41
Josey, E. J.	1969	Not indicated
McGrath, Earl J.	1965	61
Totten, Herman L.	1969	30 UNCF Institutions
Jordan, Casper L.	1970	85
Hill, Johnny Ray	1976	34 Public
Smith, Jessie Carney	1977	96
Hill, Susan T.	1985	Public HBCUs
Molyneux, Robert E.	1991	68
Gravois, Jim	1995	36 Public HBCUs

1917 to 1952

Three studies of Black colleges were conducted by the United States Bureau of Education (the latest one under its later name, the U.S. Office of Education) in 1917, 1928, and again in 1942.[22] These studies identified problems at the HBCUs and, as a result, minimal federal grants were made to assist in correcting some of the systemic problems. The first of these studies was predicated upon the fact that in the past, library facilities had only been incidental to the study of education for Black students. This observation seems to imply that earlier studies had, in fact, been conducted of these schools.

The report of the 1917 study of the collections was dismal indeed. Many of the books were deemed unsuitable and nearly worthless, and were housed in overcrowded conditions. To help correct this problem matching grants were made to eight colleges and universities (Alabama A&M, Atlanta University, Cheyney Institute, Fisk University, Howard University, Knoxville College, Tuskegee Institute, and Wilberforce University). The largest, $50,000, of these grants was awarded to Howard University and the two smallest, $10,000, to Knoxville College and Cheyney Institute.[23]

The 1928 study looked at managerial aspects with the idea that there was a need for overall improvement at these colleges and universities. Here the library was judged to be an important element and was described as a part of the educational equipment. The report stated that the collections in these libraries were built by too many donations and contained too few public documents. It was believed also that the faculty had failed to recognize the purpose of the library in educational endeavors. In comparison to the 1917 report, the findings in this study indicated a slight increase in expenditures for the libraries.[24]

The 1942 study examined the types of programs and services that were needed for these colleges and universities. As in the previous studies, the data from this study called for strong support for upgrading and improving these institutions with a particular emphasis on the physical facilities and services. One important strength did emerge from this final report. In terms of library holdings of Black books, periodicals and newspapers, these libraries surpassed other institutions used for comparative purposes. This is a strength these libraries continue today. A less encouraging finding of the study was the overall conclusion that the majority of the academic libraries received less than their share of institutional budgets, and the institutions were expending amounts insufficient to allow the libraries at HBCUs to function effectively in the educational programs of the institutions.[25]

The final study of this era, conducted by A. P. Marshall, examined the professional requirements for librarians in forty-one Black colleges. Included among the findings were the degree to which these colleges would hire recent graduates based on their experience, and whether or not there were race or gender preferences in hiring. Marshall wrote: "Twenty-six colleges reported that recent library school graduates would be acceptable for their positions, while four preferred not to accept them. In three libraries, the matter of sex was an issue; preference was given to men in one instance, while two colleges preferred women. Concerning race as a factor in the employment of librarians, seventeen colleges reported that it would be a factor, while ten indicated that it would not."[26]

1965 to 1970

In 1965, Earl J. McGrath conducted one of the most comprehensive studies of all aspects of Black academic libraries, including collections, facilities, personnel, the use of resources by students and faculty, and administrative and financial support.[27] This report exposed the differences and unevenness among Black academic libraries. McGrath stated, "the resources and services of Negro College libraries run the gamut from excellent to poor, but unfortunately the curve of quality is heavily skewed toward the lower end."[28] He concluded that the need for strong libraries in these institutions was accentuated "by their lack of sufficiently trained faculty members and their larger than normal proportion of poorly prepared students."[29] McGrath's findings confirm those of the earlier period, that there was a need to award grants to enable most of these libraries to update their collections and provide for major elements of their educational programs, and that most of these collections contained too many gift books, swelling the size while not adding to the quality of the collections.

Totten's 1969 study added additional insights into the operations of HBCUs, more specifically, the private UNCF schools.[30] His study measured reporting channels in management and the degree to which head librarians were involved in the overall operation of the institutions. His findings showed that of the thirty institutions responding there were varied patterns of administrative organization. Thirteen (44%) of the librarians reported directly to the president and seventeen (56%) reported to the dean of the college or the vice president for academic affairs. Twenty-three (77%) of the respondents reported that their head librarians served on curriculum committees while seven (23%) did not. The reporting structure of the library director and the degree to which librarians were involved in the educational pursuits of the institution were in some ways measures of the value the institution placed on the library, and, in turn, the measures the library placed on the value of its services to the institution. In terms of the budget, nineteen (63%) reported that total library expenditures were five percent or more of the educational and general expenditures of the college.[31]

In the same year, E. J. Josey, conducting a study similar to the earlier Office of Education studies, confirmed the same general findings regarding the status of the collections of the Black college libraries. Josey expanded the scope of the studies by looking also at the service ethic of the staff. He found that "staffs in these libraries were small yet dedicated to service. Even so, their involvement in clerical assignments and pedestrian activities, which was forced upon them because of insufficient numbers of library personnel, prevented them from engaging in more professional tasks."[32]

Casper Jordan's findings confirmed earlier studies in terms of the condition of the collections, but his study went a step further, noting apparent improvement.[33] Both he and McGrath concluded that there was a broad span of conditions among these colleges from near excellent to poor, but nonetheless there was some overall progress. The improvement was that, generally, the facilities of the HBCUs were in somewhat better condition than the collections they contained or the number of personnel employed. This was true of both the public and private HBCUs, with a slight edge given to the private UNCF schools.[34]

1971 to Present

The studies discussed above represent a gradually improving insight into the conditions of HBCUs in general, but particularly in their libraries. It was, however, a study conducted in 1976 by Johnny Ray Hill at the Office for the Advancement of Public Negro Colleges (OAPNC), a division of the National Association of State Universities and Land Grant Colleges (in cooperation with the American Association of State Colleges and Universities), that provided information that may have been a turning point for these colleges and universities.[35] What sets Hill's work aside from the earlier studies is his inclusion of "interinstitutional cooperation." This was not just another factor to be included as a variable, but one that was prescriptive: Cooperation could make a difference for these libraries. In addition to "interinstitutional cooperation," Hill looked at enrollment, total collection size, staffing patterns, facilities, financial support, and services to students. He conducted his study with an appreciation for the progressive and constructive changes associated with these libraries to gain insights into their progress for the previous three years. The study included thirty-four HBCU libraries and was funded in part by the Council on Library Resources.

Comparing categories over a three-year period, Hill found the enrollment of the thirty-four institutions to be 137,000 in 1976, representing a 13 percent increase over 1973/74. The total number of volumes held by all the libraries, based on data submitted to OAPNC by the chief librarians of the thirty-four institutions, was 5,532,870 volumes. This figure represented an increase of 932,097 volumes over the total number housed in 1973/74. He also found that all the libraries were accredited by their respective state, regional, and various professional accreditation agencies. Thirty-two of the thirty-four libraries had special collections of rare and historically important documents and artifacts associated with the struggles and history of Black Americans.

As stated above, of particular note in this study is Hill's emphasis on interinstitutional support and services provided by the libraries of HBCUs. Cooperation among libraries in sharing collections has long been one of the ways of strengthening their value and worth to institutions and users. The cooperative efforts that Hill found were exemplary beginnings to one of the best means of strengthening the libraries of the HBCUs. Methods of cooperation included interlibrary loan, shared collections of materials by and about Black Americans, reciprocal borrowing arrangements within a geographical area, cooperative purchase of materials by institutions located close together, publication of union lists and film catalogs, and shared personnel and library directories.

Services being provided, Hill found, included more orientation programs to the use of the library, open stacks, and a change in classification systems from Dewey Decimal to the Library of Congress. Of particular note was Project Literature-Art-Music-Philosophy (LAMP) at Jackson State University, a library-oriented teaching program for courses in the humanities and social sciences to promote greater use of library resources in the learning process.

COMPARING HBCUs WITH NON-HBCUs

The 1970s brought on a new twist in higher education affecting not only HBCUs but non-HBCUs. Just as *Brown vs. the Board of Education* improved the opportunities for Blacks to have better access to higher education, the U.S. Office of Education's Office (USOE) of Civil Rights provided a second component of integration. The USOE's mandate required that the curricula, facilities, and libraries of HBCUs be upgraded to attract White students.[36]

Jim Gravois sought to discern to what extent the various states had dedicated the funding needed to improve public HBCU libraries. He asked whether a snapshot comparison of public HBCUs with public non-HBCU libraries would verify such improvement.[37]

Gravois's study followed a similar study by Susan T. Hill who looked at a comparison of volumes per student in each of the above settings. Her study estimated that the libraries of all public four-year HBCUs in the country held sixty-five volumes per student on average, compared to sixty-two volumes for "comparable" White colleges.[38]

Gravois compared the following between HBCUs and non-HBCUs: volumes per student, salary expended per student, salary expended per library staff, total library staff per hundred students, and professional librarians as a percentage of total staff. His findings showed that HBCUs held nearly sixty-four volumes per student compared to sixty-six per student in non-HBCUs. Salary per student was $128.84 in HBCUs compared to $144.46 in non-HBCUs. HBCUs employed .547 staff and .226 professionals per student while non-HBCUs employed .544 staff and .196 professionals per student. Finally, the level of professionals as a percentage of staff was 41.2 percent in HBCUs and 36.0 percent in non-HBCUs.

In general, then, using the survey data for HBCUs and non-HBCUs, there appears to be no significant difference between HBCUs and non-HBCUs in the measurements of volumes per student, library staff per student, and professional librarians per student. The selected HBCUs, however, in these data, have an advantage in the measure of professional librarians as a percentage of the staff, while the non-HBCUs outpace the HBCUs in salary per student and salary per staff.[39]

TECHNOLOGY

There are other areas that need attention that have not been addressed in the current literature. Despite the importance placed today on the use of technology in libraries of all types, there were no studies that looked specifically at the status of technology in HBCU libraries. Beatrice O.

Agingu conducted a study to assess how useful Web pages were as tools for disseminating information and providing services to users among seventy-four HBCUs in the southeast region of the United States. Agingu's findings showed that HBCU libraries still lagged behind in terms of the resources and services they provided via their Web sites.[40]

She offered recommendations for these libraries to make their Web sites more useful. For example, those whose catalog was not Web-accessible should ensure that their catalog was telnet accessible from remote sites and linked to their Web sites. Also, HBCU libraries should provide links to databases such as *ERIC* and *PubMed* or *Grateful Med*, which were available free of charge on the Web, together with links to other Web sites relevant to their users' needs. Agingu also encouraged HBCU libraries to expand the resources available to users by linking local libraries and then making the catalogs of those libraries and other resources available to their users. HBCU libraries should post on their Web sites resources such as indexes and CD-ROM databases even if they cannot be searched through the Web sites and journal/periodical holdings. Finally, given the rich collections of African-American materials in the special collections of many of these libraries, HBCU libraries should seek to mount projects to digitize and make them available to users through the library's Web site.[41] Some of the reasons why HBCU libraries are lagging behind are some of the same reasons seen earlier-inadequate budgets and sometimes insufficiently trained staff.

CURRENT INITIATIVES

A telephone interview on March 2, 2000 with Brenda Banks, an assistant director of the Georgia Department of Archives and History, revealed exciting progress being made to improve the preservation of and accessibility to archival collections in HBCUs.[42] Banks has now written four grant proposals, three of which already have been funded by the National Endowment for the Humanities (NEH), to assist HBCUs in better preserving and making available the resources of their archives. Her initiatives provide opportunities for staff members of HBCUs to receive training in identifying and processing archival collections through the use of MAchine Readable Cataloging (MARC) records to describe their substantive collections (not their entire archival collections). A visiting trained archivist assists staff in identifying resources and creating MARC records, after which, the project director reviews the work and then returns the records to the participating library. The end result is to have these collections available to researchers online. Another part of this project is to meet with the HBCU presidents to explain the importance of the project and to gain their support for local funding to match funding from the NEH.

Banks recently submitted a grant proposal to the Southeastern Library Network (SOLINET) to seek cooperation between that organization and HBCUs. Some of the opportunities for cooperation would include work in preservation and conservation. Banks feels that one of the needs that should be addressed first is that of microfilming the archival collections of HBCUs, and then working on digitization. Her concerns center around issues of security and access.

Some of the problems Banks has encountered in her archival projects include a lack of adequately trained staff in many of the libraries, of funds to meet all the training needs, and of personnel for adequate follow-up and accountability. Her fourth grant proposal to the NEH is for conducting follow-up visits and to seek partnerships with larger universities to assist in broadening and enhancing the archival project.

ACRL and Its Contributions to HBCUs

Three projects of the Association of College and Research Libraries (ACRL) have been instituted for HBCUs: the Internship Program, the Planning Project, and the Accreditation Workshops. Casper Jordan and Beverly Lynch described the purpose of the Internship Program as a project to accelerate the development of the management ability of librarians at HBCUs by providing them with experience in the administration of strong and progressive academic libraries. Between 1974 and 1978, twenty-five managers working in HBCU libraries were identified as potential directors of libraries and were given the opportunity to learn about academic library administration in a variety of settings by working directly with experienced academic library directors. Participants completed evaluation forms, and in the final analysis, the program was highly impressive and there was a desire to have the project continued.[43]

In 1986, the Andrew W. Mellon Foundation provided ACRL with funds to undertake a planning project to consider programs for improving the libraries of HBCUs. The project committee agreed to propose to ACRL, based on the discussions, the following initiatives: collect and publish a statistical survey of the HBCU libraries using ACRL's "100" model, seek funding from the NEH to conduct a workshop targeted to the HBCUs and their communities on how to do public programming in the humanities (modeled on ACRL's program already in place), and sponsor a series of accreditation workshops for libraries conducting self-studies in preparation for accreditation visits.[44]

After the statistics were gathered, they were distributed to the president of each of the HBCUs, the HBCU libraries, and the regional accrediting associations. It was believed that one of the immediate benefits of this report was the receipt of an invitation to four HBCU presidents to attend the White House Conference on Libraries and Information Services. Moreover, the statistics were used to support resolutions for the HBCUs.[45]

Finally, John H. Waley discussed the success of Virginia Commonwealth University (VCU) in establishing a Multicultural Archives (with an emphasis first on Black archives and later including Hispanic archives) in cooperation with Virginia Union University (VUU). The project was entitled "Illusion vs. Reality: Teaching and Learning Cultural Diversity Through Archives." The purpose of the project was to improve campus race relations at VCU and VUU, an HBCU located in walking distance of VCU. More broadly the project was to bridge the gap not only between the two institutions, but also between the two institutions and the larger community. Whaley's discussion of the challenges of gaining trust between particularly the African-American community and the project directors as representatives of the non-HBCU is instructive, as is his discussion of the challenges of copyright that such a project brings. The project included borrowing documents from the African-American community, scanning those documents, and returning them so that the documents were still available in their original communities.[46]

Limitations of the Studies

HBCUs are complex and varied institutions. Unfortunately, there are no studies (historical or recent) that have made in-depth analysis of these libraries. Many of the studies deal only with the public institutions or with the private institutions, or a variation thereof, such as the private UNCF schools. There are no studies that give a current indication of the extent of technologies being used in these institutions. Moreover, there are many indications of the quantity of HBCU collections, but no studies that deal with the quality of the collections or with the quality of the data gathered. Somewhat more is known about the overall strength of the content of these collections in Black history, literature and art, and the overall dedication of the staff of many of these collections.

CONCLUSION

Synonyms for the word "story" in *Roget's Thesaurus* include chronicle, record, history, annals, ancient, medieval or modern history, biography, memoir, memorabilia, experiences, autobiography, journal, diary, letters, etc.[47] Indeed all of these synonyms describe in some way the content of the resources available in the collections of HBCU libraries. Some of the "story" remains to be told in terms of further development, preservation, access and technology. And more attention needs to be given to what Jessie Carney Smith observed decades earlier: "There is an immediate need for a clearinghouse which would record these activities, classify them, and attempt to disseminate information about Black academic libraries to foundations, to other agencies, and to the Black institutions themselves."[48]

By way of summary, one of the great strongholds of the HBCU libraries is the early and continuing work of past and present bibliophiles whose dedication and determination documented, preserved, and made accessible the "stories" of peoples of African descent. Secondly, credit must be given to philanthropic and professional organizations that have contributed capital to improve these collections. Thirdly, to those educators of vision who saw a need to provide in an academic setting a means of educating and training African-American librarians, before the integration of American library schools.

Additional studies that reflect the needs in preservation, conservation, access, and improved technology in general and special collections must be undertaken. More important is the need to replicate many of the studies conducted earlier that reflect the managerial practices of these libraries (reporting structure and involvement in the larger educational community) as well as the studies that would reflect recent findings regarding gender and race of staff. Such studies and appropriate follow-through would provide more data regarding the need for improved diversity and cooperation between HBCUs and between HBCUs and non-HBCUs.

NOTES

1. John Mark Tucker, *Untold Stories: Civil Rights, Libraries, and Black Librarianship* (Champaign, IL : Publications Office, Graduate School of Library and Information Science, 1998).

2. Rosie L. Albritton, "The Founding and Prevalence of African-American Social Libraries and Historical Societies, 1828-1918: Gatekeepers of Early Black History,

Collections, and Literature," in *Untold Stories: Civil Rights, Libraries, and Black Librarianship*, 23-46.

3. Ibid., 24-35, Appendix A, B, and C.

4. Ibid., 38.

5. James F. Hooper, "Private Dominance in Black Academic Libraries, 1916-1938," in *Untold Stories: Civil Rights, Libraries, and Black Librarianship*.

6. Robert Sidney Martin, and Orvin Lee Shiflett, "Hampton, Fisk, and Atlanta: The Foundations, the American Library Association, and Library Education For Blacks, 1925-1941," *Libraries and Culture* 31 (1996): 299-325.

7. *Higher Education Act of 1965, U. S. Code*, vol. 10, sec. 1061-2 (1965).

8. Harry A. Ploski, and James Williams, *The Negro Almanac: A Reference Work on the African-American*, 5th ed. (Detroit, Michigan: Gale Research, 1989).

9. Ibid., 762.

10. Ibid.

11. Ibid., 763.

12. Ibid.

13. Ibid.

14. Jessie Carney Smith, *Black Academic Libraries and Research Collections: An Historical Survey* (Westport, Connecticut: Greenwood Press, 1977).

15. Ibid., 12-13.

16. Ibid.

17. There are several published (usually brief) histories of some HBCU libraries. See Margaret E. Battle, "A History of the Carnegie Library at Johnson C. Smith University" (master's thesis, University of North Carolina, 1960); Anne M. Duncan, "A History of Howard University Library, 1867-1929" (master's thesis, Catholic University of America, 1951; Charles N. King, "Profile of the Edward Waters College Library, 1901-1994," *Florida Libraries* 38 (2) (1995): 26-7; William L. Olbrich, "An Adjunct, Necessary and Proper . . . : The Black Academic Library in Texas, 1876-1986," *Texas Library Journal* 62 (1) (1986): 94-103; Thelma F. Pearsall, "History of the North Carolina Agricultural and Technical College Library" (master's thesis, Western Reserve University, 1955); Joseph H. Reason, "The Howard University Libraries," *DC Libraries* 24 (2) (1953); Herman L. Totten, "The Wiley College Library," *Texas Libraries* 48 (2) (1987): 39-43; Herman L. Totten, "The Wiley College Library: The First Library for Negroes West of the Mississippi," *Negro History Bulletin* 32 (1969): 6-10.

18. Smith, *Black Academic Libraries and Research Collections*.

19. "United Negro College Fund-History" [online] available from http://www.uncf.org [cited 26 March 2001].

20. Herman L. Totten, "They Had a Dream: Black Colleges and Library Standards," *Wilson Library Bulletin* 44 (1969): 75-9.

21. "Gates Millennium Scholars" [online] available from http://www.gmsp.org [cited 26 March 2001].

22. U.S. Department of the Interior, Bureau of Education, *Negro Education: A Study of the Private and Higher Schools for Colored People in the United States*, 2 vols., Bulletin 1916, nos. 38-39 (Washington, DC: Government Printing Office, 1917); U.S. Department of the Interior, Bureau of Education, *Survey of Negro Colleges and Universities*, sections of Bulletin 1928, no. 7 (Washington, DC: Government Printing Office, 1928); U.S. Office of Education, Federal Security Agency, *National*

Survey of the Higher Education of Negroes, vols. 2-4, misc. no. 6 (Washington, DC: Government Printing Office, 1942).

23. *A Study of the Private and Higher Schools for Colored People in the United States*.

24. *Survey of Negro Colleges and Universities*.

25. *National Survey of the Higher Education of Negroes*.

26. A. P. Marshall, "Professional Needs in Negro Colleges," *College and Research Libraries* 13 (January 1952): 37.

27. Earl J. McGrath, *The Predominantly Negro Colleges and Universities in Transition* (New York: Columbia University Teachers College Bureau of Publications, 1965).

28. Ibid., 29.

29. Ibid., 128.

30. Totten, "They Had a Dream."

31. Ibid.

32. E. J. Josey, "Future of the Black College Library," *Library Journal* 15 September 1969, 94.

33. Casper L. Jordan, *Black Academic Libraries: An Inventory* (Atlanta, Georgia: Atlanta University Libraries; Chicago, IL: Association of College and Research Libraries, 1970).

34. McGrath, *The Predominantly Negro College and Universities in Transition*.

35. Johnny Ray Hill, *A Contemporary Status Report on the Libraries of Historically Black Colleges and Universities* (Atlanta, Georgia: Office of Advancement of Public Negro Colleges, 1976).

36. Jim Gravois, "Comparing Libraries of Public Historically Black Colleges and Universities with Their White Counterparts," *College and Research Libraries* 56 (1995): 519.

37. Ibid.

38. Susan T. Hill, *The Traditionally Black Institutions of Higher Education, 1860-1982* (Washington, DC: U.S. Government Printing Office, 1985).

39. Gravois, "Comparing Libraries of Public Historically Black Colleges and Universities," 522, 529.

40. Beatrice O. Agingu, "Library Web Sites at Historically Black Colleges and Universities," *College and Research Libraries* 61 (1) (2000): 30-7.

41. Ibid., 39.

42. Brenda Banks, telephone interview with author, 2 March 2000.

43. Casper L. Jordan, and Beverly P. Lynch, "ACRL's Historically Black College and Universities Libraries Projects, 1972-994," in *Untold Stories*.

44. Ibid., 160.

45. Ibid.

46. John H. Whaley, "Digitizing History," *American Archivist* 57 (1994): 600-72.

47. *Roget's II: The New Thesaurus*, ed. by the editors of *The American Heritage Dictionary*. (Boston: Houghton Mifflin Company, 1980).

48. Smith, *Black Academic Libraries and Research Collections: An Historical Survey*.

Historically Black College and University Libraries in the 21st Century: Accomplishments, Challenges and Recommendations

Elaina Norlin

Patricia Morris

SUMMARY. Historically Black Colleges and Universities (HBCUs) were established before the Civil War. Their original mission was to provide educational opportunities for African Americans who could not attend traditionally white institutions (TWIs). Today, HBCUs continue to provide a cultural and educational experience for African American students pursuing higher education. Yet what are the present state and future prospects for HBCUs? How have the constant changes within HBCUs affected libraries? Can non-HBCU libraries develop partnerships and collaborations with these very important libraries? This article will take a closer look at some of these questions and offer suggestions on how all librarians can strengthen connections with HBCU libraries. *[Article copies available for a fee from The Haworth Document Delivery Service: 1-800-HAWORTH. E-mail address: <getinfo@haworthpressinc.com> Website: <http://www.HaworthPress. com> © 2001 by The Haworth Press, Inc. All rights reserved.]*

Elaina Norlin is Assistant Librarian, University of Arizona Main Library, Tucson, AZ (E-mail: *norline@u.library.arizona.edu*).

Patricia Morris is Associate Librarian, University of Arizona Science-Engineering Library, Tucson, AZ (E-mail: *morrisp@u.library.arizona.edu*).

[Haworth co-indexing entry note]: "Historically Black College and University Libraries in the 21st Century: Accomplishments, Challenges and Recommendations." Norlin, Elaina, and Patricia Morris. Co-published simultaneously in *Journal of Library Administration* (The Haworth Information Press, an imprint of The Haworth Press, Inc.) Vol. 33, No. 3/4, 2001, pp. 183-197; and: *Diversity Now: People, Collections, and Services in Academic Libraries* (ed: Teresa Y. Neely, and Kuang-Hwei (Janet) Lee-Smeltzer) The Haworth Information Press, an imprint of The Haworth Press, Inc., 2001, pp. 183-197. Single or multiple copies of this article are available for a fee from The Haworth Document Delivery Service [1-800-HAWORTH, 9:00 a.m. - 5:00 p.m. (EST). E-mail address: getinfo@haworthpressinc.com].

KEYWORDS. Outreach, diversity, academic libraries, Historically Black Colleges and Universities, partnerships, HBCUs

HISTORY OF HISTORICALLY BLACK COLLEGES AND UNIVERSITIES

Historically Black Colleges and Universities (HBCUs) were established before the Civil War. The earliest HBCU was founded in 1837, twenty-six years before the end of slavery. The first colored school can be traced back to Richard Humphreys, a Quaker philanthropist, who founded the Institute for Colored Youth. This Institute provided opportunities to train and educate free blacks to become teachers. After the Civil War, twenty-four colleges were founded that were supported by church groups, the Freeman's Bureau and other black people in the community.[1] By 1890, the total had increased to two hundred colleges dedicated to serving the black population.[2] The Second Morril Act of 1890 also helped establish additional schools for the southern black population. According to this Act, southern states had to choose whether to provide coloreds equal access to land grant colleges or have separate schools for colored students.[3] Faced with the two options, the southern states decided to establish public and private institutions for colored students to attend.[4] Private institutions were designed for students wanting a liberal arts education. Public institutions were designed to help students get jobs in the industrial and agricultural fields.[5]

Although HBCUs were instrumental in graduating black students, most institutions were insufficiently funded from the very beginning. The decision of the Supreme Court in 1896 Plessy vs. Ferguson tried to reverse some of these inadequacies by stating that educational institutions could be segregated as long as there was some degree of financial equity. However, this ruling did not change things very much because there remained a wide gap between the funding of traditionally white and black institutions. Despite the hardships, these institutions were usually the only way for many blacks to get an education and become successful in the work world. Many HBCU graduates went on to become doctors, lawyers, teachers, preachers and educators within the black community.[6]

The 1954 Brown vs. Board of Education of Topeka decision was a pivotal ruling towards desegregation and took a closer look at some of the financial inequities. The Civil Rights Act of 1964 and the Higher Education Act of 1965 were decisions that prohibited funding to schools who participated in segregation and provided federal funding for students who could not afford the cost of education. In response to the new desegregation laws, some HBCUs started to recruit a more diverse student and faculty body with some success.[7]

In spite of all the financial challenges, HBCUs have developed a reputation for having smaller classes, more hands-on instruction and lower tuition rates. Many prominent people graduated from HBCUs including Alice Walker, Rosa Parks, W. E. B. Du Bois, Booker T. Washington, Oprah Winfrey, Toni Morrison and Martin Luther King Jr.[8]

PRESENT STATE

HBCUs are as crucial in the 21st century, if not more so, as when first created in the 19th century for the integration of under-represented citizens into the U.S. labor force and economy. The economy has become global and information-based, with information literacy skills being essential to successful integration into the modern labor force. Information technology, including the Internet, has augmented the mission of higher education to include producing an information literate workforce. The current level of undereducation in the African American community attests to the ongoing need for HBCUs, particularly in light of the affirmative action backlash. The demise of these affirmative action programs has already negatively impacted the numbers of African Americans entering many traditionally white institutions (TWIs), according to reports in publications such as the *Chronicle of Higher Education* and the *Black Collegian*.[9]

The current level of support, both publicly and privately, for these institutions of higher learning does not reflect their crucial national mission. According to a 1999 report of the President's Board of Advisors on Historically Black Colleges and Universities:

> In the environment of the 21st century the premium placed on education will continue to grow and the need to utilize our available human resources as fully as possible will increase. If this is to become a reality, it will be essential that African-Americans, as well as other groups in which relatively large numbers of individuals

currently lack the requisite education to fully develop their talents and contribute to the economy, raise their overall levels of educational attainment dramatically. Fortunately, historically black colleges and universities (HBCUs) provide a vehicle for accomplishing this goal.[10]

The successes of the present state of HBCUs include:

In 1994, nearly 300,000 students were enrolled in historically Black colleges and universities (HBCUs). The 103 recognized HBCUs constitute only 3 percent of the country's [3,688] institutions of higher education, but 28 percent of all blacks who receive bachelor's degrees get them there.[11]

The present state also includes unique challenges. One of the major challenges for HBCUs as contrasted with TWIs is:

. . . [that] states, politicians, funding sources and even some blacks are asking the question: "Do we still need historically black colleges and universities?"[12]

According to Henry Ponder, president of the National Association for Equal Opportunity in Higher Education, the question should never be asked.

No one ever asks if we need Notre Dame or Brandeis. No one ever asks if we need white schools or Hispanic schools or Native American schools, VMI or The Citadel. It is a racist question out of a racist society . . . We definitely need these institutions going into the 21st century. If we didn't have HBCUs, we'd have to invent them.[13]

As institutions of higher learning, HBCUs are facing the same challenges as TWIs. Among these challenges are increased public demands for accountability, intense competition for public funding and for top students. The lack of funding for information technology resources, such as computers, wiring, access to electronic databases, etc., has had an adverse impact on the library assets available for quality research and teaching purposes. In addition, there is an expected systematic re-evaluation of their position in terms of the contribution they make to the local economies as well as to society at large.

These institutions, however, have many traditional areas of strength, such as providing a welcoming and supportive environment which contributes to the success "of African American students who do not always 'measure up' according to standardized test scores."[14] Many have very unique and rich archival collections, and some HBCUs are expanding into new areas such as online education. Yet there are also areas requiring enhancement, for example, the need to broaden HBCU doctoral program offerings.

All of these factors-successes, challenges, areas of strength and areas needing enhancement-must be optimized by these institutions in dynamic ways to continue fulfilling their mission.

If HBCUs are to flourish in the 21st century versus merely hanging on, they must do so from a position that includes strong academic programs, visionary leadership and creative marketing strategies. Creative marketing is essential to increase the public profile of HBCUs, which in turn would engender support for their mission as well as encourage private and public funding.

HBCUs AND THEIR LIBRARIES: DEALING WITH THE DIGITAL DIVIDE

All institutions of higher learning are facing tremendous challenges to revamp their thinking and approaches to fulfilling their educational missions in large part due to advances in information technology. Today, there is so much information available, attempting to utilize this flood of information for the unprepared is like trying to take a drink from a fire hose. Computer technology and the advances in global networks, particularly the Internet, have created a global information universe, which is often only a keystroke away. Information literacy, the ability to find, analyze and utilize information, has become an essential skill set for college graduates and anyone else whose plans include active participation in the modern labor force and economy.[15]

The 21st century will continue to be an era where information is power. Those without access to information-an institution, organization or person-are often referred to as the information have-nots.[16] This chasm caused by the lack of digital resources and information technology-coined the "digital divide,"[17] puts institutions at a competitive disadvantage. It has a negative effect on the caliber of research, acquisition of grants, teaching and learning process, as well as competition for students and faculty members. Many HBCUs and their libraries are dealing with a deficit of information resources and technology due to insufficient funding.[18]

In the past libraries were viewed only as data or information warehouses and used only as reservoirs for storage and retrieval. Librarians were thought of and utilized only as gatekeepers to the wealth of information resources. At the same time the concept of teaching and learning was viewed as something that occurred outside of the library.[19] The information explosion has created the opportunity for librarians to become a part of the larger educational process in terms of providing instruction in information literacy skills. Students are taught to understand how information is generated and organized, how to critically evaluate it and how to use it to create new insights. This is how the library has transformed from a static warehouse to an important partner in the educational process. "The library is a pathway-enhancing, extending, and supporting the academic life of an institution. It is a catalyst in the learning process, the essential link in scholarship and information of endless variety."[20] HBCUs that do not have access to a robust library, one which provides access to dynamic collections and cutting-edge services, are missing a key ingredient in today's higher education environment.

The standard teaching and learning processes at most universities across the country now incorporate computer technology. To successfully integrate these new technologies, it is absolutely necessary to have funding for hardware, software and training. The Internet is used for distributing course syllabi, interactive quizzes and listservs, lecture notes, and communicating with the instructor via e-mail. More and more courses are moving to the online environment in their entirety. The ability to work in an electronic environment is an expectation for today's students when they enter the workforce. Sufficient funding for library resources and technology upgrades is one of the central areas of concern for HBCU campuses. It is essential that students receive education in a highly technical environment as they work toward their degrees.

One of the unique ways in which HBCUs have received funding is a result of federal court ordered desegregation. Public HBCUs were mandated to upgrade their curricula, facilities and libraries to attract white students. White enrollment at HBCUs increased 16% between 1990 and 1998 and at a handful of institutions the percentage of black students had dropped below 50%. This has raised concerns with some about maintaining the cultural identity and mission of HBCUs.[21]

The mission of providing black students with a quality education has remained intact at the vast majority of HBCUs. New strategies and collaborations are necessary to insure the continued success of these vital institutions. It is essential that HBCUs analyze the current fast-paced technological environment in which they compete and realize its implications for education in this information age. There are a variety of ways to insure that their campuses are providing adequate access to technology and information resources to produce information technology-literate, life-long learners.

Assessment of HBCU Libraries

Most libraries in the 21st century are becoming more familiar with assessment techniques for evaluating their products and services. In today's campus environment, university administrators are demanding to know more than how many books are circulating or how many reference questions the library gets each year. Today libraries may collect data that reflects information literacy levels, faculty partnerships, library outreach and services to remote and non-traditional students. National and international library organizations such as the Association of Research Libraries (ARL), the American Library Association (ALA) and the Association for College and Research Libraries (ACRL) organize and collect information about different types of libraries. However, are we continually gathering this same data for HBCU libraries? There were some national statistics published in the 1980s and 1990s which looked at HBCUs in relation to other institutions. In 1987, ACRL completed and later published statistics on HBCU libraries.[22] This comprehensive look was important for the progress of the 1980s, but does not reflect the change of technology and library advancements during the 1990s and beyond.

Beatrice O. Agingu recently published a paper comparing the usefulness of library Web sites at HBCU libraries with other library institutions in the southeastern part of the United States.[23] Agingu developed several questions as a criterion for evaluating library Web sites based on a thorough literature review. She concluded that HBCUs needed to obtain additional funding to get the software and other resources for Web design and maintenance and possibly subscribe to other Web based resources. She also suggested that HBCU libraries begin to recruit staff who have the technical expertise to assist with Web design and train other library staff members.[24] This article is an important start in assessing the current needs of HBCU libraries, but there is a crucial need for further research.

We recommend that a local, national or state organization revisit former library statistics on HBCU libraries and update the questions to reflect more of the librarians' work in the 21st century. Some of the areas for improvement might include scholarly communication, electronic resources, information literacy, distributed learning, faculty partnerships, digital technology and electronic information access.

RECOMMENDATIONS
FOR STRENGTHENING HBCU LIBRARIES

Methodology

During the period between 1998 and 2000, the authors communicated with approximately forty HBCU librarians through phone interviews, face to face conversations and e-mail correspondence about some of the challenges facing them in the 21st century. These responses were gathered and analyzed along with an extensive literature review in order to provide recommendations for possible collaborations among HBCU libraries. The questions below expanded upon what was available in the published literature.

Some of the questions asked were:

- Are the HBCU librarians at your university actively involved nationally, locally or state-wide?
- What is a major concern at your library for the 21st century?
- If you could develop a partnership with a national organization, what would you suggest?
- Do you know of any partnerships and projects that are going on at a national level?
- How about the ACRL/HBCU projects from the 1970s and 1980s?
- When your librarians go to a national conference, where do they usually go and in which section do they usually participate?

Collaborations with ACRL and Other Institutions

In the early 1970s, ACRL, along with proactive HBCU librarians like Virginia Lacy Jones, submitted a proposal and were awarded a $500,000 grant from the Andrew W. Mellon Foundation. The goal of the program was to improve the management skills and overall development of HBCU librarians. This proposal connected twenty-five HBCU librarians with directors of academic libraries who were known for their strong leadership and management skills. After the librarians were paired up, they worked together over a period of years to help strengthen the leadership foundation of HBCU librarians. Strong partnerships and life-long friendships were developed between HBCU librarians and the mentoring librarians. The program evaluation revealed that this mentoring internship program was a success.

Based on the success of the first project, Andrew W. Mellon Foundation awarded funds to ACRL to continue the development of HBCU librarians. With these funds, several influential black librarians were appointed to a HBCU Library Planning Project to outline potential programs and ideas to advance HBCU libraries. The ACRL and the HBCU Library Planning Project team met in Atlanta in October, 1987 for 10 days. Three initiatives resulted from this meeting:

- A statistical survey of HBCU libraries was compiled and published by ACRL: *ACRL/Historically Black Colleges and Universities Statistics 1988-89: A Compilation of Statistics from Sixty-Eight Historically Black Colleges and University Libraries* (Chicago: ACRL, 1991).
- A Humanities Programming Workshop for HBCUs and their communities was developed and conducted in Atlanta, Georgia from February 22-24, 1989.
- Two pre-conferences on accreditation were held in Dallas in 1989 and Atlanta in 1981.[25]

After the completion of the program, several librarians highly recommended that ACRL begin to work closely with HBCU presidents to inform them about libraries, current opportunities, goals, future directions and concerns.[26] In addition, at the 1987 Atlanta meeting, group sessions recommended major areas to continue promoting and developing such as image building, accreditation, staffing, facilities, network and automation, collection development and bibliographic instruction.[27]

During the 1970s and 1980s, in addition to developing concrete plans for the future, ACRL and HBCU librarians made great strides in terms of communicating, collaborating and learning from each other. However, we were unable to locate evidence of plans to implement the recommendations or continue the progress made in the initial meetings. Many of the proactive HBCU librarian leaders of the 1970s and 1980s have either retired or moved on to other libraries. Many HBCU librarians we communicated with either never heard of or vaguely remembered the ACRL/HBCU projects and programs. The authors recommend that

ACRL, state library associations, or other national library organizations take a closer look at some of the accomplishments and themes and work to develop partnerships for the 21st century. The past themes need to be revisited and current trends such as information access, digital technology and distance education should be incorporated. A good program model to take into consideration is the Association for Research Libraries Leadership and Career Development Program (LCDP). ARL's LCDP was designed to increase the number of librarians from underrepresented racial and ethnic groups in positions of influence and leadership in research libraries by helping them develop the skills needed to be more competitive in the promotion process. "This program consists of several components: two five-day institutes, the establishment of a mentoring relationship between participants and ARL deans and directors, research project development, and a closing ceremony."[28]

HBCU LIBRARIES AND THE BLACK CAUCUS OF THE AMERICAN LIBRARY ASSOCIATION

Phone interviews and e-mail correspondence with HBCU librarians revealed that many librarians felt that the lack of travel funding kept them from being active on a national level. A few librarians who did get a chance to attend conferences only did so when one was held close to their geographic area. Many libraries can only afford to pay for one or two librarians per year to attend national conferences. The main group which HBCU librarians said they were active with was the Black Caucus of the American Library Association (BCALA). One librarian stated that she especially felt comfortable and at home at BCALA meetings and functions during the very crowded annual ALA conference. In terms of national committees and educational programs, BCALA has co-sponsored various programs with ACRL groups including the African American Librarians and Women Studies sections. Throughout its history, BCALA has also had HBCU librarians on its executive board.

We recommend that BCALA develop a separate section for HBCU libraries. This section would allow a forum for HBCU librarians to get together at the ALA annual and midwinter, and the national BCALA conference to focus on future work and potential collaborations with other HBCU libraries. BCALA could also cosponsor, with other national organizing committees, programs which reflect these collaborations and future work and increase awareness on a much larger scale. This would also be beneficial to HBCU libraries that can only fund one or two librarians a year for travel. These librarians could attend ALA conferences and become active in committee work that reflects their interests, ideas and future thinking. Usually national exposure can assist in making changes within the library culture.

Library Schools and Recruitment of African American Students

HBCUs are still recruiting and graduating more African American students in all professions. Furthermore, many HBCU graduates go on to pursue graduate, doctorate and professional degrees. In 1998 HBCU undergraduates accounted for half of all African Americans with master's degrees and 45 percent of African Americans in the corporate world.[29] Many big corporations such as IBM, Hewlett Packard, Motorola and others are reaching out to and recruiting HBCU students through advertisements in black publications such as *Black Enterprise, Black Collegian, Ebony* and *Essence* in addition to attending HBCU career fairs.

Library schools and librarians can capitalize on the high retention numbers and recruit African American students into pursuing a master's degree in library and information science. Recruiting students directly can be very beneficial. This can be accomplished by marketing librarianship to HBCU students during their junior and senior year when they are starting to consider whether to continue their education. Library schools should use ALA's marketing and publicity tools which focus on the benefits of today's information science community and publish this information in top African American national magazines. Finally, for the library schools that can afford it, attending HBCU career fairs could be another step in recruiting more African American students into the profession. In 1999 the *Black Collegian* dedicated part of its October issue to helping undergraduate students learn more about graduate programs by providing background information on how to successfully complete the graduate school application.[30] Many undergraduate students probably do not know that the terminal degree for library science is a master's and that there are many options available especially with distance education and flexible class schedules. HBCU students need to be made aware of these options even if they decide to pursue a library and information science degree at a later stage in their academic careers.

Library Schools and HBCU Library Staff

Many HBCU librarians expressed the same frustration as librarians from TWIs in terms of recruiting and retaining African American librarians. The number of African American students graduating with library degrees is small and HBCU libraries are competing for these students along with other more prestigious academic, public, school and corporate libraries.[31] Consequently, when the HBCU libraries are not successful in their attempts to attract African American librarians, they hire from other ethnic groups or have their library staff take on more professional responsibilities. One HBCU librarian asserted that although people from all ethnic groups did a great job at HBCU libraries, students who attended HBCUs wanted a cultural as well as an academic experience. Therefore, she would rather recruit African American librarians when possible.

To overcome some of these barriers, one HBCU library director encourages and provides support for her library staff to attend library school. This is not a new idea. The University of Illinois at Chicago also has a program through which its library staff can attend library school at the University of Illinois in Champaign-Urbana. The library staff member is then offered a job once they complete their degree. However, what about the HBCUs that are not near an accredited library school or cannot afford to pay for library staff to attend library schools? One HBCU librarian said it would be wonderful for library schools to publicize distance education programs and scholarship opportunities. Some HBCU libraries and library staff cannot keep up with national events and could really benefit from having a comprehensive information package which explains the different options available without having to relocate to another area to complete library school. Relocation can be quite an obstacle for potential non-traditional students who earn an average library staff salary and have families to support.

Library School Internship Projects

There are a variety of library school internship programs across the country; however, very few target ethnic communities. California State University at San Marcos conducted a pilot project that placed library interns in tribal libraries or on small American Indian reservations.[32] The coordinator of this program developed relationships with tribal library managers and found out what specific activities or programs needed assistance. After organizing the program and coordinating the work activities, she put out a call for interest at the library school in the area.[33] The library school student recruited for the position worked a few hours a week at the tribal reservation and then reported the progress. This project was successful because the coordinator of the program understood some of the issues related to the tribal libraries and the politics within these organizations.

When the idea of a similar program was presented to several HBCU librarians, most felt that this would serve as an excellent collaborative program with library schools. An additional benefit of a program such as this was the opportunity it provided for students working on their degrees via distance education to assist HBCU libraries which were not located near library schools. Some of the areas HBCU librarians listed as areas of need included Web site design and maintenance, cataloging, designing marketing materials and helping with grant writing for future projects. The library school students could do this project as a practicum or independent study. E-mail, conference calls and other forms of electronic communication make this a very feasible option to help HBCU libraries that need support. In addition, these potential partnerships could strengthen the bond between library schools and minority institutions and encourage more library staff to make the decision to attend library schools.

CONCLUSION

The more all librarians understand the importance and background of HBCU libraries, the easier it will be to naturally collaborate and work together now and in the future. During the research for this paper, we were thrilled to have the opportunity to talk with other librarians who were strategically part of the HBCU projects in the 1970s and 1980s. These individuals had many recommendations on how HBCU librarians could stay proactive in the 21st century. The major theme that came up over and over again was the need for HBCU librarians to become more nationally recognized. "It's all in who you know and always insist on getting what you need from our national library organizations," a now retired black librarian said. So the major advice for HBCU librarians is if you can only send one person to a national conference, send someone who will get involved and become active in areas that matter the most to your library. A great illustration of this point is that while the authors were talking to some state library association members about HBCU librarians, many needed clarification of what the HBCU abbreviation meant. After clarification, the state library association members were still not able to supply any information about HBCU librarian members within their association. These same state library associations had a high concentration of HBCU libraries within the state. In addition, contacting national library associations revealed that membership offices did not have any current information on how many HBCU librarians were members of its association or any ideas on how they could begin developing connections. Keeping this in mind, HBCU librarians have to start obtaining more strategic library positions state-wide and nationally so they will have the power to influence and make changes within academic librarianship.

NOTES

1. Ernie Suggs, "Invisible Colleges: Steeped in History, Black Colleges Push to Find Their Place in the 21st Century," *The Herald-Sun* (9-16 February 1997): A1.
2. Ibid.
3. Ibid.
4. "The Historically Black Colleges and Universities: A Future in the Balance," *Academe* 8 (1) (January-February 1995): 49-58.
5. Harold Wenglinsky, *Students at Historically Black Colleges and Universities: Their Aspirations and Accomplishments* (New Jersey: Educational Testing Service Policy Information Center, 1987).
6. Ibid.
7. Ibid.
8. Ibid.
9. For example see William H. Gray, III, "In the Best Interest of America, Affirmative Action in Higher Education Is a Must," *Black Collegian* 29 (2) (February 1999): 144-46+; Sara Hebel, "Courting a Place in Legal History," *Chronicle of Higher Education* 47 (13) (24 November 2000): A23-4; Mary Francis Berry, "How Percentage Plans Keep Minority Students out of College," *Chronicle of Higher Education* 46 (48) (4 August 2000): A48.
10. Historically Black Colleges and Universities for the 21st Century: Annual Report of the President's Board of Advisors on Historically Black Colleges and Universities (District of Columbia: Department of Education, 1999).
11. Suggs, *Fighting to Survive*, 7.
12. Ibid.
13. Ibid.
14. Alvin J. Schneider, "The Evolving HBCU Niche," *Black Issues in Higher Education* 14 (23) (January 1998): 35.
15. American Association of School Librarians, Association for Educational Communications and Technology, "Information Literacy Standards for Student Learning," in *Information Power: Building Partnerships for Learning* (Chicago: American Library Association, 1998).
16. David Shenk, *Data Smog: Surviving the Information Glut* (San Francisco: HarperEdge, 1997).
17. See http://www.about.com for a definition of term and links to related resources; see United States Department of Commerce, National Telecommunications and Information Administration, "Americans in the Information Age: Falling Through the Net," [online] available from http://www.ntia.doc.gov/ntiahome/digitaldivide/index.html;

Mary Mosquera, "NTIA Looks to Narrow the Digital Divide," *TechWeb News* (1999) [online] available from http://www.techweb.com/wire/story/TWB19991202S0017.

18. National Association for Equal Opportunity in Higher Education, *Historically Black Colleges and Universities: An Assessment of Networking and Connectivity* (Washington, DC: The Secretary of Commerce, 2000) [online] available from http://search.ntia.doc.gov/pdf/nafeo.pdf.

19. Benton Foundation, *Buildings, Books, and Bytes: Libraries and Communities in the Digital Age: A Report on the Public's Opinion of Library Leaders' Visions for the Future* (Washington, DC: The Foundation, 1996).

20. Geoffrey T. Freeman, "The Academic Library in the 21st Century: Partner in Education" in *Building Libraries for the 21st Century: The Shape of Information* (Jefferson, NC: McFarland, 2000).

21. Tammerlin Drummond, "Black Schools Go White," *Time* 155 (11) (20 March 2000): 58.

22. Association of College and Research Libraries, *ACRL/Historically Black Colleges & Universities Library Statistics: A Compilation of Statistics from Sixty-Eight Historically Black College and University Libraries* (Chicago: ACRL, 1991); see also Casper L. Jordan and Beverly P. Lynch, "ACRL's Historically Black College and Universities Libraries Projects, 1972-1994," in *Untold Stories: Civil Rights, Libraries, and Black Librarianship* (Champaign, IL: Publications Office, Graduate School of Library and Information Science, 1998).

23. Beatrice O. Agingu, "Library Web Sites at Historically Black Colleges and Universities," *College and Research Libraries* 61 (1) (January 2000): 30-7.

24. Ibid.

25. Jordan and Lynch, "ACRL's Historically Black College and Universities," 111.

26. Ibid.

27. Jo An S. Segal, "Identifying Needs and Solutions: The Role of Librarians in Historically Black Colleges and Universities," *College & Research Libraries News* 32 (11) (December 1987): 717-19.

28. DeEtta Jones, "Leadership and Career Development Program," (Association of Research Libraries, Washington, DC, 2000) [online] available from http://www.arl.org/diversity/lcdp.html [cited 20 February 2001].

29. Robyn D. Clarke, "Partnering for Success," *Black Enterprise* 29 (2) (September 1998): 112-116.

30. Dereck J. Rovaris, Sr., "Graduate School: A Necessary Step for Your Future Success," *Black Collegian* 30 (1) (October 1999): 91-7.

31. Kathleen de la Peña McCook, and Kate Lippincott, "Library Schools and Diversity: Who Makes the Grade?" *Library Journal* 122 (15 April 1997): 30-2; Kathleen de la Peña McCook, "Diversity Deferred: Where are the Minority Librarians?" *Library Journal* 118 (18) (1 November 1993): 35-8; Kathleen de la Peña McCook, and others, *Planning for a Diverse Workforce in Library and Information Science Professions. Revised Edition*, 1997, ERIC, ED 402948.

32. Bonnie Biggs, "The Tribal Library Project: Interns, American Indians, and Library Services: A Look at the Challenges," *College & Research Libraries News* 59 (4) (April 1998): 259-62.

33. Ibid.

INSTRUCTION AND LIBRARY EDUCATION

Communication and Teaching: Education About Diversity in the LIS Classroom

Mark D. Winston

SUMMARY. Recent research findings have documented the relationship between fostering diversity in organizations and overall organizational success. From the perspective of the library administrator, it is incumbent upon those in library and information science education to provide instruction and an academic environment, which facilitates learning about diversity among those who will be expected to contribute to the success of their employing organizations. However, there are difficulties associated with communication and instruction about issues such as diversity, race and gender. The scholarship associated with communication theory provides a worthwhile basis for understanding the nature of these difficulties and for identifying factors to consider in enhancing that instruction in better preparing graduates. *[Article copies available for a fee from The Haworth Document Delivery Service: 1-800-HAWORTH. E-mail address: <getinfo@haworthpressinc. com> Website: <http://www.HaworthPress.com> © 2001 by The Haworth Press, Inc. All rights reserved.]*

Mark D. Winston is Assistant Professor, School of Communication, Information and Library Studies, Rutgers University, New Brunswick, NJ (E-mail: *mwinston@ scils.rutgers.edu*).

[Haworth co-indexing entry note]: "Communication and Teaching: Education About Diversity in the LIS Classroom." Winston, Mark D. Co-published simultaneously in *Journal of Library Administration* (The Haworth Information Press, an imprint of The Haworth Press, Inc.) Vol. 33, No. 3/4, 2001, pp. 199-212; and: *Diversity Now: People, Collections, and Services in Academic Libraries* (ed: Teresa Y. Neely, and Kuang-Hwei (Janet) Lee-Smeltzer) The Haworth Information Press, an imprint of The Haworth Press, Inc., 2001, pp. 199-212. Single or multiple copies of this article are available for a fee from The Haworth Document Delivery Service [1-800-HAWORTH, 9:00 a.m. - 5:00 p.m. (EST). E-mail address: getinfo@haworthpressinc.com].

KEYWORDS. Diversity, communication, higher education, management, teaching, instruction, organizational success, academic library management

INTRODUCTION

In many organizations and certainly in the private sector, generally, there is the realization among managers and researchers that the reasons for promoting and fostering diversity within organizations go beyond the fact that it is a good thing to do. The justification for diversity efforts is often the important consideration of the increasingly diverse population, as well as past inequities and current unfairness. However, cutting-edge research in the study of diversity has highlighted the documented connection between investment in diversity and organizational success and performance, which will be discussed below. While it is important to point out that, thus far, the direct causal relationship between investment in diversity and organizational success has not yet been determined and the research to date has focused on private sector organizations, there are important implications with regard to colleges and universities, including academic libraries. As many colleges and universities and academic libraries invest significant resources in support of diversity, one of the implications relates to the educational preparation of graduates of library and information science programs, who are expected to contribute to the organizational success of their employers.

Thus, communication about issues of diversity in the classroom represents an opportunity for instruction and discussions about these important topics to be an integral part of the educational process, as students prepare for their careers, further study, and, generally, their roles as contributing, informed members of society. One recent and significant research finding emerging in relation to diversity in higher education is based on the Ford Foundation's Campus Diversity Initiative and other research, indicating the central role of "colleges and universities [in] prepar[ing] people to function in a diverse society."[1] In other words, most people understand and value the role of colleges and universities in this regard.

As students and employers are the primary customers of colleges and universities, it is important to consider the issue of the needs of students in increasing their awareness and in preparation for their future roles in contributing to the success of organizations-organizations for which their overall success is tied to their success in relation to diversity.

This article will address the importance of organizational investment in diversity and the necessity of preparing graduates and future employees in terms of learning about diversity in order for them to contribute to the success of their employing organizations. In addition, the difficulties associated with education about diversity are considered, as are approaches and recommendations identified by library and information science educators.

INVESTMENT IN DIVERSITY
AND ORGANIZATIONAL SUCCESS

The results of a number of research studies indicate that the companies, which are the most diverse, as measured by factors such as minority employment and spending with minority suppliers, have also been identified as more successful companies overall.[2]

For example, in the 1999 *Fortune* magazine article identifying "America's Best Companies For Minorities," the researchers report that the "companies that pursue diversity outperform the S&P 500."[3] Specifically, the companies, which are the most diverse, as measured by factors such as minority representation among senior administrators, middle managers, staff and on the board of directors, as well as spending with minority suppliers and underwriting business that goes to minority-owned investment banks, have also been identified as more successful on the basis of stock performance. Generally, stock performance reflects organizational performance, the strength of the company, and investor confidence, among other considerations. Research reported by Sherry Kuczynski in *HRMagazine* shows similar results, considering related factors associated with organizational success.[4]

It is appropriate to consider the relationship between organizational performance and diversity in the context of the 122,000 libraries in the U.S., most of which are in the public sector.[5] In this regard, similar measures of diversity and organizational performance might include minority representation among librarians and staff and on library boards, spending with minority suppliers, among others.

As a part of increasing awareness of diversity and better serving user populations, libraries have implemented various types of diversity initiatives and programs that are designed specifically to achieve those ends. Generally, these programs focus on recruitment and retention of members of underrepresented groups, increasing diversity awareness in the workplace, building multicultural collections, and designing and providing library services for users from diverse cultural backgrounds.[6] Also, it is important to note that diversity-related goals are required or encouraged for many libraries, library administrators and librarians. In addition, libraries have a societal mission, which relates to the provision of information services for a diverse population.

The development of a model for the measurement of the relationship between the level of investment in diversity and organizational performance and success requires the identification of similar measures of organizational performance and of diversity efforts in the library environment. In relation to organizational performance and success, the strength of the organization and confidence among users and primary and secondary funding sources might include measures of use, quality, and user satisfaction, as well as input from actual and potential funding sources.

With regard to the identification of similar measures of the level of investment in diversity, the research related to diversity in libraries focuses generally on issues of staffing, collections, services, and organizational climate.[7] Specific considerations include recruitment and retention of members of underrepresented groups, building multicultural collections, designing and providing library services for users from diverse cultural backgrounds, and increasing diversity awareness in the workplace. Thus, building upon the Ford Foundation and related research, factors such as the number of minority professionals employed, minority participation on library boards, the allocation of resources in the development of multicultural library collections, and spending with minority suppliers are appropriate variables to consider.

Although further research is needed in order to identify a causal relationship between investment in diversity and enhanced organizational performance, a number of hypotheses related to libraries become apparent. For example, investment in diversity contributes to an organizational reputation of social responsibility, which leads to enhanced organizational performance and growth and enhanced recruitment of members of underrepresented groups. And, more broadly, those organizations, which are effective in supporting appropriate organizational priorities, such as fostering diversity, are successful and engender confidence among primary and secondary funding sources and users or customers.

There are a number of factors to be considered in relation to these hypotheses. For example, it is important to point out that the idea that most people in society are opposed to discussions of diversity or the issue of fostering diversity is simply not supported by the research. When queried about issues related to the value of diversity as a societal issue, most people indicate a realization of its importance and value.[8] Thus, it seems that social responsibility and diversity efforts, or activities, which are inconsistent with valuing diversity, are likely to be considerations for consumers who are making choices. The research also indicates that biases against members of certain groups are widespread, pervasive and are represented across the population.[9] Thus, it is important to note that the evidence related to why we should focus on diversity is substantial.

DISCUSSING DIVERSITY IN THE CLASSROOM

Success in achieving goals related to diversity and equity is far more likely to be achieved when the issues are well defined through reasoned debate, scholarly discourse, and practical discussion, in a number of settings, including the classroom, as individuals are prepared to work in and contribute to organizations. There is a need for continuing and substantive exploration of issues related to diversity. However, initiating and facilitating the discussion of these issues and placing the diversity discussion in context are tasks, which are not easily accomplished, considering the nature and complexity of the issues.

Generally, the venues for discussion or public discourse related to diversity include diversity dialogues, diversity education and sensitivity training, classroom instruction, and other discussions of race, gender, ability, orientation, racism, sexism, etc., in the workplace, and in professional and scholarly meetings. Certainly, if those who are in higher education, including those in library and information science education, do not initiate these discussions, we are not fulfilling our responsibility and we are not creating the type of learning environment, which is necessary to prepare professionals to be successful and to contribute in the larger profession.

What the research indicates about interpersonal communication related to these topics can assist in enhancing the effectiveness of education in the classroom and the effectiveness of other diversity initiatives. Communication scholars refer to issues that are identified as taboo topics and describe the nature of the difficulties associated with communication about such topics.[10] In addition, there are historical issues related to the topics that are not appropriately discussed in public or in polite society-race and related issues being among those topics.

Regardless of the nature of the discourse, it is difficult to create an environment in which individuals are comfortable in discussing issues such as race and gender, as well as seeing the discussion of diversity as relevant to them if they are not members of minority groups or women, for example. The representation of diversity as being synonymous with affirmative action appears to have led to a perception that diversity, as an issue, is relevant only to those who are women and minorities.

THE DIFFICULTY OF DISCUSSING DIVERSITY

While many scholars and practitioners have addressed the importance of the various types of discussions and exchanges related to diversity in the literature, it is not clear that such approaches have proven successful with regard to increasing awareness and improving relations and organizational climates.[11] By providing a better understanding of why people have difficulty discussing issues of race, racism, gender, and sexism, among others, it appears possible to identify approaches that will make lectures and discussions more productive in preparing graduates in terms of awareness and sensitivity and to take on leadership roles in organizations, the profession, and in an increasingly diverse society.

According to Elizabeth Arveda Kissling, a communications scholar, "Like other communication norms and rules, communication taboos and the social phenomenon of embarrassment work to preserve the expressive order."[12] Thus, there seems to be a motivation among individuals to avoid the discussion of difficult topics in order to avoid embarrassment and to maintain propriety.

Taboo topics "are generally regarded as unpleasant conversational fodder that polite people avoid,"[13] according to Kissling. The topics, which might be considered taboo, based upon the scholarship in communication, are "illegal or embarrassing activities, such as drug use and sexual behavior,"[14] including HIV risk factors and birth control,[15] alcohol use, incest, menstruation,[16] "death, illness,"[17] as well as issues of race, gender, sexual orientation, sexism, racism, among others.[18]

The issue of taboo or sensitive topics relates not only to classroom discussion and lectures, but to research that requires the posing of questions to study participants and discussions in various types of interpersonal relationships, as well. In addition, in some disciplines, professionals receive educational training with regard to how to address sensitive issues with their clients and patients. For example "modern medical training includes instruction in the sensitive discussion of terminal illness with patients and their families."[19]

In terms of interpersonal relationships, it appears that individuals often tend to identify other communication approaches, if there is the need to address difficult topics. For example, Kissling has indicated that:

Although girls frequently recognize a need to talk about menstruation, and to share information about it with each other, they are usually embarrassed to talk about menstruation, especially with adults. To avoid and prevent the embarrassment of violating menstrual taboo, girls creatively use such linguistic strategies as slang terms, circumlocutions, pronouns, and euphemistic deixis to find ways to talk about something they are uncomfortable talking about or believe they shouldn't talk about.[20]

The concept of diversity might be, in and of itself, a representation of this idea of attempting to facilitate communication about difficult subjects in a more benign, less direct, way. In this regard, it might be posited that the word diversity is a euphemism and that the concept has been watered down, as it relates to the idea of valuing differences of many types, in order to make the concepts of racism, sexism, race and ethnicity, among others, more palatable. The word diversity, which came into common usage in this context only as recently as the Bakke case in the late 1970s,[21] might be viewed as an all-encompassing term and as representation of a less direct way of communicating ideas which are uncomfortable to discuss.

In this regard, Edna Andrews addresses the potential relationship between political correctness in speech and the nature of taboo topics in "Cultural Sensitivity and Political Correctness: The Linguistic Problem of Naming."[22] In addition, Lorna Peterson cites the work of other researchers and incorporates her own analysis in indicating that "Critics of the diversity movement commonly point out that the concept of diversity includes so many groups that the terminology is rendered meaningless."[23] In addressing the fact that issues of equity and discrimination have been overshadowed by the focus on diversity, Peterson goes on to suggest that:

> Diversity is a term that is used widely, often without consideration for its meaning and roots. Scholars have analyzed the diversity movement, its definition, and the detriment that it has caused to the achievement of equity. Equity issues have become clouded by a "me too" claim to victim status, thereby diminishing the possibility of achieving equity. Diversity defaults to little progress and substantial rhetoric that many can join in on without sacrifice or regulation that the promise of equity will be fulfilled.[24]

While the components of the debate related to equity vs. diversity are complex, controversial, and not the primary focus of this article, it is important to suggest the following:

If the concept of or the terminology associated with diversity itself might be viewed as an aspect of the process of avoiding communicating about and, possibly, addressing otherwise, issues of race, gender, orientation, and ability, how does one facilitate direct communication in the context of the discussion of diversity and related topics? This issue will be addressed in greater detail below.

LIBRARY AND INFORMATION AND SCIENCE EDUCATION

In library and information science education, issues of diversity and multiculturalism are to be a part of the curricula of American Library Association-accredited master's programs. However, according to Peterson,

> [T]he interpretation of this is left up to the individual library and information science school. A school can design a curriculum which does not address issues of equity, justice, and the historical difference in treatment of particular groups; a school can define diversity simply as the quality of being different and state that their graduates are prepared to work in a multicultural environment.[25]

William Welburn and Ling Hwey Jeng decry the limited amount of library and information science research literature on diversity and library and information science education, with few exceptions. The literature related to diversity and library and information science (LIS) education focuses mainly on issues of underrepresentation among students and faculty and the importance of fostering diversity in terms of recruitment of students and faculty.[26] According to Welburn, for example,

> We lack a body of knowledge and a critical mass of scholars engaged in the kind of research that can be used in affecting a shift in pedagogy. There is a paucity of scholarship on racial/ethnic perspectives in information and library science. Contrast our predicament with law, where a body of literature has emerged in the areas of critical race theory and feminist scholarship.[27]

The literature does provide limited discussion of the inclusion of diversity in the curricula and in class lectures and discussions. Welburn addresses the factors to be considered in the development of a course in cultural diversity, as a part of the process of incorporating diversity into the curriculum.

> First, such a course would have to be considered to be an intermediate step or transitional step toward rethinking the curriculum at large. Second, a separate course should . . . revolve around the trifold concept of linkages between the multicultural contexts of information, its users, and information providers. Third, distinctions should be drawn between diversity as a workplace issue and diversity as a service issue. In my opinion, workplace concerns are more appropriately presented within the context of teaching management.[28]

Also, with regard to the issue of content, Jeng refers to the need to relate "diversity as an academic topic on the one hand, and the real life of library and information services and its people, both providers and the users, on the other."[29] She goes on to indicate that "Diversity education without a concrete connection to LIS services and people inevitably provides students with nice concepts, but with no context in which to apply them."[30] She suggests that "good pedagogy to establish the missing link in the classroom between diversity lectures and the LIS life is the 'scenario' approach: to present specific scenarios that could happen to individual librarians in real libraries."[31] In order to address one of the communication issues related to such discussions, "The instructor needs to explain that, at times, potentially offensive words and descriptions are used to present the scenarios. This is done with the sole intention of eliciting classroom discussion on diversity."[32]

In the article "Teaching the Practitioners: One Professor's Attempt at Library Education and Sensitivity to Multicultural Diversity," Peterson describes her attempts to foster learning about issues of race and gender through the use of "a questioning context, by creating curricular activities, and responding to student curricular resistance."[33] According to Peterson, her "role is to encourage analytic questioning by students."[34]

Thus, she presents to students one of the often-mentioned quotes related to the substantial increase in the minority population in the U.S. and the impact that this population shift will have on higher education, for example, as a basis for analysis, discussion and learning. "As a slogan, 'one-third of a nation' makes an excellent classroom example to question the context of multiculturalism and librarianship."[35] Peterson also makes use of guest lecturers who are members of minority groups, lecture topics that include global perspectives, and a broad array of examples in assignments to enhance the learning process.[36]

With regard to the issue of resistance to instruction about issues of race and gender, Peterson observes the following:

> Teaching involves the liberation of students' minds, not indoctrination. Students rarely view teaching this way and believe they must parrot teacher views in order to be successful. When the perceived "indoctorination" is threatening to their power, one can expect resistance in some form. This is especially true for the professor who happens to be a minority male, minority female or white female. Unfortunately, the exploration or inclusion of multicultural diversity in the curriculum, especially if it is taught by a "diversifier," is often considered mind control and indoctrination by some students. When unpopular views or new perspectives are explored in the classroom, one must be prepared for threats to the professor's authority and hostile reactions by students. . . . It is important to have rational arguments at hand when resistance to lectures occurs.[37]

In relation to concerns about broader dimensions of diversity, Belay addresses the need for instructors to have an understanding of the "cognitive styles" and approaches to learning and engagement in the classroom that are based on culture and country of origin in order to increase the likelihood of success for students.[38]

Thus, the library and information science education literature does address some considerations and approaches related to instruction about diversity.

IMPLICATIONS

A number of implications might be drawn from the research and scholarship regarding communication, education, and diversity. For example, it appears to be the case that the discussion of diversity, race, gender, and related issues requires trained facilitators and instructors. In a context in which the students, training participants, employees, or others are apprehensive and reluctant about being involved in the discussion, it is clear that the facilitators must create an environment in which participants are able to communicate openly and respectfully. However, it seems that a key issue relates to the facilitator's or instructor's ability to communicate clearly and directly, on issues that are difficult to discuss. As professionals in other disciplines are trained in communicating with their clients with regard to sensitive topics, such instruction is necessary for library and information science educators and library and information professionals. In addition, it seems quite clear that drawing upon the scholarship and professional expertise of other disciplines and professions is appropriate and necessary. The shortage of library and information science research literature on diversity and education does not justify a lack of effective instruction for students. To the contrary, such a lack of research literature is a concern and a call to action for researchers. However, the literature in other disciplines, particularly communication, as well as education and other service professions, which often focuses on instruction about difficult topics provides an important basis for the development of pedagogical approaches in library and information science education. In addition, the management literature, which has begun to address the connection between diversity and organizational success, is relevant for inclusion in readings for graduate students in library and information science programs, as well.

Acknowledgement of the difficulty associated with communication about sensitive topics is an important consideration, as curricula and coursework are designed. In-class activities and assignments should reflect the necessity of increasing the level of comfort for students, while promoting forthright and informed discussion of difficult topics.

CONCLUSION

As illustrated in the literature described above, managers and researchers in the area of organizational theory have begun to document the relationship between the fostering of diversity in organizations and the overall success of organizations. In consideration of the importance of fostering diversity in organizations, generally, and in the library and information science profession, which has responsibility for documenting much of recorded human history, instructing users and facilitating access to that information, there is the need to facilitate and engage in discussions of the complex issues related to diversity. In order to create organizational climates, which promote equity and enhance the likelihood of success of all employees and users, an understanding of diversity should be of paramount importance. Thus, we must identify the most effective ways to instruct students in a learning environment, in which the difficult issues are discussed in light of the research and theoretical literature that underlies graduate and professional education for individuals who will not only work with diverse populations, but who will serve as professionals and administrators, who are conscious of differences and who are likely to be evaluated on their efforts related to diversity.

For managers, the organizations in which graduates are employed should be such that communication is encouraged, in ways that promote best practices in the provision of information services and in which diversity is valued, supported, and rewarded. Those professionals whose educational experiences also included learning in classroom settings, with instructors who utilized effective instructional techniques, which created comfortable, sensitive, yet dynamic learning environments, are likely to be more open to participating in discussions of issues of diversity in their workplaces.

Professionals whose educational experiences have included education and learning about issues of race, gender, ability, orientation, the "-isms," and diversity are more likely to be in a position to apply their knowledge in the performance of their responsibilities and more likely to contribute to environments which foster diversity and to organizations which are successful.

NOTES

1. Daniel Yankelovich, "Campus Diversity Initiative," New York: Ford Foundation, 1998.

2. Geoffrey Colvin, "The 50 Best Companies for Asians, Blacks, and Hispanics: Companies That Pursue Diversity Outperform the S&P 500; Coincidence?" *Fortune* 140, 19 July 1999, 53-54; Sherry Kuczynski, "If Diversity, Then Higher Profits? Companies That Have Successful Diversity Programs Seem to Have Higher Returns. But Which Came First?" *HRMagazine* 44 (December 1999).

3. Colvin, "The 50 Best Companies for Asians, Blacks, and Hispanics," 54.

4. Kuczynski, "If Diversity, Then Higher Profits?"

5. "Libraries Today: Global Reach. Local Touch." Chicago: American Library Association, 1.

6. Julie Brewer, "Post-Master's Residency Programs: Enhancing the Development of New Professionals and Minority Recruitment in Academic and Research Libraries," *College & Research Libraries* 58 (November 1997): 528; Reed Coats, Jane Goodwin, and Patricia Bangs, "Seeking the Best Path: Assessing a Library's Diversity Climate," *Library Administration & Management* 14 (summer 2000): 148-54; Mark

Winston and Haipeng Li, "Managing Diversity in Liberal Arts College Libraries," *College & Research Libraries* 61 (May 2000): 205-15.

7. Winston and Li, "Managing Diversity in Liberal Arts College Libraries," 205.

8. Yankelovich, "Campus Diversity Initiative."

9. "Bias Crimes Against Jews Increase by 16 Percent," *New York Times* 25 March 1999, B10; "Studies Find Race Disparities in Texas Traffic Stops," *New York Times* 7 October 2000, A12; "Women Rise in Workplace But Wage Gap Continues," *Wall Street Journal* 25 April 2000, A12.

10. Elizabeth Arveda Kissling, "That's Just a Basic Teen-Age Rule: Girls' Linguistic Strategies for Managing the Menstrual Communication Taboo," *Journal of Applied Communication Research* 24 (December 1996): 292-309.

11. Leslie E. Overmyer Day, "The Pitfalls of Diversity Training," *Training & Development* 49 (December 1995): 25-9; Norma M. Riccuci, "Cultural Diversity Programs to Prepare for Work Force 2000: What's Gone Wrong?" *Public Personnel Management* 26 (spring 1997): 35-41.

12. Kissling, "That's Just a Basic Teen-Age Rule," 292.

13. Ibid., 293.

14. Roger Tourangeau and Tom W. Smith, "Asking Sensitive Questions: The Impact of Data Collection Mode, Question Format, and Question Context," *Public Opinion Quarterly* 60 (summer 1996): 276.

15. Ibid., 278-79.

16. Kissling, "That's Just a Basic Teen-Age Rule," 292-94.

17. Ibid., 293.

18. Malcolm Gladwell, "The Sports Taboo: Why Blacks Are Like Boys and Whites Are Like Girls," *The New Yorker* 73, 19 May 1997, 50-5.

19. Kissling, "That's Just a Basic Teen-Age Rule," 293.

20. Ibid., 292-93.

21. Idris M. Diaz, "What's At Stake: The Court Decisions Affecting Higher Education and Diversity," *Black Issues in Higher Education* 14 (25 December 1997): 19-21.

22. Edna Andrews, "Cultural Sensitivity and Political Correctness: The Linguistic Problem of Naming," *American Speech* 71 (winter 1996): 389-404.

23. Lorna Peterson, "The Definition of Diversity: Two Views: A More Specific Definition," *Journal of Library Administration* 27 (1999): 20.

24. Ibid., 21.

25. Ibid., 23.

26. E. J. Josey, "The Challenges of Cultural Diversity in the Recruitment of Faculty and Students from Diverse Backgrounds," *Journal of Education for Library and Information Science* 34 (fall 1993): 302-11.

27. William Welburn, "Do We Really Need Cultural Diversity in the Library and Information Science Curriculum," *Journal of Education for Library and Information Science* 35 (fall 1994): 329.

28. Ibid.

29. Ling Hwey Jeng, "Facilitating Classroom Discussion on Diversity," *Journal of Education for Library and Information Science* 38 (fall 1997): 334.

30. Ibid., 335.

31. Ibid.

32. Ibid.

33. Lorna Peterson, "Teaching the Practitioners: One Professor's Attempt at Library Education and Sensitivity to Multicultural Diversity," *The Reference Librarian* (45/46) (1994): 24.

34. Ibid., 25.

35. Ibid., 29.

36. Ibid., 30-31.

37. Ibid., 33.

38. Getinet Belay, "Conceptual Strategies for Operationalizing Multicultural Curricula," *Journal of Education for Library and Information Science* 33 (fall 1992): 299.

Diversity in the Classroom: Incorporating Service-Learning Experiences in the Library and Information Science Curriculum

Loriene Roy

SUMMARY. Graduate schools of library and information science (LIS) are rediscovering civic engagement. Examples illustrate how LIS students further diversity efforts through service-based learning experiences. LIS students involved in the American Library Association's Spectrum Initiative helped plan the leadership institute and the longitudinal study of scholars. Students prepared pathfinders for faculty at tribal community colleges and tribal schools. LIS students helped develop and operate "If I Can Read, I Can Do Anything," a national reading program for schools serving Native children. LIS students helped create a virtual tour of the National Museum of the American Indian (NMAI). *[Article copies available for a fee from The Haworth Document Delivery Service: 1-800-HAWORTH. E-mail address: <getinfo@haworthpressinc.com> Website: <http://www. HaworthPress.com> © 2001 by The Haworth Press, Inc. All rights reserved.]*

KEYWORDS. Library and information science education, multiculturalism, diversity, service learning, reading program

---

Loriene Roy is Professor, Graduate School of Library and Information Science, The University of Texas at Austin, Austin, TX (E-mail: *loriene@gslis.utexas.edu*).

[Haworth co-indexing entry note]: "Diversity in the Classroom: Incorporating Service-Learning Experiences in the Library and Information Science Curriculum." Roy, Loriene. Co-published simultaneously in *Journal of Library Administration* (The Haworth Information Press, an imprint of The Haworth Press, Inc.) Vol. 33, No. 3/4, 2001, pp. 213-228; and: *Diversity Now: People, Collections, and Services in Academic Libraries* (ed: Teresa Y. Neely, and Kuang-Hwei (Janet) Lee-Smeltzer) The Haworth Information Press, an imprint of The Haworth Press, Inc., 2001, pp. 213-228. Single or multiple copies of this article are available for a fee from The Haworth Document Delivery Service [1-800-HAWORTH, 9:00 a.m. - 5:00 p.m. (EST). E-mail address: getinfo@haworthpressinc.com].

INTRODUCTION TO THE PROBLEM

One of the most crucial challenges facing the library and information science (LIS) profession today is to create a workforce that reflects the communities that libraries and information settings serve.[1] In November 1998, the American Library Association's (ALA) Office of Research and Statistics released data that indicated over 85 percent of the staff in selected academic, public, and school libraries were White.[2]

LIS school graduates will be working with citizens whose backgrounds may be very different from their own. Yet graduate students in schools of LIS may be able to complete their studies without studying issues of diversity or without direct contact working with and/or for diverse communities.[3] To combat these imbalances, faculty can incorporate opportunities for students to engage in diversity initiatives through service-learning experiences. This paper describes how students in the Graduate School of Library and Information Science (GSLIS) at the University of Texas at Austin (UT-Austin) have been involved in such curricular approaches.

LIBRARIANSHIP AS CITIZENSHIP: LIS AND SERVICE-LEARNING

Service-based education has been a part of LIS curricula since the origin of formal programs for librarian education. When Melvil Dewey designed the curriculum for the first School of Library Economy at Columbia in 1896, he acknowledged that "lectures and reading alone will not achieve the best results in training for librarianship without the conference, problems, study of various libraries in successful operation, and actual work in a library."[4]

The curricula of other early LIS schools and training programs reflected Dewey's philosophy.[5] Beginning in 1907, students at the Illinois Library School at the University of Illinois were encouraged to embark on a month of fieldwork in public libraries across the state.[6] For many students, their month in the public libraries of Bloomington, Decatur, Jacksonville, Joliet, or Rockford was their first experience in a library other than that at the University of Illinois.[7] Katharine Lucinda Sharp, Director of the Illinois Library School from 1897 to 1907, predicted that the students would "look back upon these early experiences as the most interesting in [their] career[s]."[8] In 1909 Hazeltine wrote of the two-month practicum arranged for students at the Wisconsin Library School, "arrangements for field practice are not only a gain for the students, but are beneficial to general library advancement in the state."[9] Bolton, the librarian at the Brookline (Massachusetts) Public Library, reminded librarians "it is the duty of every man to set apart some of his time and strength to be devoted to the welfare of the community in which he lives."[10] He noted that service brought mutual rewards: "no librarian can enter into the improvement of the social and intellectual life of the community without gaining strength himself."[11]

Over time, many librarian educators withdrew from the service model.[12] The following statement by Raber and Connaway is an example of the denigration of service in the discipline: "The need to be of meaningful service to the profession, however, aggravates the problems library and information science education has with regard to establishing a credible position within university culture."[13] As a result, librarians, both educators and practitioners, today find themselves on the fringes of the service-learning movement, although there is evidence that this is changing. The field is ready and conducive to educational reform and a few exemplary service-learning educational experiences are beginning to be noticed.[14]

NATIONAL TRENDS: THE SERVICE-LEARNING MOVEMENT

While LIS education still wrestles with the extent of its reconciliation with experiential learning, service learning has emerged in such disciplines as education, literature, social work, medicine and religious studies as a major area of practice and investigation.[15] Ryan and Callahan noted that service-learning is described both as a philosophy or school of belief and as a pedagogy or approach to teaching.[16] Scholars describe and define service-learning in many ways. To some, it is the "pedagogy of possibility" or "an education in humanity."[17] A more formal definition of service-learning is:

> . . . a course based, credit bearing educational experience in which students participate in an organized service activity that meets identified community needs and reflects on the service activity in such a way as to gain further understanding of course content, a broader appreciation of the discipline and an enhanced sense of civic responsibility.[18]

Troppe points out that there are numerous service-learning curricular approaches.[19] For example, courses may have required, optional, or extra-credit service-based assignments. Students partner service with studying and testing research methods or enroll in a cluster of classes from different disciplines that explore a common social issue. Internships and independent studies offer students even more flexibility. Service-learning through a seminar or senior thesis can provide a capstone experience that allows students to construct contextual meaning while preparing for their departure from higher education.

Initiatives in higher education and within LIS schools are providing the impetus for LIS schools to rethink their missions. Some of these initiatives include the Kellogg Commission on the Future of State and Land-Grant Universities, the Campus Compact and the first and second Congress on Professional Education sponsored by the American Library Association (ALA).[20] As LIS schools adopt new vision and mission statements, they are seeking ways to "transform information into knowledge" as one step in "changing lives."[21] Colleges and universities are rediscovering civic engagement as a result of national educational reform movements.[22] Another indicator of the current focus on service-based learning scenarios is the upcoming international University as Citizen conference scheduled for February 2001 on the campus of the University of South Florida in Tampa.[23]

Service-learning models respond to the need to provide LIS students with experiences with diverse clientele. Four examples illustrate how students at the GSLIS at The University of Texas at Austin (UT-Austin) seeking their first professional degrees in LIS can be integrally involved in the design of service experiences that engage them in creating and furthering diversity efforts: the Spectrum Initiative; the preparation of pathfinders for diverse clients; participation in the "If I Can Read, I Can Do Anything" project to promote reading in schools serving American Indian students; and the creation of virtual museums of Native American material culture.

The Spectrum Initiative: Developing a Representative Work Force

In 1998, ALA initiated a groundbreaking and innovative attempt to change the demographics of the professional workforce.[24] ALA Council approved the expenditure of $1.35 million toward the Spectrum Initiative. Spectrum is a program combining financial support with mentoring to fast-track scholars into their careers and professional activities. Financial support in the form of $5,000 scholarships is awarded on a competitive basis each year for three years to fifty individuals. Spectrum accepts applications from individuals from the four largest underrepresented groups: African American or African Canadian; Asian or Pacific Islander; Latino or Hispanic; and Native People of the United States or Canada. The Spectrum Initiative also includes a national recruitment network, a mentoring program for current scholars, and the establishment of an annual leadership institute for scholars in 1999 and 2000.[25]

GSLIS students have participated in planning the leadership institute and in assisting in the longitudinal study of Spectrum Scholars. One student provided, through an independent study, a plan for the first leadership institute. She conducted a literature review of other leadership training programs along with telephone interviews with some twenty leaders of diversity issues within the profession. As a result, she was appointed to the first Spectrum Initiative Institute Committee, which used her findings to recommend the length and focus of the first leadership institute held in New Orleans in June 1999.

Spectrum is a high profile project. Many ALA members are interested in knowing what the impact of the program has been-whether or not the influx of Spectrum funding increased the number of professional librarians of color. An evaluation component is being built into the project and GSLIS students are involved in the data collection. The research involves gathering and interpreting both qualitative and quantitative data on the Scholars. In addition to information that Scholars provided on their application form, an annual survey will further track all Scholars. In-depth interviews are being conducted of twenty to thirty scholars in order to gather data to arrive at categories of meaning. Data from interviews will be used to identify and interpret major themes that can help assess the impact of the Spectrum Initiative.

A second UT-Austin GSLIS master's student designed a prototype Web page for the longitudinal study. The page provides background on the methodology and technology used, copies of forms tailored for the project, a bibliography of resources, links to relevant publications and organizations, information on the researcher through her resume and reflective writings, and a form for viewers to contribute comments and future questions.[26]

Pathfinders: Tailored Guides to Locating and Using Reference Sources

Students in reference courses often have the opportunity to serve users directly. The tradition of providing bibliographic service through organized courses continues, allowing LIS students to combine their growing skills in searching for and evaluating materials with library use instruction.

One approach to providing assistance to library patrons is to prepare customized bibliographies. Students in early library and information science programs prepared lists of resources for student debate teams and women's clubs involved in cultural programs.[27] Bibliographies usually enumerate a variety of resources-monographs, indexes, journal articles, proceedings, organizations, Web sites-according to some arrangement (alphabetically by author, classified by format, or chronologically) and may provide a descriptive or evaluative annotation or summary for each entry in the bibliography.

One step beyond the bibliography is the pathfinder. Information professionals have developed pathfinders since the 1970s when they were one feature of a grant-funded project at MIT.[28] Pathfinders are library instruction aids that not only identify potentially useful resources; they also outline methods to locate information on topics of interest to a particular client. Pathfinders, therefore, are tied more directly to the information professional's teaching responsibilities.

Students in the GSLIS have been preparing pathfinders for clients since 1987, following a prescribed template. Each pathfinder begins with a two-page introduction in which the student describes the nature of the topic covered and the scope of his/her pathfinder, assesses client needs, and explains the chronology of steps he or she took in identifying and evaluating relevant resources. The introduction is followed by an annotated bibliography of fifteen to twenty-five resources covering aspects of the topic. In most cases the students identify a variety of resources, including print and electronic reference sources.

The last two pages of each pathfinder is the pathfinder proper, a guide illustrating how to locate resources. Here the students describe a search process, and make suggestions on how to locate information, how to use search engines or library catalogs, how to identify relevant subject terms, and how to narrow and/or broaden a search. Students usually select one of three approaches in organizing the pathfinder. Some follow a question and answer format in which the student presents a question that is similar to one the client might have. The search process is often introduced with general questions and moves to more specific ones. A second pathfinder format follows an outline of suggested actions or moves in the search. Here the client is instructed to "narrow the search" or "browse" a given call number range. A third common pathfinder format is to organize by type of resource and/or format. Rather than considering first a broad question to answer, the client is advised to start locating information by considering a type of resource to consult, such as a dictionary, encyclopedia, or periodical index.

GSLIS students have prepared pathfinders for clientele across the country, including faculty and students at tribal community colleges, teachers at Bureau of Indian Affairs schools and tribally controlled schools, and university faculty and students engaged in work for or about diverse audiences. Pathfinders on Black Dance in America were published as an ERIC document.[29] The fall 1998 "Information Resources in the Humanities" class prepared pathfinders on international dance topics for students in theatre and dance who were preparing research papers. Summaries of pathfinders on Native Americans with disabilities were presented at a national conference. Their pathfinders were also published as an ERIC document.[30] Tribal educators requested pathfinders on cultural areas (Native American regalia), social issues (compulsive gambling and fetal alcohol syndrome), and research topics (cultural differences in learning). Student pathfinders have been published in the newsletters of the Austin Songwriters Group and the American Indian Library Association.[31] Since spring 1999, students in "Information Resources in the Social Sciences" and "Bibliographic Instruction" have been preparing pathfinders on the experiences of Latin Americans in World War II. These guides assist journalism students preparing to conduct oral history interviews. Students have presented their experiences in preparing pathfinders at the ALA annual conference, a meeting of the First American Bar of Texas, and at a national conference on U.S. Latinos and Latinas and World War II held in Austin, Texas in May 2000.[32]

The pathfinder assignment gives students first-hand experience of the wide-ranging information needs of diverse clientele. The assignment helps the students not only hone skills for locating information but also provides the opportunity to customize documents and refine writing and presentation skills.

"If I Can Read, I Can Do Anything"

Librarianship is rediscovering its historical foundations by rededicating itself to literacy, as confirmed by the growing number of organizations and publications that focus on the role of libraries in information literacy initiatives.[33] Such efforts require warrior librarians. These socially responsible watchdogs ensure that programs do not leave out underserved populations and widen the gap between user groups who do have access to the best services and those who do not. In 1998 ALA president-elect Sarah A. Long established her theme, "Libraries Build Community" and identified key areas, including literacy, that she would focus on during her presidential year, 1999-2000.[34] She was receptive to funding a demonstration project that would include library service to Native American children in national literacy efforts. Long's commitment translated to a budget line of $5,000, and she provided the initial opportunity to develop the "If I Can Read, I Can Do Anything" reading incentive project designed for schools serving Native American children.

There are 187 schools in the United States that serve over 50,000 students in kindergarten through twelfth grade.[35] Nineteen of these 187 schools participated in Four Directions, a five-year federally funded grant that aimed to assist reservation schools in developing culturally responsive curriculum using technology.[36] Shortly after Long's approval of the project in November 1998, a call for participation was submitted to selected reservation schools involved in the Four Directions grant. These schools were selected because staff were more able to communicate via e-mail. Also, the project team might be funded to travel to the sites involved in the grant. Two master's students in the GSLIS volunteered to help design the project, one as part of a for-credit independent study. The reading project is based on the successful structure of summer reading programs in public libraries. It is theme-based and provides readers with small gifts in exchange for evidence that they are spending time reading or listening to the spoken word. Library staff at the Rock Point Community School in northern Arizona assisted in designing the program and titled it, "If I Can Read, I Can Do Anything." The project was tested at the Laguna (New Mexico) Elementary School during the 1999-2000 school year.[37] Laguna Elementary is located 49 miles west of Albuquerque, New Mexico.[38] It is a kindergarten through fifth grade school, serving 365 students from 285 families. An additional six schools were added to the program in fall 2000: Browning Middle School (Montana), Red Mesa High School (Arizona), Rock Point Community School (Arizona), Sacaton Elementary School (Arizona), Saint Peters Indian Mission School (Arizona), and To'Hajiilee Community School (New Mexico). Over 2,800 children were in the project at the time of this writing and new schools were to be added in fall 2001.

In addition to assisting in the design of the project, GSLIS students also provided direct service to the librarian, the educators, and the children at the schools. Furthermore, students have solicited donations of books. Due largely to these efforts, the Laguna Elementary School received 1,000 new books, worth approximately $15,000. Students designed program materials, including membership cards, letterhead, promotional brochures, and reading logs for children and their parents. One student designed a logo for the project, featuring a tree growing from an open book. Four students developed and redesigned the Web page that includes the calendar of events, copies of documents, links to the schools, a QuickTime Virtual Reality panoramic movie of the GSLIS headquarters, streaming video of storytelling, and an acknowledgment of donors.[39]

The vision for "If I Can Read, I Can Do Anything" is to develop and implement a transferable model for a school-year-long family community reading program. The mission is to assist the Indian community to increase literacy skills while preserving Native American identity. The goals are:

1. To encourage children and community members to read for pleasure.
2. To encourage intergenerational reading in the community.
3. To provide the community with opportunities to engage in and communicate about reading.
4. To promote library usage at the school.
5. To provide children with flexible reading choices.
6. To document the impact of a culturally based reading program.
7. To provide opportunities to thematically explore reading and reading activities.
8. To increase reading skills.
9. To improve the collections at the school libraries.[40]

The program is designed to support activities around four themes, each of which can coincide with the schools' four nine-week grading periods. These themes are animals and rodeo, Native Americans, sports, and chills and thrills (science, science fiction, and horror). Each reading theme is accompanied by new reading logs, incentives, and more books. The project team, including the GSLIS students, assists the schools in planning and presenting a program kick-off event. The event involved meeting with all of the children in their classrooms or in the school media center to distribute membership cards, reading logs, and incentives such as bookmarks, stickers, posters, and book bags. The "If I Can Read" project staff, including GSLIS students and a GSLIS faculty member, also organized a meeting with school educators and a family reading event with a reception and door prizes. The team made attempts to connect the project to other reading incentive initiatives. For example, the family of each student in the Laguna Elementary School received a paperback copy of *Read to Your Bunny*, author Rosemary Wells' call for parents to spend twenty minutes a day reading to their children. The Texas State Library donated copies of a *Read to Your Bunny* poster for every teacher at Laguna Elementary. Project partners also sought ways to incorporate technology into promoting reading. A GSLIS student sponsored a series of password protected and moderated chat rooms that allowed Native children at other schools to communicate about reading. A closing ceremony included the distribution of certificates to children, their parents, and teachers.

The project now has an executive board and is acquiring other partners. The Chandler Public Library (Arizona) is sponsoring two of the project schools, dedicating volunteer staff to seek donations of books and incentives, and providing support for storytelling, cataloging, and processing.[41] Goals for the second year include providing each new project school with 1,000 new books and $500 to each continuing school. Another GSLIS student is producing a storytelling video series for the children, videotaping local storytellers telling stories. Children may be invited to contribute their own stories to the series. A GSLIS student designed a project online newsletter, which will be produced quarterly. The project team hopes to work with local educators and cultural representatives to develop culturally responsive reading promotion materials and an "If I Can Read" program manual. GSLIS students will expand the Web site to include more immersive technology, including audio and video. The project team also plans to extend the program to provide opportunities for Native adults to engage in a family literacy program that would include tutoring. One aspect of the literacy project would be to incorporate Native language revitalization approaches such as producing tapes of award-winning children's books in Native languages and producing program materials, including information on the Web page, in Native languages. Project members seek opportunities to speak to professional groups both within the Native American community and library community. They will also seek additional support to extend the program to other schools serving American Indian children.[42]

Creating a Virtual Museum of the American Indian

GSLIS students have been involved in another major collaborative project involving Native American children, their educators, and community members. GSLIS students accompany Native people to museums that house Native American art works or cultural objects in their collections. The teams of children and educators are trained in the use of QuickTime Virtual Reality Technology through the Four Directions grant. In some cases, as with the National Museum of the American Indian (NMAI), the students help create a virtual tour of the exhibitions.[43] In other cases, as with the Heard Museum, the children create digital media at the museums that they can bring back to their schools to create local virtual museums. Three schools were involved with the NMAI virtual tour project: Santa Clara Day School (New Mexico), Hannahville Indian School (Michigan), and Marty Indian School (South Dakota). Hannahville, along with Standing Rock Community School (South Dakota), Seba Dalkai Boarding School (Arizona), and Dilcon Boarding School (Arizona) traveled to historical societies or museums within their states in order to capture images of cultural objects to digitally return the artifacts to their places of origin.

The results of the collaboration with the NMAI were recently made public on the NMAI Web site.[44] Three GSLIS students were involved in planning and creating the virtual tour. The students traveled to the Santa Clara Day School, twenty-five miles west of Santa Fe, and to the Nay-Tah-Wahsh School, on a Potawatomi reservation on Michigan's Upper Peninsula. They assisted in training students and their teachers on the use of QuickTime Virtual Reality Technology and in Web page construction. Three of the students accompanied their community teams to New York City and assisted during the construction of the movies of cultural objects and the panoramic movies and in using the resources in the NMAI's library. The GSLIS students subsequently co-presented a contributed paper at the 1999 Texas Library Association Annual Conference.[45] They also participated in the 1999 ALA Annual Conference by staffing a booth at the Diversity Fair and co-presenting a poster session and a program.[46]

Rich West, NMAI Director, wrote about the virtual tour: "We have reached yet another milestone at the NMAI, one that will enable us to provide technical support to help Native people proudly describe their own communities in a virtual reality format to the world."[47]

Future plans include extending the tour within the NMAI collections, enhancing features of the tour, collaborating with other cultural museums, and producing local virtual museums. The project will provide an opportunity to develop policies, especially those pertaining to intellectual and cultural property rights, to promote a training model for others interested in virtual museum construction, and to engage in research on the use of virtual museums. These efforts could extend internationally to create an international indigenous virtual museum, allowing Native people and others an opportunity to create a universal exhibit of Native cultural objects dispersed in museums and private collections around the world. The virtual museum is an act of cultural recovery. It is a way for Native communities to digitally repatriate precious items of their cultural heritage.

LIMITATIONS, CHALLENGES, AND RECOMMENDATIONS

LIS faculty must commit to providing students with opportunities to engage in service-based diversity efforts. They must be willing, in some cases, to direct student activities outside of scheduled classes, to vary course requirements, and to seek financial support for such efforts.[48]

Successfully incorporating service-based diversity efforts into LIS curricula requires clear commitment. First, LIS faculty must acknowledge the necessity of supporting diversity efforts and service. Second, LIS administration must provide LIS students with ways to receive either academic credit or other incentives for being involved in such efforts. Third, faculty members must initiate contact with funding sources, potential clients, and students who would be willing to work on such collaborations. Fourth, in order for the models to be extended, faculty members must promote such efforts through writing and presentations. LIS educators should examine their courses and teaching styles to determine how to incorporate service-based learning experiences. They should initiate or partner with grant-funded projects that unite community members and educators in creating new educational environments.

FINDINGS AND CONCLUSIONS

Service-based diversity efforts provide LIS students with opportunities to meet with and become involved with non-majority cultures. They provide rich educational opportunities for students and a social context for students to acquire and share new skills.

There is more to LIS education than what happens in the classroom. The founders of formalized LIS education recognized the field's potential for extending systems of knowledge into systems for change. Dewey used the phrase "library spirit" to represent "the idealism, the enthusiasm and the unshakable belief in the far reaching mission of libraries which runs as an undercurrent to the work of daily routine."[49] Library and information science education is undergoing great change in the midst of great criticism. As schools of LIS are rethinking their missions and crafting vision statements, they will rediscover service as a key to "transform[ing] information into knowledge." This is how LIS educators will find themselves involved in the process of "changing lives."[50]

NOTES

1. American Library Association, "ALA Interests and Activities. ALA Key Action Areas. Diversity" [online] available from http://www.ala.org/work/[cited 3 November 2000]; Christine Watkins, "A Community Mirror: Reflections on the Color of Librarianship," *American Libraries* 30 (10) (November 1999): 64-6.

2. Mary Jo Lynch, "Racial and Ethnic Diversity Among Librarians: A Status Report," [online] available from http://www.ala.org/alaorg/ors/racethnc.html [cited 15 December 2000].

3. Lorna Peterson, "Issues of Race," *Journal of Education for Library and Information Sciences* 37(2) (spring 1996): 1972.

4. Melvil Dewey, "School of Library Economy at Columbia College," *The Library Journal* 9 (7) (July 1894): 118.

5. Loriene Roy, "Personality, Tradition, and Library Spirit: A Brief History of Librarian Education," in *Library and Information Studies Education in the United States*, ed. Loriene Roy and Brooke Sheldon (London: Mansell, 1998): 1-15.

6. Laurel A. Grotzinger, *The Power and the Dignity: Librarianship and Katharine Sharp* (New York: Scarecrow Press, 1966).

7. Loriene Roy, "Library Spirit: The Library School Experience and Early Professional Work During Progressive Era Texas and Illinois. A Reader's Theatre Performance," Texas, 1996, ERIC, ED 393467.

8. Katharine Lucinda Sharp, letter to Lucy P. Williams, 25 February 1907, University of Illinois Alumni Personnel Records, University Archives, University of Illinois at Urbana-Champaign.

9. Mary Emogene Hazeltine, "Methods of Training in One Library School," *The Library Journal* 34 (6) (June 1909): 256.

10. Charles Knowles Bolton, "The Librarian's Duty as a Citizen," *The Library Journal* 21 (5) (May 1896): 219.

11. Ibid.

12. Kathleen de la Peña McCook, "Reconnecting Library Education and the Mission of Community," *Library Journal* 125 (9) (September 1, 2000): 164-65.

13. Douglas Raber and Lynn Sillipigni Connaway, "Two Cultures, One Faculty: Contradictions of Library and Information Science Education," *Journal of Education for Library and Information Science* 37 (2) (Spring 1996): 123.

14. Kathleen de la Peña McCook, "Librarians and Comprehensive Community Initiatives," *Reference and User Services Quarterly* 40 (1) (fall 2000) (forthcoming); Kathleen de la Peña McCook, *A Place at the Table: Participating in Community Building* (Chicago: American Library Association, 2000); McCook, "Reconnecting Library Education."

15. Harry Boyte and Elizabeth Hollander, "Wingspread Declaration on Renewing the Civic Mission of the American Research University" [online] available from http://www.compact.org/news/Wingspread.html [cited 3 November 2000].

16. Lynne Ryan and Jane Callahan, "Service-Learning Competencies for Beginning Teachers," *Academic Exchange Quarterly* 3 (4) (winter 1999): 69.

17. Kelly Ward, "The Presence of This Second Volume," *Academic Exchange Quarterly* 4 (1) (spring 2000): 3; Bettina Baker and William Labov, "Raising the Roof: Expanding the Frontiers of Service-Learning in the Field of Literacy," *Academic Exchange Quarterly* 4 (1) (spring 2000): 32.

18. R. G. Bringle, and Hatcher, J. A., "A Service-Learning Curriculum for Faculty," *Michigan Journal of Community-Service Learning* 2 (1995): 112-122.

19. Marie Troppe, "Service-Learning: Curricular Options," *Academic Exchange Quarterly* 3 (4) (winter 1999): 98-100.

20. McCook, "Reconnecting Library Education."

21. Graduate School of Library and Information Science, The University of Texas at Austin, "Our Mission and Vision," [online] available from http://www.gslis.utexas.edu [cited 15 December 2000].

22. Baker and Labov, "Raising the Roof"; L-Jay Fine and Chris Fiorentino, "Service Learning in Higher Education," *Academic Exchange Quarterly* 3 (1) (spring 1999): 6-18; [online] available from http://www.newcastle.edu.au/department/ar/AEQ/V3-1/V3-1-Focus-1.htm#content [cited 18 June 2000].

23. University of South Florida. Division of Conferences and Institutes. "Call for Presentations for International Conference on the University as Citizen: Engaging Universities & Communities," Tampa, Florida: University of South Florida, Division of Conferences and Institutes, 2000.

24. Christine Watkins, "Can Librarians Play Basketball?" *American Libraries* 30 (3) (March 1999): 58-61.

25. Ibid.

26. Heather Ball, "Spectrum Initiative Longitudinal Study," [online] available from http://www.gslis.utexas.edu/~heatherb/longstudyhome.htm [cited 29 January 2001].

27. Roy, "Library Spirit."

28. Alice Sizer Warner, "Pathfinders: A Way to Boost Your Information Handouts Beyond Booklists and Bibliographies," *American Libraries* 14 (3) (March 1983): 150.

29. Loriene Roy, ed., "Pathfinders on Black Dance in America," Texas, 1991, ERIC, ED 339380.

30. Loriene Roy, comp., "Pathfinders for Finding Information on Native Americans with Disabilities," Texas, 1992, ERIC, ED351171.

31. Michelle Beattie, "Starting Your Own Oral History Project: Resources on the Internet," *American Indian Libraries Newsletter* 20 (2) (winter 1997): 1-3; Anne Burnett, "Pathfinder on Songwriting," *Austin Songwriters Group Newsletter* (October

1994): 12-14; Laura Tyner, "The Native American Boarding School Experience: Pathfinder," *American Indian Libraries Newsletter* 20 (4) (summer 1998): 1-2; Michael Ugorowski, "Economic and Regulatory Aspects of Radio Broadcasting," *Austin Songwriters Group Newsletter* (December 1994): 6-7, 8, 12.

32. Loriene Roy et al., "Teaching the Pathfinder: One Approach in Bibliographic Instruction Training," (poster session presented at the American Library Association Annual Conference, Chicago, 26 June 1995); Loriene Roy et al., "Pathfinders for Finding Information on Native Americans with Disabilities: A Panel Presentation" (paper presented at the annual meeting of the First American Bar of Texas, Wimberley, TX, 22 August 1992); Loriene Roy et al., "Pathfinders on World War II: Guides to Preparing Undergraduates to Conduct Oral History Interviews of U.S. Latinos and Latinas and World War II" (paper presented at the U.S. Latinos and Latinas & World War II: Changes Seen, Changes Wrought Conference, Austin, TX, 27 May 2000).

33. American Library Association, 21st Century Literacy (ALA Action Series No. 1) (Chicago: ALA, 2000).

34. Sarah Ann Long, "Report of Sarah Ann Long, President-Elect" (American Library Association, Council Document 1999-99, No. 29) (American Library Association Midwinter Conference, Philadelphia, PA, January 28-February 2, 1999).

35. William A Mehojah, Jr. "Director's Page: Foreword from the Director [of the Bureau of Indian Affairs. Office of Indian Education Programs]" [online] available from http://www.oiep.bia.edu/director's_page.htm [cited 3 November 2000].

36. Loriene Roy, "Four Directions: An Indigenous Model of Education," *Wicazo Sa Review* 13 (2) (fall 1998): 59-69.

37. "Reading Promo on Reservations Reaches Six Schools in NM, AZ," *Library Hotline* (14 August 2000): 4-5.

38. Laguna Elementary School, "Community Profile," [online] available from http://4d.sped.ukans.edu/lagunaelementary [cited 3 November 2000].

39. The Web site for the "If I Can Read, I Can Do Anything" project is available from http://www.gslis.utexas.edu/~ifican.

40. Ibid.

41. Carlos Miller, "Chandler Library Reads on the Rez," *Arizona Republic* (31 October 2000) [online] available from http://www.arizonarepublic.com:80/mesa/articles/1026library26Z11.html [cited 1 November 2000].

42. "Reading Promo on Reservations."

43. Loriene Roy and Mark Christal, "Creating a Virtual Tour of the American Indian," in *National Association of Native American Studies 2000 Conference Proceedings* (Morehead, KY: NANAS, 2000): 304-30.

44. The Web site for the National Museum of the American Indian is available from http://www.conexus.si.edu/main.htm.

45. Loriene Roy et al., "Take the VR Challenge! Incorporating Virtual Reality Technology into Your Web Page" (paper presented at the Texas Library Association 1999 Annual Conference, Dallas, TX, 21 April 1999).

46. Loriene Roy et al., "Take the VR Challenge! Incorporating Virtual Reality Technology into Your Web Page" (poster session presented at the American Library Association Annual Conference, New Orleans, 28 June 1999); Loriene Roy et al., "Four Directions: An Indigenous Educational Model" (paper presented at the second Annual Diversity Fair at the American library Association Annual Conference, New Orleans, 26 June 1999).

47. "Santa Clara Pueblo Students Create Virtual Museum Tour," *NMAI Runner* 99-2 (summer 1999): 6.

48. Debra K. Hearington, Phyllis E. Kirsch, JoAnne Henry and Laura M. Festa, "Process and Outcomes if Integrating Service-Learning Methodology in Nursing Curricula," *Academic Exchange Quarterly* 4 (1) (spring 2000): 33-46.

49. Arne Kildal, "American Influence on European Librarianship," *Library Quarterly* 7 (1937): 196-210.

50. Graduate School of Library and Information Science, The University of Texas at Austin, "Our Mission and Vision," [online] available from http://www.gslis.utexas.edu [cited 15 December 2000].

Race, Class, Gender and Librarianship: Teaching in Ethnic Studies

Yem S. Fong

SUMMARY. Librarians at the University of Colorado at Boulder promote diversity through activism on campus and through teaching, collaboratively and individually. This article features the experiences of a librarian who twice taught a full credit course in the Department of Ethnic Studies. The author explores the challenges of moving beyond the library to support diversity, and considers how teaching in ethnic studies informs librarianship. *[Article copies available for a fee from The Haworth Document Delivery Service: 1-800-HAWORTH. E-mail address: <getinfo@haworthpressinc. com> Website: <http://www.HaworthPress.com> © 2001 by The Haworth Press, Inc. All rights reserved.]*

KEYWORDS. Teaching, diversity, ethnic studies, tenure

LIBRARIANSHIP AND DIVERSITY

Many of us are drawn to the field of librarianship from a desire to contribute to the world we live in. As professionals we seek to meet differing needs of our multiple and sometimes disparate constituencies.

Yem S. Fong is Associate Professor and Head, Information Delivery Services, Libraries, University of Colorado at Boulder, Boulder, CO (E-mail: *judith.fong@ colorado.edu*).

[Haworth co-indexing entry note]: "Race, Class, Gender and Librarianship: Teaching in Ethnic Studies." Fong, Yem S. Co-published simultaneously in *Journal of Library Administration* (The Haworth Information Press, an imprint of The Haworth Press, Inc.) Vol. 33, No. 3/4, 2001, pp. 229-240; and: *Diversity Now: People, Collections, and Services in Academic Libraries* (ed: Teresa Y. Neely, and Kuang-Hwei (Janet) Lee-Smeltzer) The Haworth Information Press, an imprint of The Haworth Press, Inc., 2001, pp. 229-240. Single or multiple copies of this article are available for a fee from The Haworth Document Delivery Service [1-800-HAWORTH, 9:00 a.m. - 5:00 p.m. (EST). E-mail address: getinfo@haworthpressinc.com].

We often find ourselves bending over backwards in our outreach and our frontline services to be inclusive. Through a variety of activities, whether it is materials selection, library exhibits or reference assistance, we are presented with opportunities to support diversity.

These opportunities abound on campus in a number of ways. An obvious route for librarians is in the selection of materials, where we can include titles by scholars of color, and on topics related to ethnic studies, area studies, multiculturalism, sexual orientation, etc. At the University of Colorado in Boulder, librarians are involved in promoting the Libraries diversity goals in some of the following ways. The Libraries offers diversity and cultural series where faculty of color are featured speakers. Many librarians and staff volunteer for university-wide and campus committees focusing on diversity issues, such as the Chancellor's Committee on Diversity. Others seek out women's groups or student advocacy groups, and become mentors and allies for students from diverse backgrounds. At the University of Colorado, we also offer targeted freshmen orientation for first-generation students and include a library component. Library instruction in disciplines where issues surrounding race, gender and sexual orientation arise, such as ethnic studies, women's studies, sociology, journalism, history, and political science, also provides an excellent opportunity for working directly with students and faculty. Moving into team-teaching in women's studies or ethnic studies becomes a logical next step for librarians who actively support diversity.

How did I, head of interlibrary loan and the Libraries fee-based service, ultimately end up in a classroom teaching an Asian American women's studies course? As a newly hired tenure track faculty I focused on two areas in addition to my job: a research agenda on intergenerational and leadership issues for Asian American women, and campus diversity initiatives. I became a mentor to ethnic students, joined an advocacy group, was invited to join a faculty/staff committee to enhance student recruitment and retention, became a member of a new chancellor's committee on women, and generally fostered connections at all levels within and outside the Libraries. I believed, and still do, that it was important to become politically active on campus, and to support diversity through my actions. At the same time I felt I was contributing as a library faculty member, at times representing the Libraries and whenever possible promoting the Libraries' services.

Through networking and being active on campus, ethnic studies faculty learned of my research on Asian American women and invited me to guest lecture. These initial contacts led to an offer from the chair of the department to teach a class on Asian American women's history and social issues. A male faculty member had once taught this course, and the department felt that an Asian American woman could provide a more relevant framework for students. So I was asked and agreed with little knowledge of how to teach such a class or what I was getting myself into.

Teaching is an integral part of academic librarianship. Many of us, especially subject specialists, routinely teach classes in library research and information/Internet literacy. At the University of Colorado, librarians are teaching "outside the box," offering collaborative models for working with faculty in academic departments. Some examples include team teaching a course on science writing with a faculty member in biology, and team teaching a course on research methodologies with faculty in ethnic studies and journalism. At the other end of the spectrum is teaching a subject specific, non-library-related course. This personal experience of the author, who twice taught a semester course in ethnic studies, forms the basis for asking interesting questions on the role of academic librarians in actively supporting diversity.

Why teach a course in ethnic studies? What strategies does a librarian use to teach outside of librarianship? What are the risks and rewards for taking on such an endeavor? In institutions where librarians are reviewed for tenure, how is teaching in other academic departments evaluated? How can librarians integrate diversity initiatives into their jobs and professional life? This article will attempt to offer some insights for library administrators and for librarians who wish to do more than pay lip service to enhancing diversity.

A BALANCING ACT

I had guest lectured quite a bit, but found that designing and developing an entire class from day one to finals was a major undertaking. At that time no other librarians were teaching so completely outside the Libraries. My supervisor and dean were very supportive and encouraged me to teach. I negotiated release time, received support for resources from Ethnic Studies and was rostered as an adjunct faculty, in addition to being an assistant professor in the Libraries.

At the same time, I continued to be a full-time department head over three units with ten staff members and thirty plus student assistants, and was in the office four out of five days a week. One of the first challenges I faced was how to balance my job, my research for tenure, and teaching twice a week. This meant delegating more work to staff and relying on others to represent the department when I was unable to do so. This also meant working many evenings, weekends, and holidays.

I realized fairly quickly that I wasn't able to do it all, that some things in the library fell behind schedule, or didn't get my attention until the semester was over. I tried to be available for both my staff and the students in my class, and found that it just didn't always work. In retrospect I know that there were some departmental crises that could have been avoided had I been one hundred percent at my job, and some personnel issues that surfaced because I wasn't always there to intercede. Yet, on the whole, my staff was supportive and gave me the space and time I needed, and in a pinch, would help me locate resources or photocopy class assignments.

Balancing my job and teaching for Ethnic Studies forced me to consider why I was taking on such a commitment. While I was dealing with practical daily realities I was also making a career decision as a tenure track faculty that could turn out to be positive or negative. As tenure track librarians at the University of Colorado, we are reviewed for tenure on the basis of forty percent teaching/librarianship, forty percent scholarship, and twenty percent service. How would teaching outside of the Libraries be reviewed? As part of my forty percent teaching/librarianship, or under the twenty percent service category? Would university mandated student evaluations be taken into consideration? Would I be evaluated by the Department of Ethnic Studies in addition to the Libraries? Would the Vice Chancellor's tenure committee view teaching for ethnic studies as a legitimate contribution to the academy?

The notion of legitimate contributions continues to be an important question on college campuses. In the study, *Faculty of Color in Academe*, Turner and Myers note that their review of the literature "documents the pervasive theme-and our study respondents report-that the talents and contributions of faculty of color are devalued or undervalued, and that this racial and ethnic bias carries over to the tenure and promotion process."[1] The study highlights a number of issues that faculty of color face when seeking tenure, such as the additional demands and expectations placed on them as "ethnic resources," the devaluation of research interests that differ from mainstream faculty, the greater investment of time in teaching and service by faculty of color, and the campus environment that often leads to experiences of isolation and chilly classroom climates.[2] At the University of Colorado these issues have been raised in a number of high profile tenure cases involving faculty of color. The case of Dr. Estavan Flores, who was denied tenure in the sociology department in 1994 is particularly telling. Following campus protests and a series of appeals, Dr. Flores and two other Chicano faculty members in sociology were reassigned to the ethnic studies department, where he ultimately was awarded tenure.[3] However, one of the obstacles Flores faced was the charge that he hadn't published in the "right journals," although he published much of his work in the international *Migration Review*.[4]

Flores' case underscored the concern I felt about the university's commitment to promoting faculty of color, especially those who teach and research outside the norm, whatever that norm may be. Taking all this into consideration I found that I was still willing to teach the class no matter the outcome. I ardently believed in the need for a class that placed Asian American women's history and experiences at the center and not on the periphery. I also believed that librarians should extend themselves outside the libraries, and in so doing have a greater impact on the university. I also believed that teaching such a class created stronger connections and support for the library and its role on campus. At the core of all of this was a strong belief in education and the impact the process of learning could have on students. If I could contribute to this, I was willing to take the risk.

DEVELOPING THE COURSE

My course was titled *Asian American women: Historical and contemporary issues*. When I first taught the class in 1994, there were very few courses across the country that specifically focused on Asian American women's history. Ethnic studies grew out of the San Francisco student strikes of 1968.[5] The theme of bachelor societies and teaching racism and discrimination based on anti-labor movements of the early nineteenth century often formed the basis for early Asian American studies classes.[6] Over the past thirty years, Asian American studies has evolved to include aspects of community and increasing numbers of immigrant groups.[7] What is also evident in the recent literature, and highlighted in an article by Diane Fujino, is that there has been a shift in focus, and recognition by scholars on the need for integrating feminist pedagogy into Asian American and ethnic studies.[8]

As I researched my topic and searched for ethnic studies bibliographies and curricula, I found very few course descriptions that I could use as a model. A search of library literature pointed to articles on literacy, library instruction, team teaching and diversity issues, but none related to teaching ethnic studies by library faculty. I borrowed sample course descriptions from colleagues and located a number of printed syllabi for introductory classes and women's studies courses.[9] However, as I searched through numerous annotated bibliographies on Asian American studies, I realized that I would have to create my own curriculum, and identify my goals and strategies. I also examined the literature of teaching for diversity and found sources such as *Multicultural Teaching in the University*[10] and articles on classroom dynamics.[11] At the University of Colorado we are also fortunate to have a Faculty Excellence Teaching program, which generates lectures and writings by faculty on many topics, including a series entitled *On Diversity in Teaching and Learning.*[12] These sources were invaluable to me in providing a context for the classroom experience.

Course Content and Materials

My primary goal was to teach Asian American women's history, and their lived experiences in the United States. This is a history fraught with silence and oppression, where women lacked a voice and were essentially not visible. Judy Yung's pictorial history of Chinese women in America highlights this.[13] I soon realized that in order to teach this history, I also needed to address the structural features and cultural patterns that support gender, race, and class-based inequities in society. As a result, students were challenged to think critically and to analyze historic, social, and legal issues. It was my intention to present factual material on the cultural and economic circumstances that manifested in outward victimization and loss of rights, as well as women's internalized oppression. I also wanted students to learn aspects of American history that they might not learn otherwise, i.e., that there were early frontier Asian women who contributed to a new west, that the internment of Japanese American families was racially motivated, and that citizenship was denied to Asians prior to 1942.

In developing the curriculum I quickly discovered that there were few textbooks solely focused on Asian American women. I located an anthology or two of literary writings, a book on the history of Chinese women in America, one on Japanese women immigrants, a few articles on other groups, such as Korean women in the United States, and found chapters here and there on various social issues and women's labor history.[14] So I found myself using a combination of articles, short historical treatments, and anthologies as the primary readings, then adding fictional/biographical works, such as Maxine Hong Kingston's *Woman Warrior*, and Ruthanne McCunn Lum's *Thousand Pieces of Gold*.[15]

In order to engage the students and keep their interest, I located films, documentaries, and short videos, such as *Forbidden City U.S.A.* that depicted a San Francisco nightclub of the 1940s featuring Asian American singers and dancers and their stories.[16] I also invited speakers from the community, such as an activist who had been in an internment camp, and a woman who worked to help abused women brought to this country as mail-order brides.

As a librarian I felt it was important to assign a research paper, which was a large percentage of the grade. Students were encouraged to be original with this assignment. They could do traditional library research on a topic, such as feminism, or they could write a family history or an oral history, or even do a service related paper at a local social service agency. Some students even asked to do creative pieces, such as a short story written by a non-Asian male from the perspective and voice of a Korean War bride. Needless to say I had a class devoted to library literacy and to oral history research and writing. Students were asked to give presentations on their research projects, which enabled students to hear and learn other stories.

Classroom Teaching and Interaction

I consciously chose to create a student-centered classroom, to encourage discussion and to keep lectures at a minimum. In order to do this, I asked students to record thoughts and insights in journals, and to write short five-minute papers, as a basis for small group discussions. Still that meant being "on" for ninety minutes twice a week. Because of the subject matter and because I was new to teaching, I felt responsible for the well being of the classroom. I found myself constantly juggling content and classroom dynamics, and often found student interactions mentally and emotionally charged. David Schoem, in his co-edited volume *Multicultural Teaching in the University*, characterizes many of the highs and lows I experienced in the following quote:

> Imagine the most satisfying teaching experience, the most enlightening, analytic discussions. Imagine provocation, challenge, tears, anger, joy, transformation, insight. Imagine deeply hidden life stories and uncensored honesty suddenly bursting forth.

But picture, too, intimidation, posturing, denial, fragility. Picture students who can "see" only one perspective, who don't listen or read carefully except when their own group is being discussed, who are so anxious to talk about themselves and their individual ethnic/racial experience that they are ready to dismiss research findings and scholarly debate as interfering with their learning. Picture students being intellectually passive for weeks for fear of offending their classmates from different backgrounds.[17]

Discussions about gender bias or issues such as sexual harassment were often provocative. As a result students raised questions, debated, and disagreed routinely. The student ratio was generally eighty percent Asian American, mixed heritage or other racial minority and seventy-five percent female. This meant presenting material in ways that would reach white males, first-generation Hmongs, second-generation students from India or fourth-generation half-Japanese students. It was also important to not ask students to represent an entire ethnicity, such as the lone Cambodian student or the single south Asian woman. Some students had taken other ethnic studies or women's studies courses and were more comfortable with discussing concepts such as racism and oppression, while many had not, and took the class to fulfill a requirement. In the end it was important to establish a framework and common ground so that healthy dialogue could occur.

RISKS AND REWARDS

When I became a librarian many years ago, I thought that I could have a "safe" career among the stacks and card catalogs. In teaching, I discovered that I was no longer "safe." Teaching forced me to look at my own assumptions, stereotypes, identity issues, and political goals to name a few. I had never taught to this extent before, nor had I taken education courses and learned how to be a teacher. I found that I had truly moved outside the library walls and was visible and responsible in new and different ways.

Being of Asian descent, it was also important to counter racial assumptions. While silence in Asian cultures may be seen as a sign of dignity and of endurance and wisdom, it is often interpreted from a western perspective to be a sign of weakness. In teaching the class I had to find my own true voice as a teacher and an Asian American woman role model, not as a quiet librarian or silent member of a racial minority.

My rewards came from seeing students begin to shift some of their biases, broaden their worldviews, and question their own sense of self in the context of the university and community. For many students it was an opportunity to learn of their immigrant background in this country. For some the class helped shape their sense of ethnic identity. Several students talked about seeing for the first time how prevalent gender bias and racism was in their lives, and how it affected them on campus and at home. Non-Asian students related new understandings about race and gender.

I also discovered that I truly enjoyed interacting with students. I often had discussions with many of them outside the classroom, and provided personal and academic counseling. I even developed ongoing relationships with some students. My student evaluations were positive, with ratings of B+ to A-.

Was the risk worth taking? After all was said and done I did receive tenure. At that time, since I was one of the first tenure track faculty to teach outside of the Libraries, my teaching was evaluated under the service category of the Libraries tenure criteria. What was interesting, however, was that in the letter from Vice Chancellor's committee awarding me tenure, the committee made a point of commenting favorably on how my teaching contributed to the campus. So in the end the risks were worth taking.

I believe my path helped pave the way for other librarians at the university to teach outside the Libraries. It also contributed to the Libraries' most recent revision of our tenure criteria where teaching outside the Libraries is now considered part of the forty percent Teaching/librarianship category. However, I learned that teaching is a full-time occupation. While it is possible to be a full-time librarian and also teach outside the libraries, it requires a great deal of commitment. One must be willing to invest personal time and to be able to risk "safety" for public visibility. It was a personally transformative and enriching journey in many ways. In the final analysis, teaching in ethnic studies ultimately impacts librarianship and helps us better understand students' needs, perspectives, and daily lives.

NOTES

1. Caroline Sotello Viernes Turner and Samuel L. Myers, *Faculty of Color in Academe: Bittersweet Success* (Needham Heights, MA: Allyn and Bacon, 1993), 32.
2. Ibid., 33-4.
3. Hector Gutierrez, "CU President Reverses Dean's Ruling on Tenure," *Rocky Mountain News*, 28 December 1994, 14A.

4. Paul Ruffins, "The Shelter of Tenure is Eroding and for Faculty of Color Gaining Membership May Be Tougher Than Ever," *Black Issues in Higher Education* 14, no. 17 (1997): 24-5.

5. K. Scott Wong, "Our Lives, Our Histories," in *Multicultural Teaching in the University*, ed. David Schoem, Linda Frankel, Ximena Zuniga, Edith A. Lewis (Westport, CT: Praeger Publishers, 1993), 87.

6. Gary Y. Okihiro, "Teaching Asian American History," in *Teaching Asian America: Diversity and the Problem of Community*, ed. Lane Ryo Hirabayashi (Lanham, MD: Rowman & Littlefield Publishers, 1998), 25.

7. Lane Ryo Hirabayashi and Malcolm Collier, "Embracing Diversity: A Pedagogy for Introductory Asian American Studies Courses," in *Reviewing Asian America: Locating Diversity*, eds. Wendy L. Ng, Soo-Young Chin, James S. Moy, Gary Y. Okihiro (Pullman, WA: Washington State University Press, 1995), 15-31.

8. Diane C. Fujino, "Unity of Theory and Practice: Integrating Feminist Pedagogy into Asian American Studies Courses," in *Teaching Asian America: Diversity and the Problem of Community*, ed. Lane Ryo Hirabayashi (Lanham, MD: Rowman & Littlefield Publishers, 1998), 73-91.

9. Gary Y. Okihiro, ed., *Ethnic Studies: Selected Course Outlines and Reading Lists from American Colleges and Universities, Vol. I Cross Cultural, Asian and Afro-American Studies* (New York, NY: Markus Wiener Publishing, Inc., 1989).

10. David Schoem, Linda Frankel, Ximena Zuniga, Edith A. Lewis, eds., *Multicultural Teaching in the University* (Westport, CT: Praeger Publishers, 1993).

11. Becky Thompson and Estelle Disch, "Feminist, Anti-Racist, Anti-Oppression Teaching: Two White Women's Experience," *Radical Teaching*, no. 41: 4-10.

12. Deborah Flick, "Developing and Teaching an Inclusive Curriculum"; Janet Jacobs and Michele D. Simpson, "Dialogue on Diversity in the Classroom"; and Polly E. McClean, "Head Trip: A Teaching and Learning Discussion," in *On Diversity in Teaching and Learning Series* (Boulder, CO: University of Colorado Faculty Teaching Excellence Program, 1990-1999).

13. Judy Yung, *Chinese Women of America: A Pictorial History* (Seattle: University of Washington Press, 1986).

14. See Appendix.

15. Maxine Hong Kingston, *The Woman Warrior* (New York, NY: Random House, 1975); Ruthanne McCunn Lum, *Thousand Pieces of Gold* (Boston, MA: Beacon Press, 1981).

16. *Forbidden City, U.S.A.*, prod., dir., writer, Arthur Dong, 57 min., PBS Video, 1989, videocassette.

17. David Schoem, "Teaching About Ethnic Identity and Intergroup Relations," in *Multicultural Teaching in the University*, ed. David Schoem, Linda Frankel, Ximena Zuniga, Edith A. Lewis (Westport, CT: Praeger Publishers, 1993), 15-16.

APPENDIX

COURSE DESCRIPTION

AAST 3420 Asian American Women: Historical and Contemporary Issues

Placing Asian American women's experiences at the center of our interpretation, this course will introduce comparative analyses of race and gender issues in a historical, economic, political, and cultural context. Stereotypes, myths, images and realities of Asian American women across generations, ethnicities and historical periods will be critically examined from a diversity of perspectives. Thematic emphasis will be given to issues of family and community, labor, activism, feminism, identity politics and race and power relations as it specifically informs Asian American women's lived experiences.

COURSE READINGS & TEXTS

Aguilar-San Juan, Karin, ed. *The State of Asian America: Activism and Resistance in the 1990s.* Boston: South End Press, 1994.

Anzaldua, Gloria, ed. *Making Face, Making Soul: Creative & Critical Perspectives by Women of Color.* San Francisco: Aunt Lute Books, 1990.

Chan, Sucheng. *Asian Americans: An Interpretive History.* Boston: Twayne Publishers, 1991.

Hong Kingston, Maxine. *The Woman Warrior.* New York: Random House, 1975.

Kim, Elaine H. and Janice Otani. "Asian Women in America." In *With Silk Wings: Asian American Women at Work.* San Francisco: Asian Women United of California, 1983.

Ling, Susie and Sucheta Mazumdar. "Asian American Feminism," *Cross Currents*, 1983.

Lum, Ruthanne McCunn. *Thousand Pieces of Gold.* Boston: Beacon Press, 1981.

Asian Women United of California, eds. *Making Waves: An Anthology of Writings By and About Asian American Women.* San Francisco: Beacon Press, 1989.

Matsumoto, Valerie, "Desperately Seeking Dierdre: Gender Roles, Multicultural Relations, and Nisei Women Writers of the 1930." *Frontiers* 12, no.1 (1991): 19-32.

Nakano, Mei T. *Japanese American Women: Three Generations.* Berkeley: Mina Press, 1990.

Our Feet Walk the Sky: Women of the South Indian Diaspora. San Francisco: Aunt Lute Books, 1993.

Pascoe, Peggy. "Gender Systems in Conflict: The Marriages of Mission Educated Chinese American Women, 1847-1939." In *Unequal Sisters: A Multicultural Reader in U.S. Women's History*, eds. Vicki Ruiz and Ellen CuBois. New York: Routledge Press, 1994.

Policy Issues to the Year 2020. Los Angeles: Leap Asian Pacific American Public Policy Institute and UCLA Asian American Studies Center, 1993.

Poor, Grace. "Purification." In *Our Feet Walk the Sky: Women of the South Indian Diaspora*. San Francisco: Aunt Lute Books, 1993.

Quan, Kit Yuen. "The Girl Who Wouldn't Sing." In *Making Face, Making Soul: Creative & Critical Perspectives by Women of Color*. San Francisco: Aunt Lute Books, 1990.

Yang, Eun Sik. "Korean Women of America: From Subordination to Partnership, 1903-1930," *Amerasia Journal* 11, no. 2 (1984): 1-28.

Yung, Judy. *Chinese Women of America: A Pictorial History*. Seattle: University of Washington Press, 1986.

Healing Hearts, Enriching Minds:
The Multicultural Storytelling Project
and the Texas A&M University Libraries

Johnnieque B. (Johnnie) Love
Candace Benefiel
John B. Harer

SUMMARY. The growing emphasis on storytelling for instruction in a variety of settings and subjects also raises the question of training for storytellers: How is storytelling itself taught, and what research exists to aid in the development of pedagogy for storytelling? This paper will address storytelling in the context of use as an instructional tool and the development of a storytelling project specifically designed for its utilization of

Johnnieque B. (Johnnie) Love is Associate Faculty Librarian III, and Coordinator of Personnel Programs, University of Maryland Libraries, College Park, MD (E-mail: *jbl345@umail.umd.edu*). She was formerly Assistant Professor of Library Science, Curriculum Collection Librarian, and Coordinator of the Multicultural Storytelling Project, Texas A&M University Libraries 5000, Texas A&M University, College Station, TX.

Candace Benefiel is Associate Professor of Library Science and Senior Humanities Reference Librarian, Texas A&M University Libraries 5000, Texas A&M University, College Station, TX (E-mail: *cbenefie@lib-gw.tamu.edu*).

John B. Harer is Director, Corriher-Linn-Black Library, Catawba College, Salisbury, NC (E-mail: *jbharer@tamu.edu*). He was formerly Associate Professor of Library Science, Texas A&M University Libraries 5002, Texas A&M University, College Station, TX.

[Haworth co-indexing entry note]: "Healing Hearts, Enriching Minds: The Multicultural Storytelling Project and the Texas A&M University Libraries." Love, Johnnieque B. (Johnnie), Candace Benefiel, and John B. Harer. Co-published simultaneously in *Journal of Library Administration* (The Haworth Information Press, an imprint of The Haworth Press, Inc.) Vol. 33, No. 3/4, 2001, pp. 241-258; and: *Diversity Now: People, Collections, and Services in Academic Libraries* (ed: Teresa Y. Neely, and Kuang-Hwei (Janet) Lee-Smeltzer) The Haworth Information Press, an imprint of The Haworth Press, Inc., 2001, pp. 241-258. Single or multiple copies of this article are available for a fee from The Haworth Document Delivery Service [1-800-HAWORTH, 9:00 a.m. - 5:00 p.m. (EST). E-mail address: getinfo@haworthpressinc.com].

241

multicultural literature and implementation of activities to support that focus. *[Article copies available for a fee from The Haworth Document Delivery Service: 1-800-HAWORTH. E-mail address: <getinfo@haworthpressinc.com> Website: <http://www.HaworthPress.com> © 2001 by The Haworth Press, Inc. All rights reserved.]*

KEYWORDS. Pre-service teacher training, storytelling and classroom instruction, teacher education, storytelling as an art, storytelling festivals, library liaison work, storytelling event planning, interdepartmental/collaboration, professional storytellers

INTRODUCTION

As we begin a new century, it can be noted that the wonders of technology and computers have become an integral part of modern life. Politicians, pundits, and others are decrying the lack of connection and social interaction between human beings. Robert Putnam, in his study on social change in America, *Bowling Alone: The Collapse and Revival of American Culture*, devotes several chapters to the decline in participation in civic, religious, and even social activities and connections.[1] Storytellers and storytelling organizations are on the upswing, as evidenced by the growing National Storytelling Festival.[2] One of the oldest of human arts, it seems, is alive and well.

What is storytelling? As with many apparently simple questions, the answer is complex. Collins and Cooper, in *The Power of Story: Teaching Through Storytelling*, assert:

> Storytelling is an art, a science, a way of life. To define storytelling or storyteller is to try to make concrete that which is abstract. Suffice it to say that storytelling is among the oldest forms of communication. It exists in every culture. Storytelling is the commonality of all human beings, in all places, in all times. It is used to educate, to inspire, to record historical events, to entertain, to transmit cultural mores.[3]

Storytelling is a natural part of the human psyche, and humans, worldwide, are hard-wired to respond to narrative as a means of communication and teaching. Storytelling has been described as a defining human characteristic.[4] In the classroom, storytelling has long been recognized as an effective teaching tool for almost every subject, and research on storytelling in the context of instruction abounds.[5]

As growing dependence on technology threatens to cut our ties to both our past and the many traditional cultures that make up the nation and the world, storytelling serves as a means of recapturing the past, relaying values to another generation, and reconnecting humans with one another. Storytelling is a tool that can be effectively used in schools for instruction and building reading interests and skills.

WHAT DEFINES STORYTELLING AS MULTICULTURAL?

Multicultural storytelling is reflective of a people's history, cultural perspective and contributions. For the purpose of the Multicultural Storytelling Project, we seek to identify and share the stories of people whose history and cultures have traditionally been marginalized in our society.

In our opinion, multiculturalism is not a fad. It is a recognition that diversity is a fact of life and that past efforts to address racial, ethnic, cultural, religious, and other differences among people have fallen short. Storytelling can change hearts and heal old wounds. Our goal is to show how stories and the art of storytelling should become an integral fabric of life and education in our society. Mythology, folklore, fables, and traditional stories used in multicultural storytelling show that we as a people diverse with many cultures, are one country.

What defines storytelling as multicultural? Prime sources for stories are the folktales and myths of the world. Stories that illustrate the customs, beliefs, and traditions of a culture and transmit those cultural values can be termed multicultural. Whether a class of American children, regardless of their own cultural background, is listening to Navajo coyote legends, traditional Yoruba tales, or the myths of ancient Greece, they are being exposed to multicultural stories.

Harris identifies three major objectives in incorporating multicultural storytelling and/or children's literature into curricula:

1. It is important to validate minority experiences not commonly represented in literature, media, and the arts. This is crucial if the American education system is to avoid the creation and perpetuation of feelings of alienation and bitterness among "People of Color."

2. Preparing students for a life in a world characterized by diversity of race, ethnicity, culture, religion, gender so as to promote mutual respect, tolerance, and understanding, to foster greater appreciation for diversity and clearer communication among all people.
3. Cultivating and instilling in students a greater appreciation for all people and that all people are valued and are important individuals.[6]

When used in the curricula, multicultural storytelling advances literacy among ethnic groups by linking stories to culture. Secondly, multicultural storytelling also builds a greater understanding of our diverse cultures and the contributions each has made to the growth and development of America, and builds bridges among those cultures. This cultural awareness humanizes people in general and emphasizes the commonality of the human experience.

THE ACADEMIC LIBRARY'S ROLE IN STORYTELLING

When we discuss the Texas A&M University Libraries Multicultural Storytelling Project with, well, almost anyone, the first question that arises is, almost inevitably, "Why in the world is an academic library interested in something like storytelling? Isn't that more of a public library activity?" The following questions are certainly valid: (1) Why should an academic library be interested in storytelling, multicultural or otherwise? (2) How does this activity tie in with the mission and goals of a university library?

The academic library plays a significant role in the cultural arena of storytelling. Multicultural storytelling can become a vehicle for the academic library to enrich teacher preparation programs, to forge positive partnerships with teaching departments, to empower students to use library collections more effectively, and to provide a means of outreach to the community both within the university and in general.

Forging Partnerships Through Liaison

Over the past ten years, one area that has gained increased attention in the academic library community is that of active liaison with academic departments. Librarians strive to become participants in the educational process not only by providing materials, but also by forming partnerships with teaching departments. In a storytelling program, close partnership with the education department is essential since the primary focus of the program has to do with pre-service training for education professionals.

Education is not the only department that can benefit from the library interest in multicultural storytelling. Anthropology, especially in the areas of folklore and traditions, and English, in the study of children's literature and traditional literature, can also be involved with the library's multicultural storytelling initiative. Historians can be drawn into project activities as well.

Enriching Teacher Preparation Programs

One of the basic tenets of library instruction is that students become information literate in the education process, as evidenced by the adoption of information literacy standards by the Association of College and Research Libraries.[7] This goal must be even greater for colleges of education as they graduate pre-service teachers who will be leaders in the nation's classrooms. The pre-service teacher should feel comfortable enough with his/her newly acquired research skills to pass them on to the students they will be teaching. Academic librarians are equally concerned about instructional methods used to facilitate the acquisition of research skills in a multicultural education environment. Due to the proliferation of information and resources, coupled with the need to teach students, academic librarians must find ways of collaborating with faculty to help students acquire the skills for becoming teacher-researchers and lifelong learners.

Pre-service education professionals are learning the teaching skills they will use throughout a career. One of the skills is speaking before a group. Everyone has heard that most Americans fear speaking in public. College students are no exception and yet, as teachers, these students will speak all day to a class that must be kept interested and engaged. Students who learn and practice storytelling can not only build confidence through experience, but also learn that mastery of storytelling gives them the methods of preparation and skill to make effective presentations.

As the demographics of the American population shifts, teachers face classes that are increasingly multicultural. For example, California's general population has already surpassed the minority-majority status. The White population is now 49.8 percent.[8] The Texas school population has also surpassed minority-majority status.[9] It is projected that by the year 2030, the Texas public elementary and secondary school population will be 70 percent minority, while 57 percent of students of minority-majority will be enrolled in the higher education institutions of the state.[10] Teachers need to be culturally aware of the traditions of the various constituents of their classes. Through multicultural storytelling, they learn, whether consciously or not, about other cultures and become better prepared to interact with students and parents from differing cultures.

Storytelling in the Context of Instruction

The essential connection between teaching and storytelling is that storytelling is instinctually and naturally allied with learning and teaching. In an illustration of the versatility and widespread use of narrative as a teaching tool, the following examples from recently published studies reveal the ways in which storytelling is used in the classroom. Thea Canizo writes in *Science Scope* on using storytelling to teach "Myths and Legends of the Sky," combining astronomy and folklore from a variety of ethnic backgrounds.[11] Kathryn Holly Fox, in her article "Storytelling: The Real Story," writes of using storytelling as a motivational tool in high school English classes.[12] In their article "Teaching as a Sensory Activity: Making the Maya Come to Life," Dennis Banks and Deborah Gallagher describe the use of storytelling to heighten student interest in social studies.[13] "Lives and Other Stories: Neglected Aspects of the Teacher's Art," an article by John E. Wills, Jr., discusses using storytelling to make a college-level Chinese history course more "understandable and authentic."[14] Janet L. Glass, in "Everyone Loves a Good Story: Take the Time," examines the experience of using children's literature and storytelling as a part of an elementary school Spanish program.[15] "Quilts and Tangrams: Linking Literature and Geometry," an article by Gerry Bohning and Rebecca Williams, discusses the use of children's literature and the folk art of quilting to teach mathematical thinking skills.[16] In "The Art of Situated Narrative: A Tool to Teach Environmental Ethics," Danielle M. Wirth and Julia A. Gamon write about using storytelling to create psychological changes in listeners and discuss how professional storytellers select, learn, and tell stories.[17] "Teaching Stories: Viewing a Cultural Diversity Course Through the Lens of Narrative" by Ann C. Berlak illustrates one of the many programs using storytelling and narrative to promote multicultural awareness.[18] And lastly, "Reform of the College Science Lecture Through Storytelling" by John A. Knox.[19] The title says it all.

Bibliographic Instruction for Effective Library Use

Identifying stories and finding variants of familiar folktales for use in performance are basic skills for students to acquire in a storytelling program. In collaboration with an education department, a library may offer bibliographic instruction classes that provide information to students on library resources and research skills. For pre-service teachers, this skill is critical as they plan instructional units and develop lesson plans for discovery and inquiry of various cultures and disciplines.

THE MULTICULTURAL STORYTELLING PROJECT AT TEXAS A&M UNIVERSITY: DEVELOPMENT AND STRUCTURE

The mission of the Multicultural Storytelling Project is to utilize, study, promote, and research storytelling as an art and instructional tool. The Project focuses on exploring the oral and traditional literature of African American, Asian American, European American, Hispanic American, Jewish American, and Native American cultures. The Project seeks to spread understanding of how these and other traditional cultures use stories to communicate universal truths, heal hearts, enrich minds, and build a stronger community. The overarching concept and challenge for the Project is to equip pre-service teachers with valuable tools and resources to educate students to live in a culturally diverse society, while becoming productive citizens.

The Multicultural Storytelling Project, developed by education librarians in the Education and Media Services Department of the Texas A&M University Libraries, built bridges not only to the College of Education but also to the English and Anthropology departments of the College of Liberal Arts. This enabled students to use library collections more effectively. The Project has also been providing outreach services to this audience as well as the university community and the general community at large.

Preliminary research by the authors shows that no other storytelling organization exists with a mission specifically focused on multicultural storytelling as an instructional tool.[20] However, five academic institutions in the country (East Tennessee State University, University of Rhode Island, Texas Women's University, South Mountain Community College in Phoenix (Arizona), and Eastern Connecticut State University) do offer advanced degrees in storytelling, some in their schools of library science.

Academic partnerships between teaching departments and libraries are natural and critical in an age of electronic information. The Multicultural Storytelling Project has collaborated with teaching departments in several areas including:

- Training pre-service professionals and students in children's literature classes, in conjunction with the College of Education faculty, on the art of multicultural storytelling.
- Teaching pre-service and professional educators, in conjunction with the College of Education faculty, on the use of multicultural storytelling as an instructional aid and tool.
- Collaborating with school districts and schools to promote the use of multicultural storytelling.
- Incorporating multicultural storytelling in children's literature classes taught by the English Department.
- Developing efforts with Department of Anthropology faculty to promote multicultural storytelling as an aspect of oral history, folk stories, and the study of cultures.
- Aiding the Office of the English Language Institute in using multicultural storytelling to teach students learning English-as-a-second language.

Collaboration and cooperation will aid in the development of the Multicultural Storytelling Project as a nationally recognized vehicle for promoting multicultural storytelling.

The Project requires effective coordination as well as interdisciplinary consultation and guidance. An advisory committee of faculty from participating departments with expertise in related fields was established early in the Project's development. It included faculty from three teaching departments: the Department of Teaching, Learning and Culture of the College of Education, the Department of English, and the Department of Anthropology, plus administrators from the Provost's Office and the Office of Multicultural Services. As part of community outreach, the director of the local public library system, who has a strong commitment to library services to children, was invited to become an Advisory Board member. Because of the University's unique relationship with the George Bush Presidential Library, the education coordinator of the Bush Presidential Library joined the Advisory Board as well. Dr. Donna Norton, an internationally recognized expert on children's literature and liaison to the library from the College of Education, was elected chair of the Advisory Board.

THE MULTICULTURAL STORYTELLING FESTIVAL

The keystone of the year's activities of the Multicultural Storytelling Project was the first Multicultural Storytelling Festival. Planning and hosting the Spring 2000 Multicultural Storytelling Festival increased awareness of the Storytelling Project as a continuing campus initiative. After more than a year of intensive planning by the Advisory Board and Festival Planning Committee, the Festival drew together six professional storytellers from various cultures along with aspiring college student storytellers who performed for university students, local school children, and interested members of the community. The Festival lasted three days and included the following activities:

1. the grand opening ceremony;
2. storytelling performances held at area schools;
3. small tent storytelling sessions held on the Bush Library grounds;
4. workshops on storytelling;
5. a logo contest to develop a new logo for the theme, "Stories from the Heart";
6. college student storyteller performances;
7. a storytelling concert "Storytelling Jamboree" for the general public;
8. trickster tales on April Fool's Day;
9. book fair offering resources from the professional storytellers and major storytelling publishers;
10. outreach to student organizations serving as vendors at the storytelling concert; and
11. establishment of the Texas A&M Storytelling Guild to assist interested students and community members in developing their storytelling skills.

The Festival presented a research opportunity for college students as they evaluated the children's responses to the storytelling presentations. College student storytellers were also able to observe professional storytellers' techniques and methods of working with various groups while some served as assistants for presentations.

Purposes of the Spring 2000 Multicultural Storytelling Festival

The purposes identified for the Spring 2000 Multicultural Storytelling Festival were to:

- Observe and commemorate the official opening ceremonies of the Multicultural Storytelling Project with memorable events in keeping with the Project's mission and objectives.
- Offer pre-service teachers in the College of Education and educators in the field workshop opportunities and experiences with professional storytellers, illustrating both the value of storytelling as an educational tool and techniques for using it in the classroom.
- Provide students in public schools with an opportunity to hear professional storytellers from major ethnic groups, thereby encouraging appreciation of both ethnicity and diversity, and the universality of various cultures' values and beliefs.
- Provide community-wide opportunities for all ages and ethnic groups to enjoy and personally get involved with the age-old and multicultural tradition of storytelling by both listening to and engaging in storytelling activities.
- Facilitate the training of students and professionals in the education field in multicultural storytelling.
- Provide the community with a memorable introduction to multicultural storytelling.
- Encourage partnerships among and between university faculty, graduate and undergraduate students, professional educators, librarians, civic leaders, parents, grandparents, and others interested in storytelling for cultural and educational purposes.
- Demonstrate how multicultural storytelling can aid classroom effectiveness and promote understanding among different cultures.
- Enhance acceptance of the value of multicultural storytelling across age, ethnic, and institutional boundaries.
- Promote multicultural storytelling as a tool for aiding in the instruction of respectful cultural awareness as well as universal ethics and values.

Strategic Planning Concepts for the Festival

The Multicultural Storytelling Festival was a new concept to the south central part of Texas. Although there are festivals nearby geographically (such as the Tejas Storytelling Association's Texas Storytelling Festival in Denton, Texas,[21] and the George West Story Fest in George West, Texas[22]), none had an emphasis similar to the purposes of the Project. The development of the Festival was guided by five planning concepts. First, a sense of community. This is one of the most important aspects of designing a festival. The Festival was a way of launching the Multicultural Storytelling Project, and the goal was to announce the Project to the University community as well as to the cities of Bryan and College Station.

The second planning concept was to focus on performance and instruction. This was a new learning experience for everyone involved. This concept became our main emphasis for student participation for college students as well as school-aged children.

The third planning concept was that demonstrations and instruction would be implemented using the following:

- Professional storytellers would be selected from various cultural groups so that students would be able to make comparisons and contrast styles and identify cultural characteristics
- Local storytellers from the campus and community
- College student storytellers
- A workshop for seniors to tell their own stories
- Workshops on storytelling techniques for teachers
- Workshops on using multicultural stories in the classroom
- Cross purpose multicultural storytelling; i.e., oral narratives and multicultural stories
- Folklore and multicultural stories and life stories

The fourth planning concept was to provide an excellent storytelling and learning experience without cost to the participants. Building relationships with various segments of the community and various audiences was seen as critical. The desire to establish a safe environment for students, faculty and community was the fifth planning concept. As participants begin to develop storytelling skills, they need to feel free to talk, discuss and develop without inhibitions, and with knowledge of committed support. For this purpose, the Texas A&M Storytelling Guild was organized.

Artistic Vision in Selection of Storytellers

Selecting storytellers requires an artistic vision of how to utilize the talents and skills of the tellers to reach the target audiences. Storytellers are members of a unique community and are a special breed of artists who are kind, caring, and "soulful" advocates of humanity everywhere. The selected storytellers were invited to share stories that would prove to be successful demonstrations on "how to do storytelling" for first-time college student "tellers." All presentations by professional storytellers were to be interactive.

Several criteria for selection of the first featured storytellers were identified, namely: good entertainers, good interaction with the identified target audiences, good voice quality and diction, good physical poise, and good story composition.

The Project Planning Committee as well as the Advisory Board sought tellers with a variety of styles and from a variety of cultures. Storytellers all responded favorably to the fact that this was a first effort on a limited budget. Three of the storytellers were workshop presenters as well as tellers. Balance was one of the key ingredients in planning the format of the storytelling festival. Most of the selected storytellers knew one another and had worked together at other festivals. As a result, they were receptive to their order of story presentations at the "Storytelling Jamboree" and the thematic presentation of stories on "April Fool's Day." College student tellers were placed first in each presentation. The outcome was that the festival had its own story with a "beginning"-an elaborate opening ceremony held to launch the Multicultural Storytelling Project publicly; a "middle"-during the festival as the audiences and participants enjoyed many storytelling activities, and an "end"-a closure in the form of a traditional goodbye story from the Cherokee heritage.

Every aspect of entertaining the storytellers reflected respect for the art as well as for the storytellers themselves. This ensured the establishment of a lasting relationship with the presenters. A welcome luncheon was held in their honor prior to the Festival grand opening ceremony.

Target Audience

The target audience determines the success or failure of a festival. Pre-service teachers from the College of Education, professional educators, school librarians, and elementary students in grades 3 through 5 were the audience for this festival. A class of kindergartners and their teachers came unannounced to the festival but were well received by the storytellers. Identifying target audiences did not preclude other people from attending the festival. Participation by college student tellers provided opportunities for the students to showcase their growth and development as tellers.

Funding Sources for the Festival

As the saying goes, "Money makes the world go around," and funding the Project was a major activity for the administrative staff. The Texas A&M University Libraries provided staff and financial support, but this was not sufficient to provide for all of the Project activities. External funds were obtained from local and state sources with the coordinator of the Multicultural Storytelling Project leading the fundraising efforts. Gifts and grants came from both the non-profit and government sectors, especially those organizations supporting the arts. Significant support came from the University itself, especially the Provost's Office and the Office of Multicultural Services. Other sources of funding included the Texas Council on the Arts, and Junior League of Brazos Valley. For future funding, the Project seeks to secure grant funding and has submitted a proposal to the Institute of Museum and Library Services.

Publicity Strategy

The success of any special event rests heavily on the publicity it receives. The publicity strategy for the storytelling festival included the following:

- registration brochure and mailing,
- press releases to campus and local media,
- feature story in *Insite* magazine, a community-focused publication,
- television and radio interviews with festival coordinators,
- grand opening ceremony and reception,
- Web site *http://library.tamu.edu/edms/storytelling/* with photo archives of Festival events, and
- wrap-up publicity in local media and annual report.

Community Outreach

While members of the urban university community have access to regular storytelling sessions at local public libraries, in smaller cities the establishment of storytelling programs at a university provides a useful service for the community. As the face of the student body becomes more diverse, not only culturally, but also in terms of age, storytelling is a welcome addition to other cultural resources offered by the university.

International students may welcome opportunities to share traditional stories from their cultures, and this can be an important part of a multicultural storytelling program. Involvement of these student groups gives a program access to many cultures that might otherwise not be represented and adds a depth and richness, which can only be of benefit to all involved.

School children preparing for University Interscholastic League Storytelling competitions may also benefit from observing storytellers. A program such as this is a means of getting children and parents excited about storytelling and may encourage participation in storytelling activities.

Another important method of outreach to the community is for the Multicultural Storytelling Project to provide professional storytellers to local schools. In addition, many professional storytellers offer workshops on storytelling in the classroom. For example, one workshop at the Festival offered students and teachers (at no cost) instruction on storytelling techniques for use in preparation for Texas Essential Knowledge Skills (TEKS) and Texas Assessment of Academic Skills (TAAS) standardized tests used in Texas public schools.

Other opportunities for community outreach are limited only by the imagination. Programs for senior citizens to share their life stories can be initiated in conjunction with genealogy and oral history projects. Libraries may be able to use CD technology to re-record folktales on audio tapes in a more permanent form. Videotaping projects can provide a visual archive of local history materials.

Evaluation of the Festival: A Storyteller's Point of View

One of the featured professional storytellers at the festival described the event in the following manner:

> What an adventure! Texas A&M's first Multicultural, across the curriculum, Storytelling Festival, designed to give undergraduate and graduate, elementary and middle school students a look into the effective world of student/teacher communication, was an eye-opening experience into the future of education.
>
> The Library Storytelling Coordinating Team, along with its Advisory Board, brought together a mix of storytelling backgrounds,

styles, cultures, and experience, with each representative a professional storyteller in his or her own right, to demonstrate that storytelling can illustrate the value and merit of each and every
academic subject. In addition, the festival showed the inter-rela-
tionships that exist between the various academic disciplines as
they are applied in the world of work. Reading, writing, speaking,
spelling, counting, and measuring is not nearly as useful singularly
as they are in concert. So stories are told.

Using superb arrangements to engage the tellers; provide each
teller the means by which his or her story is best told, was a re-
freshing atmosphere in which to pass along a tradition as old as
drum beats and dance, yet, still communicate the truth and wisdom
of the ages. Should Texas A&M continue lighting this all but for-
gotten path of learning and teaching, they will be the "torch
bearer" which lights the way to character building, value appreciation and accurate communication.

Evaluation of the Festival: The Planning Team

As the planning team began to look back over the activities and
events planned, we had to keep in mind the strategic planning concepts
of the festival. First and foremost, we were observing and commemo-
rating the launching of the Multicultural Storytelling Project to the University community as well as to the Bryan/College Station community
with memorable events in keeping with the Project's mission and objectives. Secondly, we were also opening up a collaborative relationship
that would ensure new learning opportunities for pre-service teachers.
Festivals in the future would not be planned on as large a scale as the
first one. More emphasis will be placed on learning situations and getting more of the target audiences to attend events. In addition, recruiting
more participation by the History Department and the Anthropology
Department as well as the classes in the developing area of the arts on
campus will be addressed.

The consensus of the Festival Planning Committee was that the number of sites for activities may have hampered the number of people attending various events. Weather was also unkind on Saturday morning.
However, this did not prevent the storytellers from performing and creating a wonderful listening situation for those who attended "Trick-
sters' Tales" and other Saturday activities. Some of the Advisory Board
members were concerned about the size of the tents used. These

changes in equipment will be made for future festivals. It was also suggested that storytellers be able to share one large tent. In that way they would not appear as if they were competing with one another.

One Advisory Board member felt that "the Festival was a great success!" The storytellers were all excellent, the children and college students seemed to enjoy themselves and appreciate the presentations, the workshops were well attended, and the community came out, especially to the Palace Theatre. College student storytellers were well incorporated into the Festival and praised repeatedly for their efforts.

One of the suggestions that has been repeatedly given is the development of a course on storytelling itself, to be offered in the College of Education. The Coordinating Team and the Advisory Board are set to pursue this idea in the coming year.

CONCLUSION

There has never been a better time for storytelling. All over the world, people are re-uniting with this age-old art. The benefits of its complete usage will last a lifetime and generations to come. Storytelling is "an essential element in our apparent purpose for being, which is to understand and articulate life, to make creation conscious of itself."[23]

Again, we ask, "Why is an academic library interested in multicultural storytelling?" The university community is where students expand their learning opportunities and make critical decisions about and for the future. By initiating and pursuing a program of multicultural storytelling aimed primarily at teachers in training, the academic library can strengthen its capability and impact on students and generations to come. The library will serve as a change agent by its participation in storytelling on how people live and communicate. It will be able to reach and touch hearts the way no video, CD, or DVD possibly could. The academic library-the center of the university community-provides short- and long-term benefits by enriching teacher training, which benefits all citizens of the state.

The success of the Multicultural Storytelling Festival has shown that a university community can be an appropriate venue for storytelling activities that serve the goals of education. Pre-service teachers gained valuable experience that was linked directly to their academic preparation for instruction on children's literature and storytelling in the classroom. Valuable partnerships were begun among the public schools and the College of Education. The workshops on multicultural storytelling techniques and applications for the classroom provided unique opportunities for the academy to enrich the skills of professional educators, extending theory into practice.

NOTES

1. Robert D. Putnam, *Bowling Alone: The Collapse and Revival of American Community* (New York: Simon and Schuster, 2000), 31-133.

2. Storytelling Foundation International, "About the Festival: A Little History," [online] available from http://www.storytellingfestival.net/festival2000/history.htm [cited 15 December 2000].

3. Rives Collins and Pamela J. Cooper, *The Power of Story: Teaching Through Storytelling* (London: David Fulton Publishers, 2000), 1.

4. David Adams Leeming, "Once Upon a Time," in *Storytelling Encyclopedia: Historical, Cultural, and Multiethnic Approaches to Oral Traditions Around the World*, ed. David Adams Leeming (Phoenix, AZ: Oryx Press, 1997), 3.

5. For examples see Thea L. Canizo, "Legends and Myths of the Sky," *Science Scope* 17, no. 6 (March 1994): 31-3; Kathryn Holly Fox, "Storytelling: In the Real Story," *Reading Improvement* 30, no. 3 (fall 1993): 171-55; Dennis Banks and Deborah Gallagher, "Teaching as a Sensory Activity: Making the Maya Come to Life," *Social Studies and the Young Learner* 5, no. 4 (March-April 1993): 11-12; John Wills, Jr., "Lives and Other Stories: Neglected Aspects of the Teachers' Art," *History Teacher* 26, no. 1 (November 1992): 33-49; Janet L. Glass, "Everyone Loves a Good Story: Take the Time," *Hispania.* 77, no. 2 (May 1994): 295-97; Gerry Bohning and Rebecca Williams, "Quilts and Tangrams: Linking Literature and Geometry," *Childhood Education* 73, no. 2 (winter 1996-97): 83-7; Danielle M. Wirth and Julia A. Gamon, "The Art of Situated Narrative: A Tool to Teach Environmental Ethics," *Journal of Vocational Education Research* 24, no. 1 (1999): 45-61; Ann C. Berlak, "Teaching Stories: Viewing a Cultural Diversity Course Through the Lens of Narrative," *Theory into Practice* 35, no. 2 (spring 1996): 93-101; John A. Knox, "Reform of the College Science Lecture Through Storytelling," *Journal of College Science Teaching* 26, no. 6 (May 1997): 388-92.

6. Violet J. Harris, ed., *Using Multiethnic Literature in the K-8 Classroom* (Norwood, MA: Christopher-Gordon, 1997), 122.

7. Association of College and Research Libraries, "Information Literacy Competency Standards for Higher Education: The Final Version, Approved January 2000," *College and Research Libraries News* 61, no. 3 (March 2000): 207-15.

8. United States Census, *USA Counties 1998 California General Profile* [online] available from http://www.census.gov/statab/USA98/06/000.txt [cited 11 January 2001].

9. Texas Education Agency, Division of Performance Reporting, *Pocket Edition, 1999-2000 Texas Public Schools Statistics* [online] available from http://www.tea.state.tx.us/perfreport/pocked/2000/index.html [cited 3 April 2001].

10. Texas State Data Center, *Texas Population Projections Program* [online] available from http://txsdc.tamu.edu/tpepp/txpoprj.html [cited 11 January 2001].

11. Canizo, "Legends and Myths of the Sky."

12. Fox, "Storytelling: In the Real Story."

13. Banks and Gallagher, "Teaching as a Sensory Activity."

14. Wills, "Lives and Other Stories."

15. Glass, "Everyone Loves a Good Story."

16. Bohning and Williams, "Quilts and Tangrams."

17. Wirth and Gamon, "The Art of Situated Narrative."

18. Berlak, "Teaching Stories."

19. Knox, "Reform of the College Science Lecture Through Storytelling."

20. Johnnieque Love, John Harer, and Candace R. Benefiel, "Storytelling: Resources, Collections, Programs and Services," (manuscript, 2000).

21. Tejas Storytelling Festival, "Texas Storytelling Festival 2000" [online] available from http://www.tejasstorytelling.com/ [cited 15 December 2000].

22. George West Texas, "George West Story Fest" [online] available from http://www.georgewest.org/storyfest.htm [cited 15 December 2000].

23. Leeming, "Once Upon a Time," 3.

Aboriginal Students in Canada: A Case Study of Their Academic Information Needs and Library Use

. Deborah A. Lee

SUMMARY. This study involved the use of personal interviews of six Aboriginal students at the University of Alberta in the fall of 1999. This

Deborah A. Lee is of Cree, Iroquois and European ancestry. She undertook this research for partial fulfillment of her course-based MLIS degree at the University of Alberta, Edmonton, Canada. Ms. Lee is Reference Librarian in Training, National Library of Canada, Ottawa, Ontario, Canada (E-mail: *deborah.lee@nlc-bnc.ca*).

The author wishes to acknowledge her gratitude for the conscientious participation of the six Aboriginal students interviewed for this research project and the assistance of the Office of Native Student Services at the University of Alberta. She would also like to thank Dr. Olive Dickason for her review of the section on "The Indigenous perspective."

Acknowledgement also goes to Dr. Alvin Schrader, Director of the School of Library and Information Studies at the University of Alberta; Dr. Olenka Bilash, Associate Professor, Department of Secondary Education, University of Alberta; Gwynneth Evans, Director General, National and International Programs, National Library of Canada; Mary Bond, Acting Manager, Public Services, National Library of Canada; and Teresa Y. Neely, University of Maryland, Baltimore County, MD and Janet Lee-Smeltzer at Harris County Public Library, Houston, TX.

Ms. Lee is grateful for the financial support received from the Department of Education at the University of Alberta, the Faculty of Graduate Studies at the University of Alberta, the Library Association of Alberta, and the National Library of Canada in order to complete this research and present it at the Big 12 Plus Libraries Consortium Diversity Now Conference in Austin, TX, April, 2000.

[Haworth co-indexing entry note]: "Aboriginal Students in Canada: A Case Study of Their Academic Information Needs and Library Use." Lee, Deborah A. Co-published simultaneously in *Journal of Library Administration* (The Haworth Information Press, an imprint of The Haworth Press, Inc.) Vol. 33, No. 3/4, 2001, pp. 259-292; and: *Diversity Now: People, Collections, and Services in Academic Libraries* (ed: Teresa Y. Neely, and Kuang-Hwei (Janet) Lee-Smeltzer) The Haworth Information Press, an imprint of The Haworth Press, Inc., 2001, pp. 259-292. Single or multiple copies of this article are available for a fee from The Haworth Document Delivery Service [1-800-HAWORTH, 9:00 a.m. - 5:00 p.m. (EST). E-mail address: getinfo@haworthpressinc.com].

259

article includes a brief literature review of other articles that consider adult Aboriginal people as library patrons and a section on Indigenous knowledge and values. Findings include three main concerns: a lack of Indigenous resources in the library system; a lack of resource or research development concerning Indigenous issues; and a lack of services recognizing the Indigenous values of "being in relationship" and reciprocity. *[Article copies available for a fee from The Haworth Document Delivery Service: 1-800-HAWORTH. E-mail address: <getinfo@haworthpressinc.com> Website: <http://www.HaworthPress.com> © 2001 by The Haworth Press, Inc. All rights reserved.]*

KEYWORDS. Aboriginal, Indigenous, Native, minorities, college and university libraries-services to North American Indians, multiculturalism, Indigenous knowledge, Indigenous epistemology, personal interviews, library anxiety, use studies

INTRODUCTION

This research was driven by several questions: How were Aboriginal students coping with a possible lack of library resources encapsulating a holistic worldview? Did they feel that most mainstream sources did not support their Indigenous worldview? How were they accessing meaningful articles and texts to assist with their coursework assignments and research? Was the University of Alberta library system meeting their academic information needs? If so, how? And if not, how might it do so? This project, then, had two intentions. One was to provide a venue to explore Aboriginal students' experiences in an academic library setting. The other was to demonstrate how these students were or were not coping with relevant and meaningful information retrieval to succeed in their academic programs. What occurred, however, was that the information gathered turned out to be very rich in content and far more than anticipated. Indeed, the participants were frank in their discussions of not only their academic information needs and their library use but also their insights into concerns regarding the impact of library administration decisions on students and suggestions for improving library services.

The value of this research is threefold. First, there is a paucity of library and information studies (LIS) literature which considers Aboriginal adults as library users; thus, this research is an attempt to partially fill an unacceptable gap in the literature. Second, there is a growing Aboriginal student population at post-secondary institutions across Canada who have not had an opportunity to express their concerns about academic library resources and services. In the fall term of 1999, the population of this student group at the University of Alberta in Edmonton, Alberta, Canada was approximately 900 students, about three percent of the total student population. Furthermore, published statistics on the growth of Aboriginal post-secondary student populations across Canada offer some revealing information:

> Post-secondary enrollments [of Native people] have increased dramatically, with 60 Indian students going to university in 1960, 432 in 1970, 4455 in 1980 and 5800 in 1985. In 1989, 18,535 Indian students were enrolled in colleges and universities in Canada.[1]

Moreover, with the very low representation of Aboriginal people in the field of librarianship in Canada, there has been little advocacy done on behalf of Aboriginal people in general and their information needs. And third, if there is, indeed, a lack of representation of the Indigenous perspective in library resources, this would mean that non-Aboriginal faculty and students are missing the opportunity to explore or study this material and become more inter-culturally aware. It is all the more crucial given that this university offers both undergraduate and graduate programs in Native Studies and First Nations Education respectively.

LITERATURE REVIEW

A few recent and relevant resources on the topic of library services to Aboriginal people do exist. I have chosen the term Aboriginal to represent those people Indigenous to the land of North America and Australia, including those also known as Native, Indian, Métis, Inuit, First Nations and Indigenous. The following list is by no means exhaustive but includes most recent (from 1995 to the present) surveys that concern adult Aboriginal patrons. Hannum's 1995 article is the most relevant and recent Canadian source that considers adult Aboriginal people as a target user group.[2] There are two other more dated Canadian sources: a 1990 article on bookmobile services by Skrzeszewski, Huggins-Chan and Clarke,[3] and Bright's 1992 work on the policy of five Canadian provinces in serving on-reserve populations.[4] Hannum's study surveyed librarians at public libraries across the province of British Columbia regarding library use by Native people. Some interesting observations were presented in this study, such as the kinds of library services used and factors which influenced Native peoples' use of the library. For instance, Hannum's analysis of the data indicated some rather sophisticated public library usage by Aboriginals such as use of interlibrary loan services and microform readers for historical research purposes. As for factors influencing this usage, the most telling were examples of commitments made to Aboriginal people, both by library personnel and by leaders in the Aboriginal communities. Some libraries consulted with Aboriginal people for their input into collection development procedures and initiation of culturally-oriented library programs. A few such examples included First Nations storytellers/writers events, puppet shows of legends, and the involvement of Native children in summer reading programs. In addition, two libraries had active Native board members soliciting materials for the library. Wherever this collaboration was in place, library usage by Aboriginal people was higher than in libraries which did not use such relationship-building practices. The primary drawback to this study, however, is that Native people were not surveyed for their input, something Hannum recognized and recommended for future research. She suggested querying both Native users and non-users.[5]

Patterson's 1995 study looked at information needs of and services to Native Americans but from the perspective of tribal libraries, of which very few exist in Canada. This study provides an historical overview of how Native libraries came to be, including reference to New York state legislation in 1977 which provided "permanent support for Indian libraries, allowing them to become full members of public library systems."[6] Patterson also reviewed tribal library information needs studies and categorized the earlier information needs as falling into two categories: problem-solving knowledge and resources dealing with cultural heritage, i.e., Native language materials and various formats of oral histories. Her own experience told her there were many other information needs, including a need for theses. The following quote from a Navajo elder explains why:

> People are always coming out here studying us. They ask us questions. We tell them what they want to know we give them our time, then they go away and write their dissertations and theses. But we

never know what they write. We want copies of their studies so we can see what they write about us. We want our young people to see what others say about us.[7]

She concluded the article with some suggestions for future resource access for Native Americans via the use of technology and public awareness. Some of these included distance education for training staff, full-text CD-ROMs, publications and video productions in Native languages, access to tribal documents and photographs housed in national repositories and resource sharing by way of networked tribal libraries.[8]

The most helpful study I found is a more recent article by Novak and Robinson who used the focus group method to capture Aboriginal students' voices at a particular campus of the Queensland University of Technology in Australia.[9] This campus was chosen because it was one where Indigenous students had a lower profile and where a higher proportion of Aboriginal students were non-borrowers than at other campus locations. The library administration focused on cultural and motivational issues, with a secondary goal to explore academic library usage. Some areas covered by the study were:

> . . . student consideration of their own learning strategies and possible links to library usage, attitudes to authority and how these might influence relationships with the library . . . and needs of [Indigenous] students in relation to library services.[10]

Efforts made to incorporate Indigenous values into the methodological procedures used in this research were of particular interest. For instance, the project was announced at a social gathering of Indigenous students and staff. Also, two community-based consultants were hired to see the project through: One was a storyteller whose role was to inspire everyone involved, including students, library staff and funding bodies, to tell their stories in an atmosphere of mutual respect. This occurred by having the storyteller explore her own vulnerabilities through story and then by having the others tell the stories back in a way that each would understand. The other consultant was an Indigenous theatre director and a graduate of the university with many contacts at the Indigenous unit on campus. He was successful in encouraging participation in the project.[11]

The results spoke of both a physical and psychological intimidation experienced by Indigenous students in the library. Students felt that the intimidation was brought on by a denial of their history and current existence and by evidence of racist graffiti. These students also expressed that "positive recognition would help to balance the cultural face the library represents."[12] Other areas of concern included several dimensions of alienation felt by students. One dimension was that of alienation of culture, especially in learning a new language which made key word searching difficult. Another was alienation from staff because some students felt that staff had no time for them and some were ashamed to ask for help. Students also mentioned difficulties in finding specific Aboriginal and Torres Strait Islander materials and a desire to be able to access other universities' collections.[13]

Perhaps the most inspiring aspect of this article was the commitment of the Queensland University of Technology's library to the Indigenous students evident in the recommendations formulated by the library as a result of the information gathered by this project. Some of these are listed below:

- pursuit of Indigenous artworks for installation in the libraries;
- library maintenance with an emphasis on removal of the racist graffiti;
- greater networking with the Indigenous unit on campus;
- a shift in the nature of bibliographic instruction for Indigenous students and in the location (to be delivered within the Indigenous unit) of the training;
- organization of awareness training for librarians to increase their sensitivity to the issues faced by Indigenous students;
- improvement of the library's Indigenous collections;
- renewed efforts to employ Indigenous persons within the library.[14]

THE INDIGENOUS PERSPECTIVE

In order for the reader to more fully appreciate the value of the information provided by the participants in this study, it is necessary to provide some background information on the Indigenous perspective. This task, for the most part, entails some exploration of Indigenous knowledge and values. The following text is based on my own experience as well as the work of others who are more accomplished writers in this area. A primary component of the Indigenous perspective is the importance of "being in relationship" to everyone and everything in one's environment. Related to this is the concept of inclusion. For a better understanding of the concept of being in relationship, I draw on the following passage by Thomas King:

> "All my relations" is at first a reminder of who we are and of our relationship with both our family and our relatives. It also reminds us of the extended relationship we share with all human beings. But the relationships that Native people see go further, to all the animals, to the birds, to the fish, to the plants, to all the animate and inanimate forms that can be seen or imagined. More than that, "all my relations" is an encouragement for us to accept the responsibilities we have within this universal family by living our lives in a harmonious and moral manner (a common admonishment is to say of someone that they act as if they have no relations).[15]

It seems to me that Indigenous people, being tribal people living within a community-oriented mindset (and a small community at that, where everyone knows everybody), are generally apt to spend more time and energy in maintaining "good" relations, perhaps as a means of survival. For instance, we may be more generous with what little we may have because our future may depend on it. Many Indigenous people are influenced by the saying, "What goes around comes around," such that we are generous because we strongly believe that the generosity will come back to us tenfold. At the same time, however, it seems that Indigenous people are also adamant about autonomous modes of being, which may also influence the ways in which they interact with people. By this I mean that Indigenous people are interested in self-determination; we want to tell our own stories using our own voices, and to find our own solutions to our problems. In the process, we resist and reject the paternalistic and arrogant approaches used by many non-Indigenous people. This sentiment is well expressed by Smith:

> It appalls us that the West can desire, extract and claim ownership of our ways of knowing, our imagery . . . and then simultaneously reject the people who created and developed those ideas and seek to deny them further opportunities to be creators of their own cultures and own nations.[16]

Closely connected to the concept of being in relationship with one's environment is the concept of reciprocity. In the Indigenous world view, reciprocity in relationships is often expected. Values of generosity and sharing are inherent in reciprocity, as is the responsibility of being concerned for others and the well-being of the community. A common motivation for any interaction in the community is the "win-win" situation. When both parties are concerned about beneficial interaction, they will be more interested in perpetuating ongoing interaction. Another factor to consider is that one's reputation in the community is largely based on one's service and commitment to the community; therefore, developing reciprocal relationships is paramount to one's own well-being. As the stakes are high for not cultivating these relationships, Indigenous people often take this way of thinking for granted and are amazed when they encounter situations with non-Indigenous people who are not this way inclined.

Also implied in reciprocity is the notion that there is a preference for interpersonal interaction rather than interaction with automation or other inanimate entities, because the quality of interaction with people has the potential to be more satisfying. For instance, there is more opportunity for humorous, fun, trickster-like and, especially, synergistic interaction, when people bounce creative ideas off of each other. This does not preclude, however, Indigenous people's use of automation for fun, creative and synergistic interaction, for instance, as occurs with their participation in e-mail, chat groups, listservs, etc.

Also paramount in Indigenous thought is the concept of "the circle," a concept perhaps best known through Paula Gunn Allen's *The Sacred Hoop*.[17] What follows is a brief explanation of the concept of the circle based on my own participation in the circle. The circle can be seen as a practical exercise for understanding the concept of "being in relationship," as it encapsulates the Indigenous values of respect, kindness, honesty, patience and equality. Furthermore, the cultural understanding of the concept of the circle is that everyone who comes to sit within the circle is a valued member and is there for a reason, regardless of the extent of their externalized participation. The spiritual power of what is said in the circle generates much understanding and healing for those who absorb the words, thereby fostering an internalized participation for those who listen. It is often said within the circle that it is enough for people to simply be there, as they will benefit simply from listening. This understanding also demonstrates the inclusive nature of the circle.

Respect is shown to each person in the circle by offering each person an opportunity to speak, without interruption, as his or her turn comes up. This is usually indicated by the passing and holding of a feather or "talking stone." Respect is also shown by honoring the understanding that each person has the choice to pass up the opportunity to speak and that each person is unique and has some quality or gift to contribute to the circle. Another way that respect is demonstrated is by understanding that what is said in the circle remains in the circle and is not to be repeated outside of the circle. The value of kindness is reflected in the welcoming nature of the opening remarks of the person facilitating the circle as well as in the tone used by participants in the circle. Participants understand that what is said in the circle is said in such a way that everyone's integrity is left intact. Furthermore, there are times when tears and manifestations of various emotions are expressed within the circle and it is understood that when this happens, kindness and respect are demonstrated for the courage shown by the participant in sharing these emotions.

The value of honesty is reflected in what is said in the circle. There is an understanding that each person who speaks must speak from the heart. It is often stated within circles that the most difficult journey a person makes is travelling from the mind (from intellectualizing) to the heart (to the honesty of sharing feelings). Balanced with this honesty, however, is the responsibility of maintaining everyone's integrity so that communication is done honestly and directly but also with compassion. A speaker demonstrates compassion by subtly acknowledging some understanding that everyone makes mistakes, including him- or herself.

The value of patience is evident in that accommodation is made for the varying amounts of time required by people within the circle to both express themselves and to feel comfortable in doing so. For instance, some people may not speak at all in the first few circles they attend and no one is pressured to speak if they don't yet feel comfortable. In other cases, people may speak for quite some time. Regardless, it is recognized that people are in varying stages of their healing and the presence or absence of a patient environment is one factor influencing their healing journey. On the other hand, the person who is speaking for quite some time must also balance their need to speak with their understanding of respect for others, in that the circle may have some time limits and it is essential that all people in the circle have the opportunity to speak. Finally, the value of equality is demonstrated in the understanding that no one person in the circle is more important than another. The structure of the circle is conducive to this understanding in that all people are able to see each other's faces and no one is afforded a priority position.

As is evident from this discussion, the circle has many facets and complexities, especially given that so many values are interlaced throughout the governance of the circle members' participation. In addition, one value often influences others so that a balancing act between values is often at work in the decisions participants make about what they say inside the circle. Thus, there are many checks in place to provide a safe environment. One last form of governance is that if the values of the circle are not respected, the circle will fall apart and few people would want to be responsible for this happening.

This section is by no means a comprehensive presentation of the Indigenous perspective; however, it does provide a basis for understanding something about the values of Indigenous people and how we think and interact in our communities. With this foundation in place, the reader can now better appreciate the value of the research undertaken with this group of Aboriginal students. In addition, many of the values discussed in this section are reflected in the studies presented in the literature review. For instance, Hannum found that where there was collaboration between the library and the Native community, participation in library programs and other use of the library by Native people increased.[18] This situation points to the values of respect and reciprocity, whereby the library management respected the input of Native people as well as the importance of establishing good relations through communication with the local or nearby Native people. Another example is provided by Patterson who wrote of the need, by the Navajo people, for theses and dissertations so that their youth had insight into what non-Indigenous people were writing about them.[19] This fact indicates a lack of reciprocity in the actions of non-Indigenous people. Clearly, if the researchers wanted to continue a relationship with the Navajo people they were researching, they would have supplied the people with copies of their theses and dissertations. Other examples of the Indigenous perspective can be seen in the Novak and Robinson study, such as the respect shown for Indigenous protocols and values by announcing the project at a social gathering of Indigenous people. Another show of respect in this study was the decision to employ the storyteller and community developer as a valid methodology for eliciting valuable information from Indigenous people.[20]

Throughout the remainder of this paper, I will attempt to relate various decisions made and responses provided to some of the values of the Indigenous perspective.

RESEARCH METHODOLOGY

Qualitative interviewing seemed to be the most effective method of collecting data for this research project, primarily because it offers person-to-person contact, which, as has been illustrated, is important for most Aboriginal people. Also, personal interviews are advantageous in that they can be done in a less formal and intimidating manner than other methodologies such as experimental. The focus group method might also be a consideration for future research with this target group; however, this method posed some drawbacks to this study. For instance, trying to gather all participants with busy schedules together simultaneously can seriously delay a research project. In addition, a skilled focus group facilitator who is also culturally sensitive is needed. As well, the common expectation that participants will be paid monetarily and receive refreshments at focus group gatherings may prove prohibitive without necessary funding in place. Because of the limited time and funds available to carry out this project, the personal interview method was determined to be the most suitable.

The most serious drawback with interviewing is that only a few participants can take part and share their thoughts and "voices" because of the time it takes to conduct and transcribe the interviews. Mail-in surveys have the potential to involve more participants, but are generally well-known for their low response rate.[21] In the case of Aboriginal people, without the personal contact, the response rate would most likely be even lower. This would be the case especially with studies done by emerging and less-established researchers, like myself, and on topics considered low priority by Aboriginal people. Unfortunately, libraries fall into this category at this point in time, as compared to land claim, poverty, unemployment and other social and political issues in the communities. Furthermore, the interviews were more likely to generate more in-depth responses. Thus, obtaining a few, qualitative and insightful interviews would be better than possibly even fewer responses and less probing survey data. Consequently, I developed a comprehensive interview schedule of 22 questions, some of which were multi-part (see Appendix).

Once the project was approved by the Ethics Review Committee of the School of Library and Information Studies program at the University of Alberta, the main obstacle to overcome was to find participants for the study. My first attempt was to present the project and solicit participants at an undergraduate Native Studies class on Research Methods. Although students in this class were keen to ask me questions about the project, none came forward to participate. A simultaneous approach was to develop an eye-catching poster and display it at six relevant locations on campus to attract Aboriginal students. Locations included the School of Native Studies bulletin board, the Office of Native Student Services bulletin board, the Aboriginal Students' Council lounge, and the First Nations Education Graduate program bulletin board. Posters were also left with representatives of the Aboriginal Law Student program and the Aboriginal Health Careers program. Only one student responded to the posters, a student who noticed them in the Aboriginal Students' Council lounge. My third and final approach was to present the project and solicit participants at a staff meeting of the Office of Native Student Services because many of the part-time staff were also students. This method attracted five participants, bringing the total to six students.

These methods reflect the Indigenous perspective and an Indigenous way of making contact. The local Native community on campus was approached in several ways and places, providing an opportunity for discussion in two of the three instances. My understanding of the Indigenous perspective manifested itself in my intent to be respectful of the students by approaching them in their space, with familiar surroundings and at times convenient for them, and by providing them with an opportunity for dialogue and reciprocity. The poster was developed with a Native art motif border which would be appealing to the target group. In addition, it was necessary for me to meet with the gatekeepers of two Indigenous programs on campus in order for them to spread the word in their respective programs about the project through the poster I left with them. It was important to take the extra time to meet with many people. In so doing, I was hoping to achieve the goal of attracting participants from all disciplines so that the research could be as inclusive as possible and thereby reflect multiple points of view.

Most of the taped interviews were conducted in the quiet room or Meditation Room at the Office of Native Student Services, which was offered by the coordinator of this office. This was satisfactory because many of the participants felt comfortable in this "familiar space" and because it was generally quiet and conducive to interviewing. One student, however, was interviewed in her office on campus because her schedule did not allow for interviewing at a quiet time at Native Student Services. It would appear that this different location did not have any significant impact on the study as all participants appeared comfortable with the taped interview session. More specifically, no participant asked to have the tape recorder turned off during the interview.

As for the interview schedule itself, time restraints did not allow the opportunity to pilot it prior to interviewing the study participants. As a result, there were a number of problematic questions that were asked of all participants. Question 11, for example, concerned Aboriginal-content periodicals which were not a part of the University of Alberta collection. Almost all participants responded that they could not think of many titles during the interview but that they would be willing to provide a list at some point in the future. A list of only five titles was generated during the interviews.

Question 14 asked about library services used and the responses are presented in Table 1; however, some aspects of the qualitative responses do not lend themselves well to the table format. Consequently, the value of some responses becomes lost in the translation, although I will attempt to expand on some of these during the discussion and in the interpretation of related survey data.

In addition, responses to some questions overlapped. For instance, question 10 asked about information that would be most useful in the participants' current studies. Often, answers also included services associated with providing certain types of information. One example was the response of "Native content in non-academic periodicals," followed by "and having these periodicals indexed in databases." In this case, I would transfer these answers to other questions, such as question 21, which asked for "suggestions for improvement."

RESEARCH FINDINGS

Due to the limited scope of this research paper, only the most salient sections of the information collected are discussed.

Demographics

Of the six participants, four were male and two were female. Three identified themselves as Cree, one as Ojibway, one had ancestry from a reserve in Eastern Quebec and one identified as a Native American. There were three doctoral students from the First Nations Education Graduate program, two Master's students (one MA and one MEd), and one second-year nursing student who had almost completed a science degree.

Earliest Memory of University of Alberta Libraries

Almost all participants stated that their earliest memories of the University of Alberta libraries were usually associated with fear. Terms used by participants included overwhelming, confusion, intimidating,

TABLE 1. Library Use of Aboriginal Students at the University of Alberta (Use of Type of Service by all 6 Participants)

Type of Service	A	B	C	D	E	F	# of Yes Responses
Circ. Desk Checkout	Y	Y	Y	Y	Y	Y	6
GATE Catalogue	Y	Y	Y	Y	Y	Y	6
Online Databases	Y	Y	Y	Y	Y	Y	6
Info/Reference Desk	Y	Y	Y	Y	Y	Y	6
Photocopying	Y	Y	Y	Y	Y	Y	6
Library Pamphlets	Y	Y	Y	Y	Y	Y	6
Inter-Library Loan	N	Y	Y	Y	Y	Y	5
Remote Access	Y	N	Y	Y	Y	Y	5
Microform Readers	Y	N	Y	Y	Y	Y	5
CD-ROMs	Y	N	Y	Y	Y	Y	5
Callbacks	Y	Y	N	Y	Y	Y	5
Reserve Readings	N	Y	Y	Y	Y	Y	5
Reference Books	N	Y	Y	N	Y	Y	4
Study Space	N	Y	Y	N	Y	Y	4
Instruction (B.I.)	N	N	Y	Y	Y	Y	4
Suggestion Box	N	N	Y	N	Y	Y	3
Print Indexes	N	N	Y	Y	N	Y	3
Music Listening Room	N	Y	N	N	N	N	1
Automated Checkout	N	N	Y	N	N	N	1
One-on-One Appt. w/ a Librarian	N	N	N	N	N	N	0
Total Yes Responses	10	12	17	14	16	17	

Legend: Y = Yes   N = No

scary, difficult and fearful. On the positive side, one student said he loved libraries and was content to explore the online catalogue, the table of contents of selected periodicals and how the library was set up. In this case, the participant had previously attended other post-secondary institutions.

The library locations used most by participants during their current program of study were the education library (four participants), the humanities and social sciences library (one participant) and the health sciences library (one participant). The reasons given for using these libraries generally concerned content of individual library holdings related to each student's program of study. In addition, convenience was a factor. For example, four students had courses and/or offices in the same building as the education library.

Most Useful Information Sources

The most useful information sources identified by this sample of students centred around those with Native or Indigenous content. Some examples of resources were current publications on Native Studies or by Aboriginal authors, Canadian videos with Aboriginal content, resources dealing with Indigenous methodologies and on Aboriginal post-secondary education, Aboriginal theses and dissertations and a bibliography of forthcoming Aboriginal literature. Half of these students noted that much of the information they needed was in journals whose subscriptions had been cancelled. Also, most of these students mentioned that they would prefer "research coming from another Native person."

Currently, the University of Alberta humanities and social sciences library lists a selection of six Native-content journals on its Web-site for Guides to Resources by Subject for Native Studies: *American Indian Culture and Research Journal, American Indian Quarterly, Canadian Journal of Native Education, Canadian Journal of Native Studies, Inuit Studies* and *Native Studies Review*. This does not appear to be a very comprehensive collection of journals given that this library currently provides access to approximately 4500 electronic and print periodical titles. The Native-content journals most recommended by the participants in this study to be acquired by the University of Alberta were: *Tribal College, Winds of Change: A Magazine for American Indian Education and Opportunity*, and *Indigenous Knowledge Monitor*. However, as mentioned previously, these participants would have liked to have been able to provide a more comprehensive list, if given the time, tools and opportunity to do so.

Given these responses, it is not surprising that most participants spoke of a lack of resources on Native or Indigenous issues when asked about their overall impression of the University of Alberta libraries. Four participants stated that they bought a lot of their own books for research purposes as a result. One in particular questioned why, if the University Bookstore carried copies of textbooks, could not the library provide one or two copies of textbooks for Native-content courses. Having library access to textbooks is important to most Aboriginal students because, generally, they are on a lower budget and face many economic difficulties.

In general, the textbook acquisition policy for the humanities and social sciences library at the University of Alberta is not comprehensive. Textbooks are considered to be an individual decision, depending on the needs of the discipline; therefore, only about one to five percent of the monograph budget is spent on textbooks. Also, other factors influence the purchase of textbooks. For instance, there is a high risk of theft and they date quickly. Usually, textbooks are purchased specifically to support the reserve collection. It has not been determined what percentage of Native-content textbooks has been purchased by the University of Alberta library system and if this percentage is at par with other subjects or disciplines or adequate to meet this particular need of Aboriginal students.

Types of Library Services Used

Responses about the types of library services used were varied and informative. As is evident from Table 1, the services used by all or almost all of the participants included the circulation desk checkout, the online catalogue, the information or reference desk, online databases, photocopying, unassisted loading of CD-ROMs, remote access to the online catalogue and databases, interlibrary loan, microform readers, callbacks (requesting material already out on loan) and library pamphlets and pathfinders. This includes twelve of the twenty services listed, although all participants added other services to the list. These other services include: printing of database abstracts, use of audio-visual material, Internet searching, electronic journals, borrower information, phone-in renewal, ordering theses through UMI, use of the change machine (for photocopying) and the washroom. Interestingly, one participant commented that he rarely used Circulation because books were generally considered too old for research papers in the health sciences; consequently, this student's focus was on periodicals.

The one service that no participants used was the one-on-one appointment with a librarian. Most respondents indicated that they were not aware of this service, a finding which seems unfortunate given that almost all are graduate students. Another service not used by this sample was the automated checkout. Although one participant indicated that he had used it once, he has never used it since because the security buzzer beeped as he was leaving. Likely, this lack of use of automated service is indicative of Aboriginal people's preference for interpersonal interaction and perhaps a distrust of some automated services. For instance, one participant referred to this preference in other areas such as banking, stating that she did not often use the automated teller either. Also, only one student had used the music listening room; others indicated that they knew about it but had not "needed" to use it yet. Lastly, in looking at the table vertically, it is apparent that two of the participants, A and B, do not appear to be using library services to their potential, as they have answered affirmatively to only ten and twelve of the twenty listed services. It is likely that these participants prefer to rely on people resources instead, again reflecting the Indigenous values of "being in relationship" and reciprocity. However, there may be other factors involved, such as feelings of intimidation about consulting with library staff, and these should be investigated further.

Frequency of Library Use

When asked about the frequency of library use during the last twelve months, participants generally responded with complex answers. One student said almost every day for half of the semester while in tutorials, but only two or three times in the other half of the semester while in clinical courses. Another participant answered three times a week on average but this was less than usual because he was collecting his own research data. Another student said once per week on average, although he might not use the library at all for a month or so. Yet another participant stated that she would go to the library for several hours a day for the first two weeks of every term, specifically in January, May and September, then about twice per month the rest of the term.

Other libraries or information centres used by these students were the Edmonton Public Library, specifically for music and videos, the Physical Education Learning Lab, the mini-library at the School of Native Studies, the Office of Native Student Services for a few subscriptions to Aboriginal-content periodicals, community organizations, such as the Diabetes Association and the Canadian Lung Association, and bookstores because "it's easier to find new stuff there." In addition, one participant said he relied on the Internet and listservs for current information.

Assessment of Help at the University of Alberta Libraries

Generally, the participants were quite positive in their assessment of help at the University of Alberta libraries. Responses were as follows: "excellent" (one response), "very good" (three responses), "good" (two responses). No participant rated help at the University of Alberta libraries as fair or poor. When asking for guidance on finding information, these participants were most likely to approach faculty, although most also found classmates generally helpful. Four of the participants said they approached librarians for guidance fairly regularly, but usually when they were not helped by faculty or classmates. Two participants also found researchers in the field, such as people they had met at conferences, to be a valuable resource.

Guidance to Find Available Information

I also asked participants about their general opinion of various information providers and the information provided. Almost all participants respected librarians for providing a valuable and essential service but they sometimes qualified their responses. The following comments reflect some of this ambivalence:

Librarians

- I have a high regard for librarians but they can't know specifics in Phys. Ed. They can show you how to look for stuff but my classmates and profs will give me names.
- [Librarians] provide an important function. But they don't have the same perspective as I do. They are helpful to the extent that they can be. I don't fault them for it-my research topic isn't generally well-known so I can live with that.
- [Librarians] provide a very vital service and have very vital skills, being able to assess information. But I access information from everyone, not just academic folk. Because information comes from unlikely places.
- The reference people are very good but the circulation people aren't helpful.
- Librarians are essential. They can make the difference for students having a pleasant or very unpleasant experience.

Comments about other information providers were also thoughtful, informative and varied in their degree of enthusiasm:

Faculty

- So-so, because I'm working with non-Native faculty and my subject area is in a Native field. A lot of them haven't read much on Native issues. I find I'm teaching them.
- I love the people in my faculty. They love what they do, they make an effort to know what's going on, the latest thing. They're opinion leaders so I get a lot of really good info from them.

Field Researchers

- It depends on who they are and where they position themselves, the type of methodology they use. It depends on what they say and whether their research comes from their cultural base.
- The information provided by researchers is good, contemporary, bringing bits and pieces together into one place. You have to approach them differently, they're not as far-reaching as librarians. [Instead] they're very focused on one thing.

Classmates

- They're really helpful. They've been out in the field. Two students from [a small Northern community] with quite a few doctoral graduates gave me a copy of one graduate's dissertation. I wouldn't have found it otherwise.
- The First Nations program may be unique-we share information and we're encouraged to share information. There's no competition-hoarding is unheard of. Also, I owe a lot to my classmates for giving me feedback. I consider my topic and methodology to be a group process, group generated.

From these comments, many Indigenous values can be observed. For instance, the concept of inclusivity rings loud and clear in the statement about accessing information from everyone because "information comes from unlikely places." This also reflects the concept of equality because the speaker is open to listening to and approaching all people for information. In addition, the concept that all people have something of value to contribute to the circle is evident. Often, Indigenous people prefer to remain low key or humble about their gifts and accomplishments, and loathe to attract attention, opting instead to mingle with "the masses." Perhaps this explains why Indigenous people often encounter useful information serendipitously, particularly at social events. (Interestingly, many librarians value the information they come across serendipitously as well.) People from all walks of life will attend such social events as pow wows or gatherings of drummers, dancers and onlookers usually in circle formations. Hence, it is not unusual to encounter someone there who will inform you of something you need to know at that point in time. This is the magic of community and the magic of the circle. In addition, the value of generosity has come into play because the information one receives at such events is a reflection of how generous one has been in helping others and this generosity is coming back to you. Similarly, even though an Aboriginal individual may be "just" an undergraduate at a university, this does not mean that he or she has nothing to contribute. Most likely this individual has a good deal of community-based involvement and life experience which provide useful insights into the Indigenous way of being and interacting.

Also apparent in some of these comments is the notion of reciprocity necessary for maintaining "good relations" which is so important to most Indigenous people. For instance, the student who spoke of the First Nations graduate program and its encouragement of information-sharing between classmates, also saw that this generosity and responsibility extended to providing feedback to each other and the group process of generating ideas for research and research methodology.

Some of these comments also have implications for library service at the University of Alberta. Primarily, librarians are not the sole, or even the first choice of, providers of information for this group of participants. One student mentioned the different perspective that librarians had in their manner of searching and that he did not have very high expectations of a librarian being able to help him with his obscure and perhaps foreign, from the viewpoint of the librarian, research topic. This differing perspective stems from each searcher's epistemological view or knowledge base and influences the access to and evaluation of resources. Consequently, this factor makes a good case for the hiring of Aboriginal staff, whose experience and epistemology would likely be more in tune with the Indigenous student or researcher. Another student was more reliant on professors or classmates for obtaining specific names of people/authors for his research. Perhaps librarians need to advertise their abilities and research findings more in order to gain the confidence of Aboriginal students. For instance, if a librarian comes across a mainstream periodical with a special issue on Aboriginal concerns, the librarian could showcase this information in some way, or otherwise let the Aboriginal community on campus know about this finding. Similarly, creating and showcasing a bibliography of other periodicals highlighting Aboriginal issues would also likely be useful and appreciated.

The Library Is the Heart of the University

Another question asked of participants was somewhat hypothetical in nature. This question asked their opinion of the quote: "The library is the heart of the university." Responses again were varied; some agreed but qualified their agreement, while others disagreed:

- I think it's true because it brings out that the information is the "blood" and libraries circulate that.
- I'd have to agree with it from an educational standpoint. The whole university revolves around the library.
- I want to change it to be more accurate. I think the library is the core-the brain, not the heart. I think the heart and soul are the part of the community that comes from people. The libraries would then be the mental or the brain functions. But they should be the most important part of the university. They're almost inseparable from the classroom and everything else.
- I would agree except that I'm not sure if that's the case at this university.
- I don't quite agree. I'd say the classroom is-the dynamic between the prof and the students is the heart of the university. But the library is a reflection of that.
- I don't agree. I think the students are the heart of the university. Of course, I'm biased because I work at Native "Student" Services and because I'm a student. [Student's emphasis]

My first interpretation of these comments is that most of these students see the library as a vitally connected part of the university system. They also see the library's relationship to the classroom and the interaction between professors and students as important. Again, the concept of relationship is a focus of the students' responses. Yet, on closer examination, the students appear to be saying something more. The metaphor about the "information" being the "blood" and that it circulates through the university system paints a portrait of libraries as being very dynamic, leaving the reader with a thought-provoking image. In addition, this metaphor can be interpreted as a teaching tool, providing some insight into the Indigenous way of thinking. For instance, this quote attributes animate qualities to something usually considered inanimate, i.e., the library system, in the Western mode of thinking. Because of its reference to animation, this metaphor also brings attention to the people who make the library system work, and how important this interpersonal interaction is to Indigenous people. This is also reflected in the lack of use of the automated checkout system by this sample of students. Another insight provided by these responses is that there seems to be a feeling that the library does not value people interaction, the kind that represents the soul of the university community. Perhaps this is not something that can be changed, given the high percentage of repetitive transactions that occur in the library, such as circulation desk activities, and the lack of funding experienced by many libraries for much in-depth consultation with patrons.

Suggestions for Library Improvement

Possibly the most illuminating and insightful answers were those in response to the question about suggestions for improvement at the University of Alberta libraries. The suggestions were, again, varied in the range of services touched upon. Many related to increased collection of resources with Aboriginal content, especially current materials and databases. One improvement mentioned by most of the participants was the possibility of renewing cancelled subscriptions. Other suggestions were specific to individual libraries, such as taking out the entry turnstiles in the education library, and scheduling reference staff at the health sciences library on Sundays, a service offered at other campus libraries. Also of interest were suggestions for an increased commitment by the university administration to the library and increased commitment by the library to the Aboriginal community on campus. Some of these suggestions were expressed and interpreted as follows:

1. One participant suggested: "An Aboriginal Resource Centre or Learning Lab would take this university to a new level of service delivery."

The idea here would be to have easier, one-stop access to Indigenous resources, rather than to be spread out all over campus. These resources could be compiled by staff who are more in touch with the academic in-

formation needs of Indigenous students because this would be the focus
of the collection. Also an Aboriginal Resource Centre would be a more
comfortable place for Aboriginal students to learn because it could display Aboriginal motifs and art and it could be located close to other services provided for and by Aboriginal people. In addition, library
orientations could be offered here, a more welcoming and comfortable
environment, which would enhance learning.

2. Another participant made this suggestion: "Have the administration really recognize the importance of the library and not just pay
   lip service to that sentiment-what I've noticed is important to this
   university is money and capital improvements while at the same
   time the library is cancelling subscriptions."

Some explanation is due here. One issue is the corporate sponsorship
of the capital improvements currently being undertaken at the University of Alberta. The other consideration is the falling value of the Canadian dollar which has influenced the cancelling of many American and
European journal subscriptions. However, this does not preclude the
possibility of seeking out some additional funding, perhaps by way of
corporate sponsorship or endowments, for maintaining the journal subscriptions most in demand.

One solution may be to consider having Aboriginal students do some
fund-raising for subscriptions of Native-content journals, at least for the
first year. Some of these subscriptions cost less than $50 U.S. per year
and may not be that much of a hardship if several students are willing to
chip in. Another possibility is to consider requesting specific funding
for journal subscriptions from the First Nations bands and Métis settlements which have a higher representation of students on campus from
their communities.

Another suggestion here would be to have the library rep for the
School of Native Studies or for the First Nations Education graduate program really lobby for increased funding. This could come from the project funding, available for the humanities and social sciences library, to
support either large or expensive one-time purchases or to purchase "regularly priced materials which further develop or fill gaps in a specific
subject or interdisciplinary collection."[22] Perhaps there are other funding
sources, similar to the Equity Grant Project fund accessed by the
Queensland University of Technology Library for the Novak and Robinson study.[23] Other options may be funding sources external to the university, such as the Millennium fund offered by the federal government of

Canada, a fund supporting many cultural projects. At any rate, it would take some time, commitment and energy to explore these suggestions.

3. Yet another participant suggested: "Having Aboriginal staff within the libraries would go a long ways to making new Aboriginal students feel more comfortable and more confident."

This participant saw a huge need for Aboriginal students to see themselves reflected on campus, in various positions of authority, such as professors, administrators, business-owners and even library staff. These people serve as role models given the state of Aboriginal (dis)comfort levels in academia. Seeing that other Indigenous people have made it to these positions offers hope and confidence that current students can survive the struggle inherent in these achievements too. Interestingly, one of the studies discussed in the literature review also presented the idea of hiring minorities to work in libraries.[24]

4. One other suggestion made by a participant calls for: "More of a commitment to the Aboriginal student population-by asking Aboriginal student groups, staff and faculty to help library staff enhance the collection and provide input into the collection development process."

The liaison librarian for Native Studies did purchase a considerable amount of Aboriginal-content material in the late 1980s when this undergraduate program first started. The initial purchase was made after consultation with Aboriginal-focused libraries such as the Saskatchewan Indian Federated College Library and the Gabriel Dumont Institute Library, both in Saskatchewan. However, it is only very recently that the selection process for Native Studies has been influenced by any other additional funding, over and above the small, annual budgetary allocations. Certainly, there are some very current and high-demand titles. Two examples are Taiaiake Alfred's *Peace, Power, Righteousness: An Indigenous Manifesto*, a title held on reserve, and Linda T. Smith's *Decolonizing Methodologies*. But according to the students, there are not enough such titles and not enough copies, usually only one, of each title. The policy that collection development funding is guided by the size of the user community and the amount of material published in that discipline can be disadvantageous to marginalized groups who face exceptional barriers to university enrollment and publication in the first place. There is a danger that collection development librarians face in not being aware of the "ways in which libraries contribute to the maintenance of an elite heritage."[25] Manoff successfully articulated and reminded us of the politics of collection development as follows:

> Most of us don't think much about how our reading functions pro-
> vide us with reassuring images of ourselves and those like us. Nev-
> ertheless, we need to acknowledge the kind of delegitimizing
> functions libraries perform in their exclusion of certain kinds of
> materials-be they certain kinds of subject matter . . . or material ad-
> dressed to certain minority or ethnic groups . . . the refusal of li-
> braries to acknowledge, through their collections as well as their
> services, the multi-ethnic nature of their communities, are convey-
> ing a not particularly subtle message about who are the legitimate
> heirs to the knowledge they contain and whom they assume they
> are serving. The question of what libraries do not purchase has
> similar implications for scholarly as well as general materials. Li-
> brary collections not only shape research patterns, but they affect
> the way library patrons view themselves and their relation to their
> academic community as well as to the larger culture.[26]

Other suggestions were community-oriented in nature, such as a Canadian dissertations abstract service which would benefit all graduate
students on campus and the sponsoring of Aboriginal students to go to
library school. This latter was felt to be a way to empower communities
because information is seen to be an access point to power. The Aboriginal communities were not seen to have this access to information and,
consequently, power, due to the absence of Aboriginal librarians in
communities. Another student suggested that the Aboriginal community on campus should help produce a list of books and/or journals for
the university library system as an ongoing process. This student also
felt that it would be important for the Aboriginal community to critique
some of the resources listed. One other student felt that the most helpful
action the library could take would be to provide some staff with training in interpersonal skills and user-friendliness because he felt if this
was in place, then it would also increase access to resources.

RECIPROCITY AND RELATIONSHIP

Not only did these participants express concern for their fellow students and for members of their communities, many comments also re-

flect the reciprocity and expectation of reciprocity so inherent to their interactions with others. Generally, participants spoke of many positive reciprocal interactions when they discussed interactions with other Indigenous people. However, comments about interactions with non-Indigenous people generally reflected a negative reciprocity, in that there was an expectation that a reciprocal interaction would occur but it did not happen. Some examples of anecdotes indicating positive reciprocity are as follows:

- I try to find what's contemporary-journals and Websites are fairly current editions of information. They give you a sense of what's happening and what's not happening, so you can anticipate what's going to be coming out. I look for expanded book reviews or article reviews or people having a debate. I want to see what people are saying-pro and con. That's the great thing about listservs and Websites.
- If people [in our cohort group in the First Nations Education Program] know what your research interest is, we help each other find information that's valuable. It may not be what I want to use but someone else could use it.
- [I ask for guidance to info from] Everyone, not just academic folk . . . I ask everyone, students, undergrads because info comes from unlikely places. We'll exchange info that way. I even get information from administrators about relevant books.
- To see some brown faces-we need to see ourselves reflected in this institution, I think especially in libraries. That would be interesting to have Aboriginal librarians, Aboriginal people working in the libraries. I suspect Aboriginal students would be drawn to them . . . and feel much more comfortable going to them.
- Attending conferences like the World Indigenous Peoples' Conference on Education brings Indigenous and Native educators together from around the world. While we are all different, the information and data and writing that's coming out of these different places is very similar, tells a similar story. So we can get support in our writing and research through what's happening in these other countries . . . It's exciting to network with others who are looking at the same kinds of things. The sharing, networking, exchanging names and addresses-that was empowering.

On the other hand, a sample of negative reciprocity is evident in the following passages:

- Aboriginal scholars can't get our papers published in "status quo" publications like *Education Today* because they don't want this kind of new look at education because it's not following the orthodoxy. Yet we need to be published. It's a Catch 22 situation. A contradiction. So we end up being published in Aboriginal-based magazines [which aren't indexed in mainstream databases].
- [Question 12: articles accessed through interlibrary loan?] No, I get them through Native Student Services or School of Native Studies, they have [subscriptions] to these. Or else I'll dig them up through some other process. First because reference isn't being made in the ERIC database, so you have to go somewhere else. But I bet there's other really good publications that we don't even know about because they're not plugged in.

In addition, comments about the importance of being in relationship were also made. Here are some of the most salient of these comments:

- If [the University of Alberta library] is prepared to meet the needs of Aboriginal students [Aboriginal students generating a list of Aboriginal resources] would be a good idea. Each time I come up with that frustration [of the library not carrying Aboriginal content materials], it would have been nice to be able to tell someone who cared, or who might do something about it. To say, "We really need this publication" and to think that someday we might get it.
- As an Aboriginal student, I have to wonder about the other non-European Canadian population here on campus, whether they'd find the same thing. There is general information about topics, nothing necessarily well-chosen. Where do they go to get their current new material? How do they get that? Are they Aboriginal people that they're going to? To ask what's new out there that's of interest to us. Because Aboriginal people at this university will tell you that they're not getting what they need from the non-Aboriginal authors. We're finding with the increasing number of Aboriginal students in grad studies that the worldviews are different . . . The research that's out there doesn't fit for us. It's frustrating for us to qualify new methodologies or new ways of doing things that don't restrict us.
- Sometimes you feel like you're stumbling around and no one's gone there before. But there's people out there who've done it and there's books that have been written about it but you don't know about it. Native people are starting to create their own links.

- When you write your thesis, you have an idea, but you have to support it with additional research. I can have an idea but if I have nothing to support it with, then it's just me speaking. But if other researchers or grad students have found the same thing, then it's not just me speaking but this body of knowledge saying that this is so [that's why it's important to have access to other theses written by Native people].
- But I do [look for Aboriginal authors and subject material] just in my circle of friends, which includes a lot of Aboriginal people. Because I've been a student for so long, I have a lot of academic people within the institution with connections. So, I think we get a lot through word of mouth and sharing information. In terms of what is new out there, what is current. What have other people come across?

These examples reinforce the importance of the concepts of reciprocity and "being in relationship" in the Indigenous worldview. It is a logical progression, then, to think that incorporating relationship-building practices into library services would strengthen the role libraries have when serving Indigenous people. Two such practices might involve a willingness to counter negative stereotypes of Aboriginal people and the implementation of effective cross-cultural training programs.[27]

CONCLUSION

The information gathered through the course of this study has much in common with the few but related studies presented in the literature review. For instance, in the Queensland study, respondents expressed the need for increased access to Indigenous resources.[28] The Hannum study discussed the increased usage of libraries by Aboriginals when there was collaboration between the library and the Aboriginal communities.[29] Related to this were the positive effects that occurred when a commitment was made to relationship-building practices and the importance of Aboriginal people having input into collection development. Patterson also referred to the need for access to theses and dissertations.[30] In addition, these studies revealed Indigenous values in their participants' responses.

Furthermore, four main themes have emerged from a rudimentary analysis of the data from this study:

- Most of these participants were developing their own libraries for research purposes due to a lack of Aboriginal resources at the University of Alberta libraries.
- The use of people resources was common and perhaps necessary for these students' academic survival and success.
- Some participants had attended other post-secondary institutions and had made recommendations for improvements at the University of Alberta based on their experiences at these other universities.
- Most of these participants indicated a community-mindedness and reflected the concept of reciprocity (positive and negative) in their comments and recommendations. Interwoven throughout the data was a pattern of responses that often pointed towards the importance of "being in relationship."

In conclusion, there are two recommendations. The first is that broader research is needed. This study expresses the voices of only six students and cannot be taken to represent the whole University of Alberta Aboriginal student population, let alone Aboriginal students across Canada or North America. Therefore, it is recommended that future research into library use and information needs of Aboriginal adults be undertaken, particularly at academic and public libraries and at various locations across Canada. The sparse body of research in this area leaves an unacceptable gap. The idea here is to involve Aboriginal people in the studies and not to ask other people to speak on their behalf.

The second recommendation is for library administrators to consider acting on suggestions offered by the participants in this study. In response to the four main themes which have evolved from this study, it would help to alleviate the intimidation and frustration these participants feel about using the library if administrators would communicate an understanding of the participants' situation. Basically, there are three main concerns:

- A lack of holdings of Indigenous resources, evident in that students are buying their own books for research purposes and the common request to re-subscribe to cancelled journal subscriptions.
- A lack of resource or research development concerning Indigenous issues, as well as a need for support of this resource and research development.

- A lack of services recognizing the Indigenous values of "being in relationship" and reciprocity.

The next step would be to develop a process for accessing Aboriginal input into collection development. Two possibilities for such a process might be requesting a list of resources and organizing a forum/circle for representatives of all Aboriginal groups on campus to contribute to collection development procedures. In fact, there is such a Council already organized. As well, library outreach to the existing infrastructure, such as the Office of Native Student Services, would help to create a sense of trust. Other library outreach examples might include offers to customize library orientations and requests for guidance as to methods of contacting the Aboriginal community. Two other suggestions would help to create a more amicable climate of cooperation and "being in relationship." One would be to have open discussion of the financial pressures faced by the library. Another would be to provide an opportunity to brainstorm solutions, such as those funding arrangements discussed earlier in this paper, by the Aboriginal community. Surely, if a small academic library in Australia can make such a commitment,[31] then the University of Alberta and the Province of Alberta, with their combined substantial resources, should also be able to take similar progressive action. Following through on some of these suggestions would indicate an appreciation of what Aboriginal students bring to this university. One of the participants in this study expressed this notion best in the following passage:

> I'm not sure about other Aboriginal students doing their studies here, but I recognize that my particular interest is very specialized and very narrow. So I don't expect the U of A to have what I need. But then again, if other Aboriginal students are having the same problem, because they come from the Northwest Territories or the Yukon or wherever, and the material is not available, then that's a problem. We're one segment of the student population but we bring something to the university as well. The theses and dissertations that we're going to produce will bring, I think, honour and recognition to the university. And so if the university is intent on being a leader in the area of Native and Indigenous education, then they need to do something about increasing the collection to support programs.

The University of Alberta and other libraries can choose to respect inter-cultural knowledge and practices by making some accommodations for Aboriginal students. Libraries can also choose to acknowledge the importance of staff becoming culturally competent, a sentiment expressed by others in the library field:

> We have outreach programs and minority recruitment drives, and we spout endless words in tribute to diversity. Yet, in a major error of omission, our otherwise enlightened profession takes little truly affirmative action to develop in all its members the genuine cultural competency to make serving all Americans, not just the white middle class, commonplace in our society . . . If librarians don't become culturally competent to effectively serve all the people in ways that are meaningful to them, we will become politically irrelevant.[32]

NOTES

1. Duane Champagne, ed., *The Native North American Almanac: A Reference work on Native North Americans in the U.S. and Canada* (Detroit: Gale Research, 1994), 890.

2. Nancy Hannum, "Do Native people use public libraries?" *BCLA Reporter* 39 (4) (September 1995): 25-9.

3. Stan Skrzeszewski, June Huggins-Chan, and Frank Clark, "Bookmobile services to Native people: An experiment in Saskatchewan," in *The Book Stops Here: New Directions in Bookmobile Service*, ed. Catherine Alloway (Metuchen, NJ: The Scarecrow Press, 1990), 312-21.

4. Donna Bright, *The Provision of Public Library Services to First Nations Communities Living on Reserves in Ontario, Manitoba, Saskatchewan, Alberta and British Columbia* (London, ON: School of Library and Information Science, University of Western Ontario, 1992).

5. Hannum, "Do Native people use public libraries?" 25.

6. Lotsee Patterson, "Information needs and services of Native Americans," *Rural Libraries* 15 (2) (1995): 38.

7. Ibid., 40.

8. Ibid., 43-44.

9. Jan Novak and Gail Robinson, " 'You tell us': Indigenous students talk to a tertiary library," *Australian Academic and Research Libraries* 29 (1) (March 1998): 13-22.

10. Ibid., 14.

11. Ibid., 16.

12. Ibid., 19.

13. Ibid., 20.

14. Ibid., 21.

290 Diversity Now: People, Collections, and Services in Academic Libraries

15. Thomas King, ed., *All My Relations: An Anthology of Contemporary Canadian Native Fiction* (Toronto: McClelland and Stewart, 1990), ix.

16. Linda T. Smith, *Decolonizing Methodologies: Research and Indigenous Peoples* (London: Zed Books Ltd., 1999), 1.

17. Paula Gunn Allen, *The Sacred Hoop: Recovering the Feminine in American Indian Traditions* (Boston: Beacon Press, 1986).

18. Hannum, "Do Native people use public libraries?" 26-9.

19. Patterson, "Information needs," 40.

20. Novak and Robinson, "'You tell us,'" 16.

21. Ronald Powell, *Basic Research Methods for Librarians, 2nd ed.* (Norwood, NJ: Ablex Pub. Corp., 1991), 107-109.

22. University of Alberta, Rutherford Library, "Collection Development Policy."

23. E-mail correspondence between the author and Jan Novak, February, 2000.

24. Novak and Robinson, "'You tell us,'" 21.

25. Marlene Manoff, "Academic libraries and the culture wars: The politics of collection development," *Collection Management* 16 (4) (1992): 2.

26. Ibid., 3-4.

27. For further discussion on relationship-building practices with Aboriginal people in the Canadian context, see Gilles Rhéaume, "A new spirit of partnership," *Canadian Business Review* 21 (2) (summer 1994): 6-11.

28. Novak and Robinson, "'You tell us,'" 21.

29. Hannum, "Do Native people use public libraries?" 26-9.

30. Patterson, "Information needs," 38.

31. Novak and Robinson, "'You tell us,'" 21.

32. John N. Berry, "Culturally competent service," *Library Journal* 124 (14) (1 September 1999): 112.

APPENDIX

Student Interview Schedule for Research Project

1. Tell me a bit about yourself and your current studies at the University of Alberta. Do you identify with a particular Aboriginal tribe or as a Métis or Inuit? ___ Yes ___ No. If so, which one(s)?

2. What program of study are you taking?

3. What year of the program are you in?

4. Think back to when you began university and when you first used the library. What is your earliest memory of the University of Alberta Libraries?

5. Which U of A library location was it?

6. What was your impression of the library then?

7. Has your impression changed since then? If so, what factors do you think contributed to that change?

8. Which U of A library locations have you used since?
   [prompt: *Rutherford (Humanities and Social Sciences), Cameron (Science and Technology), John W. Scott (Health Sciences), the Law Library, the Business Library, Coutts (Education) Library*]

9. What library have you used the most during your current program of study?
   Is there a particular reason (or reasons) why you frequent this library?

10. What kinds of information are or would be most helpful for you in your current studies? [prompt: certain kinds of periodicals or literature, material of a certain nature, . . .]

11. Are there journals dealing with Aboriginal issues that exist that you have needed for your studies but are not a part of the University of Alberta Library collection? ___ Yes ___ No. If yes, what are they?

12. If yes, have you accessed the articles through inter-library loan?
    ___ Yes ___ No. If no, why not?

13. What is your overall impression of the collection at the University of Alberta Library?

14. What library services have you used at the University of Alberta during your current program?

__ Circulation desk checkout
__ the GATE (catalog)
__ Inter-library loan
__ Microform readers
__ Online databases
__ One-on-one consultations
   with a librarian
   (appointment necessary)
__ Print indexes
__ Reference books (including
   encyclopedias, dictionaries,
   almanacs, etc.)
__ Requesting material already
   out on loan (Callbacks)
__ Study space

__ Automated checkout
__ Remote access to the Gate
__ Library aids (pamphlets, instruction
   printouts, pathfinders)
__ Music Listening room
__ Unassisted loading of CD-ROMs
__ Photocopying
__ Suggestion box
__ Formal instruction (B.I.)__
__ Information / Reference desk
__ Reserve readings
__ Other

15. In the last twelve months, how often have you used the university libraries?

16. How would you assess the University libraries in terms of helping you obtain the information you need to do assignments or research?
    __ excellent   __ very good   __ good   __ fair   __ poor
    Please provide reasons for your answer.

17. In your current program of studies, do you access other libraries or information centres?   __ Yes   __ No. If yes, please name them and for what purpose. If yes, please state why you access them.

18. In your current program of studies, whom do you prefer to ask for guidance to find available information?
    __faculty __classmates __librarian __researchers in the field __other

19. What is your general opinion of librarians and the information they provide?
    What about faculty and the information they provide?
    What about researchers in the field and the information they provide?
    What about classmates and the information they provide?

20. What is your opinion of this quote: "The library is the heart of the university."

21. What suggestions do you have for improving library services for this university?

22. Is there anything else you would like to say regarding the University of Alberta libraries or the kinds of information you need for your studies?

Thank you for your participation.

Index

Page numbers followed by "t" indicate tables; page numbers followed by "f" indicate figures; and page numbers followed by "n" indicate notes.

Leadership in Academic Libraries: Proceedings of the W. Porter Kellam Conference, The University of Georgia, May 7, 1991, edited by William Gray Potter (Vol. 17, No. 4, 1993). *"Will be of interest to those concerned with the history of American academic libraries." (Australian Library Review)*

Collection Assessment and Acquisitions Budgets, edited by Sul H. Lee (Vol. 17, No. 2, 1993). *Contains timely information about the assessment of academic library collections and the relationship of collection assessment to acquisition budgets.*

Developing Library Staff for the 21st Century, edited by Maureen Sullivan (Vol. 17, No. 1, 1992). *"I found myself enthralled with this highly readable publication. It is one of those rare compilations that manages to successfully integrate current general management operational thinking in the context of academic library management." (Bimonthly Review of Law Books)*

Vendor Evaluation and Acquisition Budgets, edited by Sul H. Lee (Vol. 16, No. 3, 1992). *"The title doesn't do justice to the true scope of this excellent collection of papers delivered at the sixth annual conference on library acquisitions sponsored by the University of Oklahoma Libraries." (Kent K. Hendrickson, BS, MALS, Dean of Libraries, University of Nebraska-Lincoln) Find insightful discussions on the impact of rising costs on library budgets and management in this groundbreaking book.*

The Management of Library and Information Studies Education, edited by Herman L. Totten, PhD, MLS (Vol. 16, No. 1/2, 1992). *"Offers something of interest to everyone connected with LIS education-the undergraduate contemplating a master's degree, the doctoral student struggling with courses and career choices, the new faculty member aghast at conflicting responsibilities, the experienced but stressed LIS professor, and directors of LIS Schools." (Education Libraries)*

Library Management in the Information Technology Environment: Issues, Policies, and Practice for Administrators, edited by Brice G. Hobrock, PhD, MLS (Vol. 15, No. 3/4, 1992). *"A road map to identify some of the alternative routes to the electronic library." (Stephen Rollins, Associate Dean for Library Services, General Library, University of New Mexico)*

Managing Technical Services in the 90's, edited by Drew Racine (Vol. 15, No. 1/2, 1991). *"Presents an eclectic overview of the challenges currently facing all library technical services efforts. . . . Recommended to library administrators and interested practitioners." (Library Journal)*

Budgets for Acquisitions: Strategies for Serials, Monographs, and Electronic Formats, edited by Sul H. Lee (Vol. 14, No. 3, 1991). *"Much more than a series of handy tips for the careful shopper. This [book] is a most useful one-well-informed, thought-provoking, and authoritative." (Australian Library Review)*

Creative Planning for Library Administration: Leadership for the Future, edited by Kent Hendrickson, MALS (Vol. 14, No. 2, 1991). *"Provides some essential information on the planning process, and the mix of opinions and methodologies, as well as examples relevant to every library manager, resulting in a very readable foray into a topic too long avoided by many of us." (Canadian Library Journal)*

Strategic Planning in Higher Education: Implementing New Roles for the Academic Library, edited by James F. Williams, II, MLS (Vol. 13, No. 3/4, 1991). *"A welcome addition to the sparse literature on strategic planning in university libraries. Academic librarians considering strategic planning for their libraries will learn a great deal from this work." (Canadian Library Journal)*

Personnel Administration in an Automated Environment, edited by Philip E. Leinbach, MLS (Vol. 13, No. 1/2, 1990). *"An interesting and worthwhile volume, recommended to university library administrators and to others interested in thought-provoking discussion of the personnel implications of automation." (Canadian Library Journal)*

Library Development: A Future Imperative, edited by Dwight F. Burlingame, PhD (Vol. 12, No. 4, 1990). *"This volume provides an excellent overview of fundraising with special application to libraries. . . . A useful book that is highly recommended for all libraries." (Library Journal)*

Library Material Costs and Access to Information, edited by Sul H. Lee (Vol. 12, No. 3, 1991). *"A cohesive treatment of the issue. Although the book's contributors possess a research library perspective, the data and the ideas presented are of interest and benefit to the entire profession, especially academic librarians." (Library Resources and Technical Services)*

Training Issues and Strategies in Libraries, edited by Paul M. Gherman, MALS, and Frances O. Painter, MLS, MBA (Vol. 12, No. 2, 1990). *"There are . . . useful chapters, all by different authors, each with a preliminary summary of the content-a device that saves much time in deciding whether to read the whole chapter or merely skim through it. Many of the chapters are essentially practical without too much emphasis on theory. This book is a good investment." (Library Association Record)*

Library Education and Employer Expectations, edited by E. Dale Cluff, PhD, MLS (Vol. 11, No. 3/4, 1990). *"Useful to library-school students and faculty interested in employment problems and employer perspectives. Librarians concerned with recruitment practices will also be interested." (Information Technology and Libraries)*

Managing Public Libraries in the 21st Century, edited by Pat Woodrum, MLS (Vol. 11, No. 1/2, 1989). *"A broad-based collection of topics that explores the management problems and possibilities public libraries will be facing in the 21st century." (Robert Swisher, PhD, Director, School of Library and Information Studies, University of Oklahoma)*

Human Resources Management in Libraries, edited by Gisela M. Webb, MLS, MPA (Vol. 10, No. 4, 1989). *"Thought provoking and enjoyable reading. . . . Provides valuable insights for the effective information manager." (Special Libraries)*

Creativity, Innovation, and Entrepreneurship in Libraries, edited by Donald E. Riggs, EdD, MLS (Vol. 10, No. 2/3, 1989). *"The volume is well worth reading as a whole. . . . There is very little repetition, and it should stimulate thought." (Australian Library Review)*

The Impact of Rising Costs of Serials and Monographs on Library Services and Programs, edited by Sul H. Lee (Vol. 10, No. 1, 1989). *". . . Sul Lee hit a winner here." (Serials Review)*

Computing, Electronic Publishing, and Information Technology: Their Impact on Academic Libraries, edited by Robin N. Downes (Vol. 9, No. 4, 1989). *"For a relatively short and easily digestible discussion of these issues, this book can be recommended, not only to those in academic libraries, but also to those in similar types of library or information unit, and to academics and educators in the field." (Journal of Documentation)*

Library Management and Technical Services: The Changing Role of Technical Services in Library Organizations, edited by Jennifer Cargill, MSLS, MSed (Vol. 9, No. 1, 1988). *"As a practical and instructive guide to issues such as automation, personnel matters, education, management techniques and liaison with other services, senior library managers with a sincere interest in evaluating the role of their technical services should find this a timely publication." (Library Association Record)*

Management Issues in the Networking Environment, edited by Edward R. Johnson, PhD (Vol. 8, No. 3/4, 1989). *"Particularly useful for librarians/information specialists contemplating establishing a local network." (Australian Library Review)*

Acquisitions, Budgets, and Material Costs: Issues and Approaches, edited by Sul H. Lee (Supp. #2, 1988). *"The advice of these library practitioners is sensible and their insights illuminating for librarians in academic libraries." (American Reference Books Annual)*

Pricing and Costs of Monographs and Serials: National and International Issues, edited by Sul H. Lee (Supp. #1, 1987). *"Eminently readable. There is a good balance of chapters on serials and monographs and the perspective of suppliers, publishers, and library practitioners are presented. A book well worth reading." (Australasian College Libraries)*

Legal Issues for Library and Information Managers, edited by William Z. Nasri, JD, PhD (Vol. 7, No. 4, 1987). *"Useful to any librarian looking for protection or wondering where responsibilities end and liabilities begin. Recommended." (Academic Library Book Review)*

Archives and Library Administration: Divergent Traditions and Common Concerns, edited by Lawrence J. McCrank, PhD, MLS (Vol. 7, No. 2/3, 1986). *"A forward-looking view of archives and libraries. . . . Recommend[ed] to students, teachers, and practitioners alike of archival and library science. It is readable, thought-provoking, and provides a summary of the major areas of divergence and convergence." (Association of Canadian Map Libraries and Archives)*

Excellence in Library Management, edited by Charlotte Georgi, MLS, and Robert Bellanti, MLS, MBA (Vol. 6, No. 3, 1985). *"Most beneficial for library administrators . . . for anyone interested in either library/information science or management." (Special Libraries)*

Marketing and the Library, edited by Gary T. Ford (Vol. 4, No. 4, 1984). *Discover the latest methods for more effective information dissemination and learn to develop successful programs for specific target areas.*

Finance Planning for Libraries, edited by Murray S. Martin (Vol. 3, No. 3/4, 1983). *Stresses the need for libraries to weed out expenditures which do not contribute to their basic role-the collection and organization of information-when planning where and when to spend money.*

Planning for Library Services: A Guide to Utilizing Planning Methods for Library Management, edited by Charles R. McClure, PhD (Vol. 2, No. 3/4, 1982). *"Should be read by anyone who is involved in planning processes of libraries-certainly by every administrator of a library or system." (American Reference Books Annual)*

☐ YES, please send me **The Practical Library Manager**
___ in hard at $34.95 ISBN: 0-7890-1765-2.
___ in soft at $24.95 ISBN: 0-7890-1766-0.

- Individual orders outside US, Canada, and Mexico must be prepaid by check or credit card.
- Discounts are not available on 5+ text prices and not available in conjunction with any other discount. • Discount not applicable on books priced under $15.00.
- 5+ text prices are not available for jobbers and wholesalers.
- Postage & handling: In US: $4.00 for first book, $1.50 for each additional book. Outside US: $5.00 for first book; $2.00 for each additional book.
- NY, MN, and OH residents: please add appropriate sales tax after postage & handling. Canadian residents: please add 7% GST after postage & handling. Canadian residents of Newfoundland, Nova Scotia, and New Brunswick, also add 8% for province tax. • Payment in UNESCO coupons welcome.
- If paying in Canadian dollars, use current exchange rate to convert to US dollars.
- Prices and discounts subject to change without notice.

Signature _____

☐ PAYMENT ENCLOSED $ _____
(Payment must be in US or Canadian dollars by check or money order drawn on a US or Canadian bank.)

☐ PLEASE BILL MY CREDIT CARD:
☐ AmEx ☐ Diners Club ☐ Discover ☐ Eurocard ☐ JCB ☐ Master Card ☐ Visa

Account Number _____

Expiration Date _____

Signature _____

☐ BILL ME LATER ($5 service charge will be added).
(Not available for individuals outside US/Canada/Mexico. Service charge is waived for/jobbers/wholesalers/booksellers.)
☐ Check here if billing address is different from shipping address and attach purchase order and billing address information.

FAX

Please complete the information below or tape your business card in this area.

NAME _____

INSTITUTION _____

ADDRESS _____

CITY _____

STATE _____ ZIP _____

COUNTRY _____

COUNTY (NY residents only) _____

E-MAIL _____
[type or print clearly]

May we use your e-mail address for confirmations and other types of information?
( ) Yes ( ) No We appreciate receiving your e-mail address and fax number. Haworth would like to e-mail or fax special discount offers to you, as a preferred customer. We will never **share, rent, or exchange** your e-mail address or fax number. We regard such actions as an invasion of your privacy.

☐ YES, please send me **The Practical Library Manager** (ISBN: 0-7890-1766-0) to consider on a 60-day **no risk** examination basis. I understand that I will receive an invoice payable within 60 days, or that if **I decide to adopt the book, my invoice will be cancelled.** I understand that I will be billed at the lowest price. (60-day offer available only to teaching faculty in US, Canada, and Mexico / Outside US/ Canada, a proforma invoice will be sent upon receipt of your request and must be paid in advance of shipping. A full refund will be issued with proof of adoption.)
This information is needed to process your examination copy order.

Signature _____

Course Title(s) _____

Current Text(s) _____

Enrollment _____

Semester _____ Decision Date _____

Office Tel _____ Hours _____

THE HAWORTH PRESS, INC., 10 Alice Street, Binghamton, NY 13904-1580 USA
May we open a confidential credit card account for you for possible future purchases? ( ) Yes ( ) No

(10)   02/02   BIC02

FAX